Farm Policy

Farm Policy

The Politics of Soil, Surpluses, and Subsidies

Congressional Quarterly Inc.
1414 22nd Street N.W.
Washington, D.C. 20037

Congressional Quarterly Inc.

Congressional Quarterly Inc., an editorial research service and publishing company, serves clients in the fields of news, education, business, and government. It combines specific coverage of Congress, government, and politics by Congressional Quarterly with the more general subject range of an affiliated service, Editorial Research Reports.

Congressional Quarterly publishes the *Congressional Quarterly Weekly Report* and a variety of books, including college political science textbooks under the CQ Press imprint and public affairs paperbacks designed as timely reports to keep journalists, scholars, and the public abreast of developing issues and events. CQ also publishes information directories and reference books on the federal government, national elections and politics, including the *Guide to Congress*, the *Guide to the Supreme Court*, the *Guide to U.S. Elections,* and *Politics in America*. The *CQ Almanac*, a compendium of legislation for one session of Congress, is published each year. *Congress and the Nation*, a record of government for a presidential term, is published every four years.

CQ publishes *The Congressional Monitor*, a daily report on current and future activities of congressional committees, and several newsletters including *Congressional Insight*, a weekly analysis of congressional action, and *Campaign Practices Reports*, a semimonthly update on campaign laws.

CQ's online Washington Alert Service provides government affairs specialists with details of congressional action on a continually updated basis.

Copyright © 1984 Congressional Quarterly Inc.

Printed in the United States of America

Library of Congress Cataloging in Publication Data
   Main entry under title:

   Farm Policy

      Bibliography: p.
      Includes index.
         1. Agriculture and state — United States. 2. Soil conservation — Government policy — United States. 3. Surplus agricultural commodities — Government policy — United States. 4. Agricultural price supports — United States. I. Congressional Quarterly, inc.
   HD1761.F323 1985   338.1'873   84-16982
   ISBN 0-87187-286-2

Editor: Nancy A. Blanpied

Contributors: Tom Arrandale, Mary Ames Booker, Marc Leepson, John L. Moore, Roger Thompson, Elizabeth Wehr

Cover: Belle Burkhart

Photo Credits: p. 11, UPI; p. 17, 25, 33, 97, U.S. Department of Agriculture-Soil Conservation Service; p. 29, Arthur Rothstein/Farm Security Administration; p. 31, 57, 60, 81, 85, 91, U.S. Department of Agriculture; p. 41, Migrant Action League; p. 67, 71, 113, Congressional Quarterly Inc.; p. 79, Larry Morris and Doug Chevalier/*The Washington Post*; p. 105, Library of Congress; p. 115, World Wide Photos; p. 125, Jacques E. Levy; p. 140, AP; p. 150, David Hutson/*The New York Times*; p. 154, Jack Kightlinger/White House.

Table of Contents

Preface

When President Ronald Reagan lifted the grain embargo that Jimmy Carter had imposed against the Soviet Union in retaliation for its invasion of Afghanistan, the farm community thought it had an ally in the White House. But the goodwill toward the new president proved to be short lived. When Reagan, later in 1981, unveiled his proposals for renewal of the four-year omnibus farm bill, it became clear that his administration wanted to end production controls and target prices, the very mechanisms that had helped to sustain the U.S. agricultural economy since New Deal days of the 1930s.

Farmers and their allies in Congress reacted with a vengeance and, with help from Nature, forced the administration to back away from its proposals. Huge price-depressing surpluses and legislative threats from Congress prompted the administration to initiate a temporary program far removed from its free-market policies. The 1982 Payment-in-Kind (PIK) program, a novel production-control method, enabled farmers to take no more than 50 percent of their cropland out of production in return for commodities equal to up to 95 percent of their per-acre crop production. Ronald Reagan, the enemy of price supports, wound up paying more to farmers not to grow crops than had any other president.

The costly PIK episode sharply illustrated the limits of national policy when it comes to the agricultural economy. The rise in surpluses, and the on-again, off-again capabilities of foreign markets to absorb these commodities, helped to bring into focus the farm community's growing vulnerability to world markets.

Nevertheless, the American farmer has continued to be the most productive in the world. The scientific and technological advances of the past century have dramatically increased farm output while lessening man-hour requirements. Agricultural research has produced highly productive, disease-resistant plant species. But the increase in crop yields has slowed its phenomenal climb so much that advanced technology perhaps has reached the "point of diminishing returns," according to an Agriculture Department official.

Some of the new technology, in addition, is proving to have its drawbacks. The modern development of chemical pesticides, while doubling crop yields, also has created pesticide-resistant insects and spread lethal compounds beyond the farm, killing wildlife, contaminating soil and water sources, and posing a serious threat to human health.

The most obvious victims of pesticide contamination are migrant workers, most often illegal aliens, who toil in the fields for substandard wages and living conditions. Their plight was closely tied up with controversial immigration-reform legislation that was reported "hanging by a thread" as Congress prepared to adjourn for the 1984 elections.

Another threat to the farming community was soil erosion. While a certain amount of soil inevitably is washed or blown away, losses have increased dramatically with deforestation and the stepped-up plowing of land to feed the world's growing population. The problem of balancing present human needs with the long-term prospects of food production continues to be a concern throughout the world.

Farm Policy: The Politics of Soil, Surpluses, and Subsidies examines these issues and others that continue to divide and concern farmers, exporters, national policymakers, and the millions who depend on American farmers for the food they eat every day.

Nancy A. Blanpied
August 1984

ix

Part I:

Agricultural Issues

Farm Policy's New Course

As planting season got under way in spring 1980, President Jimmy Carter's secretary of agriculture, Bob Bergland, announced the federal government saw no need to pay farmers to take a single acre of crop land out of production. What could not be sold at home could be shipped abroad to satisfy a seemingly insatiable world market that already was claiming one-third of this country's grain production.

Such optimism seemed like ancient history by the mid-1980s. Bumper crops in 1981 and 1982, falling demand, rising export competition, and the dollar's strength abroad left farmers and the government stocked with price-depressing surpluses.

Market prices for wheat, corn, and other important grains shrank by one-third between 1981 and 1982. Farm income nosedived along with prices, from $32.3 billion in 1979 to $22.1 billion in 1982, when income amounted to less than the interest payments on outstanding farm debt of $215 billion.

The magnitude of the farm problem forced the Reagan administration in the spring of 1983 to reach for a bold new program to cut production and boost prices. Bergland's successor at the Agriculture Department, John R. Block, offered for one year to pay farmers in surplus grain and cotton if they agreed to plant less. The program was dubbed Payment-in-Kind, or PIK for short. Farmers responded by with-

drawing a surprising 75.6 million acres from production for which they pocketed $9.8 billion in surplus commodities. Government surpluses plunged, and farm prices rose as much as $1 a bushel for corn. PIK's true impact on cutting production, however, was obscured by the summer drought that devastated crops across the Midwest.

The sharp decrease in surpluses helped pull net farm income for 1983 to a 12-year low estimated at $16 billion by the Agriculture Department. Adjusted for inflation, that was the lowest farm income total since 1933. Concern over a continued wheat glut caused the Agriculture Department to continue the wheat PIK program in 1984. But few farmers signed up because, they said, the financial incentives were too low.

The outlook in 1984 was that farmers would return to the land left idle the year before and reap a harvest that could rival the record-setting crop of 1982. The Agriculture Department's Economic Research Service projected net farm income to double to between $30 billion and $34 billion, based on improved prices, ample harvests, and continued benefits from federal programs. June 1984 floods in the Midwest, however, may cause analysts to reassess early optimistic projections. Damage was estimated at nearly $1 billion by the American Farm Bureau Federation.

Adding to the farmers' plight has been a reversal in the steadily upward rise in land values. The price of prime farm land is tumbling across the Midwest. As land values fall, so does the equity farmers need in order to borrow money for machinery, seeds, fertilizer, and chemicals. Hardest hit are the young farmers who borrowed heavily at high interest rates to get started during the 1970s farming boom.

The Department of Agriculture estimates that about 5 percent of the nation's farmers — about 120,000 farms — are in serious financial trouble. According to their figures, at least 50 percent of the nation's farmers are doing well, 25 percent are getting by, and 20 percent are hurting — leaving 5 percent on the edge of bankruptcy. In general, producers of meat animals are faring better than grain farmers.

A farmer who finds his line of credit at the local bank abruptly cut short may turn to the Farmers Home Administration (FmHA), the federally supported lender of last resort for about 12 percent of all farm operations. Even with below-market interest rates, more than a quarter of the agency's 271,000 loans in 1982 were overdue, up from just 12 percent in 1979. The Agriculture Department reports that 7,529 farmers went bankrupt in 1983, down 700 from the year before. The improvement came about largely because federal officials restructured loan payments for 65,022 farmers, up from 20,000 in 1982. While thousands of farmers have gone out of business, the number still is far below the Depression levels of the 1930s.

Federal Efforts to Reduce Crops

Fewer farmers succumb to hard times in the 1980s because price support and production control programs begun in the Depression era hold out a financial safety net. Government commodity loan programs guarantee farmers a minimum price for their crops while attempting to keep production in balance with demand. Production

controls, however, have a poor track record. A notable failure was Block's appeal to farmers to reduce 1982 wheat plantings 15 percent and other crops by 10 percent to avert back-to-back bumper crops and their disastrous effect on farm prices. Less than one-third of the farmers cut production. *(Farm commodity programs, p. 3)*

The remainder took their chances with the market, and lost. The 1982 crop produced a record harvest of 2.8 billion bushels of wheat, 8.4 billion bushels of corn, 2.3 billion bushels of soybeans, and 1.9 billion bushels of oats, barley, and sorghum. Even before the first bushel was harvested, one-half of the abundant 1981 wheat crop and one-quarter of the corn crop remained in storage.

As market prices sank in response to the glut, government loan and price supports soared. The 1981 bumper crop cost $11.9 billion in fiscal year 1982 in loans and price supports. Program outlays lag a year behind the harvest. The 1982 bumper crop cost far more — $18.8 billion in federal support in fiscal year 1983. Support costs dropped to an estimated $6.6 billion in fiscal 1984 as a result of the PIK program having been dropped, except for wheat producers, and the 1983 drought.

Many farmers trace their current difficulties to the Carter administration's embargo on grain sales to the Soviet Union, announced Jan. 4, 1980, in retaliation for the Soviet invasion of Afghanistan. The embargo was lifted by President Ronald Reagan the following year, but not before the U.S. portion of Soviet grain imports had dropped from 70 percent to 27 percent. However, American grain found other foreign markets. Export sales continued upward in 1980 despite the embargo, peaking at $43.3 billion in 1981 and dipping in 1983 to $36.1 billion. But the dependence on outside markets continued to be shaky.

Most analysts contend that worldwide recession in 1981-83 and a strengthened

Farm Commodity Programs

The Department of Agriculture is directed by Congress to support farm income through loans, target prices, subsidies, grain reserves, and production limits. Minimum prices are guaranteed for wheat, corn, barley, oats, rice, cotton, and dairy products.

Loans obtained from the Commodity Credit Corporation (CCC) are the chief market price-support mechanism. A farmer agrees to put a specified amount of his commodity in a government-approved storage facility in exchange for a loan, generally set well below the market level. At the end of the loan period, the farmer may repay the loan with interest and retain the commodity, or forfeit the commodity as payment for the loan. CCC loans are available for wheat, corn, sorghum, barley, oats, rice, cotton, rye, soybeans, peanuts, sugar, honey, and tobacco.

Target prices are set higher than loan rates and are intended as income supplements. Target price levels are calculated to reflect the national average cost of producing a crop. If the market price fails to reach the target price, farmers are entitled to collect a "deficiency payment." It represents the difference between the target price and the market price, or between the target price and the loan rate, whichever is smaller.

Subsidies are used to support dairy prices only. The government buys what dairy farmers cannot sell at a rate of $12.60 set in 1983 for each one hundred pounds of milk, cheese, and butter. There is no limit to the amount dairy farmers may sell to the government.

The *grain reserve* was introduced during the Carter administration as a way of storing food to offset crop failures in the United States or abroad. Farmers may have their grain stored for three years in exchange for a per bushel loan rate slightly higher than CCC commodity loans. In addition, the government pays the farmer an annual storage fee of 25.6 cents a bushel. If prices rise, farmers may take their grain out of reserve storage in less than three years by repaying the loan but with no loan penalty.

Production limits may be announced at the discretion of the secretary of agriculture. While compliance is voluntary, only those farmers who sign up are eligible for commodity loans or supports. In addition, the secretary of agriculture may offer farmers cash to take land out of production.

---

dollar account for the slip in farm exports. Others point to an additional factor—export subsidies offered by the European Common Market countries and a handful of others enabling their farmers to undercut American food prices in world markets.

Threat of Farm Trade War

American agriculture decries Common Market food export subsidies — amounting to an estimated $6 billion in 1982 — as unfair and is pressing Congress to retaliate with U.S. subsidies. A number of food export subsidy bills were before Congress in 1983, but no legislation made it out of the House Agriculture Committee. *(Export subsidy program, p. 96)*

Common Market representatives defended their export subsidy practices at a meeting in November 1982 of the 88 nations subscribing to the General Agreement on Tariffs and Trade (GATT), an international trade organization that oversees tariffs, subsidies and other aspects of trade among its members, including the United States. The Common Market contends its food export subsidies do not violate a GATT agreement — an agreement that permits such subsidies if they do not result in the takeover of traditional markets of other GATT nations. The United States claimed that Common Market wheat exporters violated that agreement. But a special GATT judicial panel announced in 1983 it could find no evidence to support the U.S. charge.

President Reagan preaches the gospel of free trade for all exports, but the administration has been giving out mixed signals on trade issues. In October 1982, the administration began to underwrite farm export sales with a $500 million "blended credit" program. It offers foreign food buyers loans with interest rates two percentage points below market rates. The lower rates are achieved by combining interest-free loans by the Agriculture Department's Commodity Credit Corporation with federally guaranteed commercial loans. In January 1983 Reagan announced the program would receive $1.25 billion more lending funds.

The same month the administration negotiated the sale of one million tons of subsidized flour to Egypt, long considered one of France's markets for farm goods. The government will give U.S. millers enough surplus wheat to reduce the net per ton price to the Egyptians by $100, bringing it below the prevailing U.S. price of $255 a ton. The net cost to the government was expected to be about $130 million. Agriculture Secretary Block said the deal showed, "We mean business when we talk about competing for export markets."

The Common Market argues it is no more guilty of unfair farm export subsidies than the United States. The main difference, said Ella Kruchoff, a spokeswoman for the European Community office in Washington, D.C., is "the U.S. government has a less transparent system of subsidies" than the Common Market. "Most congressmen are ignorant of the facts," she added. She pointed out that the Common Market is the American farmers' biggest export market. It bought $9 billion in agricultural products in 1981, primarily soybeans and feed grains, while the United States bought only $2 billion in European farm products that year.

PIK Program for Temporary Relief

The domestic version of PIK was the government's primary assault on price-depressing surpluses. It represented an about-face in the administration's farm policy. President Reagan came into office favoring less, not more, government regulation of farming. He sought unsuccessfully to eliminate from the 1981 farm bill the Agriculture Department's discretionary authority to control farm production.

Just two years later, Reagan stood before the American Farm Bureau Federation convention in Dallas on Jan. 11, 1983, and portrayed PIK, a novel production control program, as the farmer's road to salvation — though admittedly a temporary expedient. The program enabled wheat, corn, sor-

Agricultural Exports

	U.S. Farm Exports *(in billions)*	Percent of all U.S. Exports	Percent of World Farm Exports
1970*	$ 7.3	17	14.3
1975	21.9	21	18.1
1980	41.3	19	18.4
1981	43.3	18.9	19.5
1982	36.6	17.7	17.3
1983	36.1	18	N.A.

* calendar years

Source: U.S. Agriculture Department, Trade and Economics Division

ghum, rice, and upland cotton farmers to take up to 50 percent of their cropland out of production. *(PIK program, p. 15)*

To participate in the program, farmers were required to sign up for a previously announced acreage diversion ("set-aside") program in which they agreed not to plant 20 percent of their land. They had to do that to become eligible for federal commodity loans, better known as price supports, and direct cash payments.

For example, wheat farmers receive cash for 5 percent of the land they take out of production. Payment is based on average per acre yield, at $2.70 a bushel. Corn farmers receive cash on 10 percent of their diverted acreage, figured at a rate of $1.50 a bushel.

Under PIK, farmers could leave idle an additional 10 to 30 percent of their cropland. In return, wheat farmers received an amount of wheat equal to 95 percent of their average per acre production. This came from surplus U.S. stocks or the farmer's own prior crops, which were placed in government hands as collateral for loans he obtained. Farmers were permitted to store or sell the PIK crops.

Corn, sorghum, rice, and cotton farmers received an amount equal to 80 percent of the per acre production of those crops. Wheat farmers were offered the higher incentive — 95 percent — because the winter crop in states south of the Dakotas already was in the ground. Agriculture officials figured it would take a greater crop guarantee to entice winter wheat farmers to sign up since most of their investment was already committed.

"This plan is aimed at bringing supply more in line with demand, and strengthening farm income in the future," Reagan said in Dallas. "It makes our problem the solution." Block had estimated that PIK would take 23 million acres out of production but the actual amount far exceeded expectations. Farmers put 47.3 million acres under PIK and 28.3 million acres under the acreage diversion program. Together the 75.6 million acres represented nearly 43 percent of the farm land eligible for the two programs.

PIK and the drought substantially cut production from 1982 totals in all the affected crops except wheat. Wheat production dropped from a record 2.8 billion bushels in 1982 to 2.4 billion bushels 1983, still the nation's third largest harvest. Most wheat is harvested by early summer, before droughts can affect the crop. Corn production, however, fell from a record 8.4 billion bushels to 4.2 billion bushels; sorghum from 841 million bushels to 479 million bushels; rice from 154 million 100-pound sacks to 100 million; and cotton from 12 million bales to 7.8 million bales.

Between January 1983, when PIK was announced, and June 1984, farm commodity prices moved upward. Corn, for example, increased from $2.36 a bushel to $3.36. The continuing wheat surplus apparently had a negative impact on its price, which fell from $3.57 a bushel to $3.45 during the same period.

While farmers stood to benefit from PIK, it posed frightening prospects to agriculture-related businesses. Farmers did not just cut back on planting. They reduced purchases of seed, fertilizer, farm equipment, and storage bins. University of Missouri economist Abner Womack calculated the nationwide impact on farm supply manufacturers and dealers in 1983 added up to a loss of $4 billion.

Food Giveaways for U.S.

The administration argues that only drastic measures, such as PIK and increased exports, can reduce the American stockpile of surplus commodities. Domestic giveaway programs also can help. By law they were limited to dairy products prior to 1983, when Congress authorized distribution of rice, flour, corn meal, and honey.

The cheese and butter giveaway program that was begun in 1982 to aid the poor cost the government $287 million that year. In calendar year 1983, the Agriculture Department's Food and Nutrition Service, which provides funds and food for school breakfast and lunch programs and nonprofit groups, gave away more than $1 billion in surplus commodities, including 392 million pounds of processed cheese, 92 million pounds of cheddar cheese, 174 million pounds of butter, 45 million pounds of powdered milk, 25 million pounds of honey, 25 million pounds of corn meal, 15 million pounds of flour, and 14 million pounds of rice. With the exception of butter, the projected surplus giveaways in 1984 were greater.

Despite these donations, the government's stockpile of surplus dairy products remains considerable. In May 1984 the government owned 850 million pounds of cheese and 375 million pounds of butter and 1.4 billion pounds of powdered milk.

The high cost of processing and shipping limits food donations to the poor overseas, Secretary Block told the congressional Joint Economic Committee in January 1983. The federal government spent $557 million in fiscal 1983 for Food for Peace program donations abroad. Congress increased that amount to $770 million in fiscal 1984, including more than $100 million in African drought assistance. The fiscal 1985 budget projects $680 million in Food for Peace donations.

CARE (Cooperative for American Relief Everywhere) and other international aid agencies have lobbied Congress to make more surplus stocks available. CARE receives government grants to purchase the commodities it distributes overseas. In addition, the agency hopes to obtain surplus food to give away, sell, or barter. Richard Loudis, a CARE spokesman, said he was not impressed with official excuses for limiting the distribution of food surpluses. "It is the principal irony of our times that when America is drowning in overproduction, millions of people are starving," he said in an interview. *(UHT milk donations, p. 8)*

Government's Role

The independent family farm has long held a special place in American political thought. Thomas Jefferson expressed it this way in *Notes on the State of Virginia*: "Those who labor in the earth are the chosen people of God, if ever he had a chosen people, whose breasts he has made his peculiar deposit for substantial and genuine virtue." Similar thoughts continued to find expression throughout the following 200 years. The post-Revolutionary ordinances of 1785 and 1787 provided for the sale of public land for farming, opening up the upper Midwest — the Northwest Territory — to settlement.

President Lincoln rededicated the nation to a belief in the family farm when he signed the Homestead Act of 1862, starting the process that gradually transferred 147 million acres of frontier land to 1.6 million families. Each settler was allowed 160 acres of public land by paying a small filing fee and living on and working the land for at least five years.

Once the government opened the West to the farm family, it induced railroads to follow by giving them vast tracts of land. It also encouraged, under the Morrill Act of 1862, the states to establish land-grant colleges to teach agriculture and mechanical arts. They became the centers of agricultural research.

As late as 1910, one third of the people lived on small family farms. By 1980, 2.4 million farms remained, averaging 430 acres — nearly triple the size of 50 years earlier. Still, 95 percent of the farms in the mid-1980s could be called family farms.

Farms perished but farm production rose. Improvements in machinery, fertilizers, pesticides, and plant varieties increased per acre yields and reduced labor needs. In the early 1900s it took 106 hours of labor and seven acres to produce 100 bushels of wheat. By the 1980s it took only nine hours of labor and three acres. Similar advancements have been made with other crops.

Production efficiency gradually has narrowed the gap between farm and non-farm income. In the 1930s, farmers earned one-third to one-half the amount that non-farm workers did. In the 1960s, they were earning three-quarters as much. By 1979, the best year ever for American farmers, their income was on a par with urban workers'. Since then, farmers have lost ground.

Tradition of Depression-Era Aid

From the Agriculture Department's inception in 1862 until 1933, it functioned primarily as a booster of research and education through the land-grant colleges. The government let farmers and the free market system make production and pricing decisions.

That changed in the Depression. Between 1929 and 1932 farm prices dropped 56 percent; net agricultural income fell from $6.3 billion to $1.9 billion. Farmers were desperate for help, and the New Deal came forth with a program to prop up prices and control production. Franklin D. Roosevelt, echoing Jefferson, said: "The American farmer living on his own land remains our ideal of self-reliance and spiritual balance."

The new farm program, detailed in the Agricultural Adjustment Act signed into law May 12, 1933, aimed to control the supply of six basic crops: wheat, corn, cotton, rice, peanuts, and tobacco. The concept of "parity" was introduced in farm policy as a means of setting the first price support levels, and it has been at the center of farm policy debate ever since.

Parity is the relationship between the price of farm commodities and the cost of goods that the farmer buys. The base years initially used were 1910-14, a period of farm prosperity. One farmer explained the

The Milk of Human Kindness...

Doing well by doing good appeals mightily to members of Congress. But balance between the two occasionally eludes them. Consider a project to give a new milk product to starving, Third World babies. It has a fine ring to it. Who would deny America's agricultural abundance to the less fortunate overseas? As for doing well, the project gives the U.S. dairy industry a way to unload a product that isn't doing so well here at home.

The plan, a minor footnote that was included in the farm bill Congress passed April 3, 1984, sounded fine to almost everyone except a couple of liberal Democrats from the House Foreign Affairs Committee. The milk is very expensive, and that is what stuck in their throats. These Democrats worry that the high cost could tarnish all overseas aid programs, which have never enjoyed wide popularity in Congress. And, they say, the federal government is already sitting on a huge surplus of dry milk, which could be donated to poor nations a whole lot easier and more cheaply than the new milk.

The product, "ultra high temperature" (UHT) milk, is specially processed and packaged to last as long as six months without refrigeration. It is widely used in parts of Europe where refrigeration capacity is limited and fresh milk is of poor quality. Market statistics are sparse, but Agriculture Department and dairy industry officials say the UHT milk is not popular here — not yet, anyway. Just three U.S. plants — in Georgia, California, and Washington — have gone into UHT production, and at least one of these expensive facilities is said to be running far below capacity.

The UHT milk costs as much as $1 a gallon more than fresh milk and it was that price differential, plus the appearance of bailing out a faltering product, that bothered Peter H. Kostmayer, D-Penn., and Sam Gejdenson, D-Conn. The two attacked the project in a House-Senate conference on the farm bill — and the experience left them shaking their heads.

Gejdenson speaks as a parent of milk-guzzling kids and as a man who grew up on a dairy farm. He says the UHT milk was great for his children during a family vacation in Mexico. But the United States has a "15-minute milk supply" — meaning that families are rarely far from convenience stores, supermarkets and other outlets for cheaper, fresh cold milk. "I don't think there's a market out there. There's production capacity and no demand," he says.

concept this way: If a bushel of wheat in 1910 sold for enough to buy a pair of overalls, then wheat prices should have risen enough to make the same purchase today. That is what farmers call 100 percent of parity.

Parts of the 1933 farm bill were struck down by the Supreme Court. But another law, in 1938, expanded the program, extending loans to farmers to store surpluses and release them during lean years. By the time the United States entered World War II in 1941, the government had made $5.3 billion in direct payments under the program.

...A Dairy Industry Outlet?

"Sales are not as good as we originally thought," concedes Joseph Westwater, senior vice president for public affairs of Dairymen Inc., the Southeastern dairy cooperative that owns one of the UHT plants. But, Westwater added, it takes time to build a market for a new product.

Meanwhile, Westwater and sympathetic members of Congress thought to ship American UHT milk to the Third World, arguing that it would ease the risk of contamination posed when powdered milk is mixed with local water. Thus was born the pilot project, in which the industry would "sell" the federal government UHT milk in return for some of the powdered milk surplus that the government owns.

The UHT milk to be donated — 40,000 metric tons over two years — is "a good chunk" of U.S. UHT production, according to Westwater. But it is a mere drop in the bucket compared with the 7.5-million-ton dairy surplus U.S. dairymen produced in 1983. The initial program is pure charity, Westwater insists. He hopes it will broaden to develop markets in nations that could afford UHT, thus siphoning off some surplus U.S. production. "Remember," he says, "food stamps began as a pilot project."

But, as Kostmayer told conferees, the federal government already owns a whopping seven-year supply of surplus powdered dry milk that can do the same job as UHT for a lot less money. He told conferees that UHT shipping costs were 10 times those of powdered milk because of the bulk of the water that makes up 89 percent of fluid milk. And he repeatedly warned that the media would blow the high cost of UHT into a scandal that would damage other foreign aid programs.

These arguments did not cut much ice with Agriculture Committee members, who dominated the conference. When Kostmayer suggested reducing the pilot program by half, Rep. James M. Jeffords, R-Vt., gasped, "I just can't believe what I'm hearing — that you only want to save half as many people. . . ."

Kostmayer says he knew he would lose before he and his colleagues from Foreign Affairs waded into the farm bill conference. But he adds, he would be most unhappy if Agriculture Committee members "came charging in after" foreign aid programs.

As for doing well by doing good, the twin objectives "are compatible, feasible purposes in most cases" related to foreign food aid, Kostmayer says. "But not milk. Not this milk."

New Deal farm programs remained virtually intact long after the Depression ended. But they failed to keep surpluses in check. In 1953, for example, the government acquired 486 million bushels of wheat, 41 percent of the year's bumper crop. A year later Congress launched a new program to help absorb food surpluses. It passed Public Law 480 authorizing donations or low-interest loan sales to needy countries. By 1980, the government had put more than $30 billion into the program, $11.4 billion in donations and $19 billion in loans for food purchases.

But exporting food to the needy did not eliminate surpluses. The growing stores of commodities and food needs of poor Americans spotlighted by the Kennedy administration brought forth an experimental food stamp program for low-income families in 1961. People could use the stamps in stores to purchase certain kinds of food. The food stamp program became permanent in 1964 and remained relatively non-controversial until four years later with the publication of *Hunger, USA*. The report, compiled by an advocacy group called the Citizens' Board of Inquiry into Hunger and Malnutrition, stated that one-half of all households in the United States had poor diets and only one-fifth of those, about five million, were reached by food programs.

The political fallout from the report triggered rapid growth in food assistance programs, primarily food stamps. Those lobbying on behalf of the poor received a sympathetic hearing, and considerable publicity, as they appeared before the Senate Select Committee on Nutrition and Human Needs, under the chairmanship of George McGovern, D-S.D. Food stamp assistance rose from $250 million in 1969 to $11 billion in 1982. The program, however, has had negligible impact on depleting government-stored surpluses.

Cutting Surpluses

It was not charity at home or abroad that finally rescued farmers from chronic surpluses in the 1970s. It was the Soviet Union, which in 1972 negotiated the first of several massive grain purchases with the United States and set farm prices soaring. The deal ushered in a new era for American farmers.

Against this backdrop, Congress in 1973 passed an omnibus four-year farm bill that put an end to direct payments for taking acreage out of production and to guaranteed price supports. The mood at the

time was that farmers needed less government assistance. However, the "target price" system was created as a concession to those who argued that farmers needed protection in the unlikely event that market prices again fell below production costs.

That is what happened in 1976 when bumper crops in the Soviet Union and other grain-importing countries drastically cut demands for U.S. grains. American farmers were left with huge surpluses and depressed prices. The target price-support mechanism came into play for the first time. As a consequence, farmers collected $1.2 billion in support payments in 1977.

They besieged Congress with pleas for a return of more government support programs as the farm bill came up for four-year renewal in the 1977 session. Farmers counted on the newly elected president, a peanut farmer from Georgia, to give them a sympathetic hearing.

Jimmy Carter proved, however, to be more adversary than compatriot. He repeatedly threatened to veto any farm bill that exceeded spending levels he set — in the hope of achieving a balanced national budget by 1981. In the end, the president compromised and signed a farm bill that increased loan and target price levels beyond his wishes, created a farmer-held grain reserve and extended the secretary of agriculture's authority to mandate an acreage set-aside programs.

Farmers complained that the bill did not do enough, and the following winter the new, militant American Agriculture Movement staged public demonstrations, including a "tractorcade" into Washington, blocking city traffic with tractor parades. Carter's trouble with the farmers deepened when he reneged on a campaign promise never to use food as a diplomatic weapon and clamped an embargo on most grain shipments to the Soviet Union. Farm prices tumbled as a result and stayed low for months.

Inability to Curb Supports

Farmers, dismayed and angry, carried their grudge against the president to the ballot box in November 1980. Ronald Reagan, a man who told a farm audience he was not familiar with parity, carried the farm vote. Fulfilling his own campaign promise, he lifted the embargo scarcely more than three months after taking office, on April 24, 1981. By that time it was clear the Soviet Union had been able to satisfy most of its grain needs through other suppliers.

Some analysts contend that the embargo had a beneficial effect. U.S. exports became more widely dispersed and therefore less susceptible to the on-again, off-again demands of the Soviet market. Since the embargo was lifted, the Soviets have resumed purchasing large quantities of American wheat and other grains: 39.9 million tons in 1981-82 and 32.5 million tons in 1983-84.

Whatever good will Reagan earned in the Farm Belt by ending the embargo, it was quickly expended in the administration's farm bill. The farm programs were up for another four-year extension, beginning in September 1981. Secretary Block shocked the farm community with his major proposals: an end to production controls and the target prices, broad discretionary power to set commodity loan rates rather than fixing them in law, and drastic cuts in dairy subsidies.

In short, the administration wanted Congress to begin weaning farmers from government income supports and production controls. To underscore its commitment to limit farm spending, the administration persuaded Congress to place a ceiling on spending.

The spending level for the four-year farm bill, roughly $11 billion, had the desired effect of causing a breakdown of the usually harmonious relationships among farm commodity groups. Instead of joining

John R. Block

forces for mutual benefit, the traditional method of shaping farm legislation, lobbyists for grain, dairy, tobacco, sugar, peanut, and other commodities were openly fighting one another for their share of diminished agriculture expenditures. *(Farm lobby, p. 77)*

The final bill cleared Congress Dec. 16, 1981, by a two-vote margin in the House, reflecting the lingering resentment stirred by months of debate. The bill preserved and authorized gradual increases in loan and target price rates, although at lower levels than farmers wanted. It froze the dairy price support of $13.10 for every hundred pounds of unsold products rather than allowing it to rise as previously authorized to $14 on April 1, 1981. Ironically, an administration that tried to curb farm support spending settled for a farm bill that has allowed a stream of payments to expand into a torrent.

Changes were made in the dairy programs in 1983 when the price support level was reduced to $12.60 per hundred pounds. Also included in the legislation was a 15-

month paid diversion program, from Jan. 1, 1984 until March 31, 1985. Producers who participated by cutting production by 5 to 30 percent from their previous yields would be paid at a rate of $10 per hundred pounds.

With each new farm bill debate, members of Congress have a renewed opportunity to frame their actions in terms of preservation of the family farm. Yet many farm policy analysts argue that federal farm programs have had the opposite effect on the agricultural community.

When Bob Bergland was secretary of agriculture (1977-80), he launched a series of nationwide hearings on survival of the family farm — in the aftermath of the American Agriculture Movement's "tractorcade" to Washington. The results of those hearings and Agriculture Department studies were published in 1980 in a report entitled "A Time to Choose: Summary Report on the Structure of Agriculture." It suggested that federal farm policies had hastened the demise of small farms while encouraging larger operations.

This does not mean that farm ownership is concentrated in the hands of giant corporations. In fact, the study found that only 12 percent of all U.S. crop land was farmed by corporations. And nearly nine of every 10 of those corporations were family held. Clearly, families still are the primary force behind American agriculture, but there are fewer of them than ever, working larger farms than ever.

Farm economists point out that federally supported research has generated the new technology and plant hybrids that push farmers inexorably toward larger and larger operations. And commodity programs offer rewards by the bushel, thereby channeling more to those who are the largest. In 1980 roughly one-quarter of the farms, those with sales of over $40,000 a year, took in two-thirds of all government farm program payments.

Beyond Today's Farm Problems

After PIK, then what? The American Farm Bureau Federation contends that the administration's farm programs are a failure and need revision. Washington office spokesman Mike Durando said in an interview, "We see continued incentives to overproduce."

The grain glut and depressed prices have underscored for farmers the need to declare their independence from ineffective government programs, said Orlen Grunewald, an agricultural marketing economist at Kansas State University. "The agriculture policies we have today were put in place in the 1930s. Most farmers have come to realize that it needs to be changed," Grunewald said in an interview.

Soil Erosion and Water Scarcity

The commodity program is not the only farm problem that awaits solution. Soil erosion and water scarcity have worsened during a decade of all-out farm production. Some farm economists worry that the nation is depleting its soil and water resources to achieve short-term export gains.

Since President Roosevelt signed the Soil Conservation Act in 1935, the federal government has channeled $25 billion into conservation programs through the Soil Conservation Service. Erosion was thought to be under control until millions of acres of marginal land were returned to production in the 1970s. Cultivated land rose from a post-World War II low of 333 million acres in 1969 to 391 million acres in 1981. A hidden price paid for this expansion was a sharp increase in topsoil erosion.

A General Accounting Office survey in 1977, "To Protect Tomorrow's Food Supply, Soil Conservation Needs Priority Attention," reported that random visits to 283 farms in eight states revealed 84 percent were suffering from unacceptably high rates of soil erosion. An Agriculture Department study in 1980, "Appraisal 1980: Soil and Water Resources Conservation Act," estimated that soil erosion was a major problem on more than 20 percent of the nation's crop land.

Erosion is not being ignored. The 1981 farm bill authorized a number of new conservation measures. And the PIK program required farmers to plant their fallow crop land in an erosion-controlling ground cover such as clover or alfalfa. But great concern over poor soil conservation techniques remains. *(Soil erosion, p. 23)*

Water depletion is the big problem in western Texas, Oklahoma, Kansas, Nebraska, the Dakotas, and westward to the Pacific mountain ranges. In those states, 80 to 90 percent of the water is used for agriculture.

Irrigation, much of it provided by the federal government since passage of the 1902 Reclamation Act, has made arid land bloom with a steady flow of cheap water. It is estimated that 50 million acres receive irrigation water in 17 Western states. The government typically pays 80 to 90 percent of the cost of dams, canals, and other water projects. Since operating subsidies help keep water prices low, there has been little incentive for farmers to conserve.

Farmers who depend on irrigation can look to a future that offers less water at higher costs, and to more competition for available supplies. Based on present levels of use, almost every region west of the Mississippi has insufficient water from all sources for future agricultural production, according to the "Second National Water Assessment" published in 1978 by the U.S. Water Resources Council.

The biggest issue is competition from municipal and industrial users. While agriculture's demand for water is projected to rise only 6 percent by the year 2000, other uses are expected to increase demand by 81 percent.

World Challenge of Feeding Billions

The depletion of natural resources affects not just the American farmer. Worldwide degradation of land, forests, lakes, rivers, and oceans caused by rapid population growth portend a decline in living standards for millions of people, argues Lester R. Brown, president of Worldwatch Institute, an environmental-minded policy research organization in Washington, D.C.

Brown makes what might be called the ultimate Malthusian argument: the Earth's biological systems eventually will break down under constant abuse by too many people. Only war, famine, disease or some form of "moral restraint" could bring the population into equilibrium with the food supply, and then only at a bare subsistence level.

The wild card that Brown has not taken into consideration is the possibility of a second "Green Revolution" by creation of new kinds of plants through genetic engineering. The first Green Revolution blossomed in the 1960s, resulting from years of concentrated effort in traditional plant breeding. New strains of corn, wheat, and rice developed through cross-pollination produced stunning increases in yields when combined with chemical fertilizers. Newly developed pesticides and herbicides helped protect the hybrid crops from pests and weeds. *(Pesticide controversies, p. 65)*

The Green Revolution spread quickly where farmers could afford the agricultural chemicals and the soil was favorable. Many developing countries, however, had a difficult time affording the petroleum-based chemicals as costs soared along with world oil prices. Without fertilizer, the new grain varieties produced yields only slightly above the traditional varieties.

Some argue that the first Green Revolution merely delayed a collision between population and food supply. Despite its successes, food production in developing countries increased little in the past decade and actually declined in Africa. Genetic engineering holds the potential of picking up where traditional plant breeding left off. Scientists hope to create custom-made plants that thrive in poor soil without fertilizer. Although research is proceeding at a fast pace, scientists predict it will be years before genetic tinkering lives up to its advance billing. *(Agricultural research, p. 51)*

Meanwhile, as many as 100 million people are considered "desperately hungry," according to Harvard researcher Nick Eberstadt. The world produces enough to feed everyone, but it is not evenly distributed — primarily because of economic and political considerations.

Aside from distribution, Eberstadt writes, poor countries seem intent on taking the great leap into the industrial age while neglecting agriculture. As a result, India's cheap labor enables it to produce a ton of steel one-third cheaper than at Bethlehem Steel, while the cost of growing a ton of wheat is 40 percent more in India than in Kansas. Eberstadt's thoughts provide yet another reminder that American farm policy, like the American economy generally, affects and is affected by the global market place.

2

Payment-in-Kind Program

A deteriorating farm economy forced President Ronald Reagan to take a startling mid-term detour from his "free market" farm policy. In 1983 the administration paid U.S. farmers more, to stop growing crops on more land, than in 50 years of federal efforts to manage agricultural output.

Under the administration's Payment-in-Kind (PIK) program, farmers agreed to idle one in every three acres of cropland normally devoted to growing wheat, feed grains, cotton, and rice. In return they received cash payments and "in kind" bonuses of surplus stocks worth more than $9 billion.

The PIK program had two major goals: to shift financial responsibility from the federal government to farmers for a huge surplus of major crops and to curb further excess production. Agriculture Department (USDA) officials hoped to shrink the total supply of agricultural commodities and thereby push market prices up and costs of federal farm programs down. A major reason the administration went ahead with the PIK program was its fear that Congress would enact even stronger "crisis" farm legislation, boosting farm program spending and imposing stringent, mandatory controls on how much farmers could grow.

For an administration averse to such interventions, the PIK program was an extraordinary step. Top USDA officials, such

as Deputy Secretary Richard E. Lyng, acknowledged that when they took office in 1981 they hardly expected to preside over sweeping — if temporary — production curbs. Agriculture Secretary John R. Block deeply believed that all-out farm production for export markets was far better than federal programs to match supply with demand.

Block's objections were founded as much on the disappointing realities of acreage reduction programs as on philosophy. The programs tend not to make much dent in output because farmers usually retire their least productive land and intensify cultivation of the remainder. In 1982 nearly half the nation's wheat farmers entered a modest federal acreage-reduction program, and then produced the biggest wheat crop in U.S. history.

As late as June 1982, Block vowed that "We aren't going to be providing any encouragement to idle land or divert it from food crops. I hope we never again find ourselves in the position we were in during the early 1970s, when 62 million acres of farm land were out of production." But huge surpluses of major crops forced him to abandon that philosophy, at least temporarily. The glut was expensive evidence that American farmers were growing far more than the world could — or would — buy. *(Farm exports, p. 89)*

U.S. farm productivity had peaked in

two back-to-back bumper crop years, in 1981 and 1982. At the same time, international export markets stopped growing because of economic problems abroad. The productive capacity of American agriculture exceeded demand by about 10 percent overall. As one congressional aide remarked, "We've got 93 million acres of wheat production, and 60 to 70 million acres of market." With differing numbers, the same could be said of corn, cotton, and rice.

The Road to PIK

In 1982 American farmers brought in the largest combined crop of grain and oilseeds they had ever harvested — nearly 500 million metric tons. At the time, the nation's storage bins still held substantial, unused "carryover" stocks from the previous record harvest of 1981. One USDA official wryly observed that the surplus was so large that, in theory, American farmers could take a vacation the following year and the nation could still keep eating.

The surplus accumulated because global markets for American farm goods had weakened after a decade of booming growth in the 1970s. The volume of U.S. farm exports increased in that decade by more than 150 percent. Export market growth had become critical to the economic health of American agriculture. With the U.S. population growing at 1 percent or less annually, domestic demand was virtually fixed. Yet overall, the nation's agricultural productivity was growing by 2 percent or more each year between 1970 and 1980.

Foreign Markets

By the mid 1980s U.S. farmers depended on foreign customers for marketing about 60 percent of their wheat, 45 percent of their soybeans and rice, and more than half their cotton, according to USDA chief

economist William G. Lesher. For more than 10 years, U.S. farm policy and individual farmers' decisions to gear up production had been based on an assumption that the world would buy as much as the United States could grow.

But in 1982, for the first time in a decade, U.S. farm exports did not grow and instead declined in value to $36.6 billion, from a record 1981 level of $43.3 billion. The dropoff in exports was attributed to factors beyond the control of either farmers or Washington policymakers. Worldwide recession dramatically reduced the purchasing power of agriculture's foreign customers. Massive levels of debt, especially in middle- and lower-income countries, combined with interest rate increases forced these customers to devote more of their income to servicing their loans. The high level of outstanding debt also meant that there was less new credit to finance purchases.

The situation was aggravated by the high value of the U.S. dollar compared with other currencies. For instance, between 1980 and 1984 the value of the dollar increased by nearly 50 percent compared with the German mark. That meant that even though surplus conditions pushed prices of U.S. farm goods down to bargain-basement levels, these prices translated into high, uncompetitive levels in foreign currencies.

The Economic Research Service at USDA calculated that in 1982 and 1983 as much as $6 billion in foreign sales of agricultural products were lost because of the strength of the dollar. The direct loss to farmers was calculated at $2 billion.

Another problem was heated competition from other nations for agricultural markets. European Market countries and other nations aggressively pursued farm sales, using subsidies and similar measures to promote purchases of their products instead of those coming from America. Other

The Payment-in-Kind program was designed to eliminate grain surpluses.

factors weakening foreign demand were the lingering impact of President Jimmy Carter's partial embargo in 1980 on grain sales to the Soviet Union and credit problems of East European countries.

By 1982 these conditions had brought farmers to their third consecutive year of low farm income. The outlook was so gloomy that the Agriculture Department, to the consternation of farm-state members of Congress, simply stopped publishing its routine estimates of net farm income. By midyear the income estimate was said by congressional sources to have dropped as low as

$15 billion to $16 billion — below estimated federal spending on farm programs.

Not until September, when it could include some $4 billion in early federal payments to farmers, did USDA produce a farm income figure. When the final numbers were in, the 1982 net income figure showed a decline to $22.1 billion, from $30.1 billion in 1981. Adjusted for inflation, the $22 billion figure was the lowest since 1933. Nevertheless, as Congressional Research Service (CRS) analysts noted, income per farm was about three times higher than during the Depression years of 1930-

34. That was because there were far fewer farms than in the Depression. Even so, on a per-farm basis, net income had not dropped so low since 1959.

Members of Congress did not make such fine distinctions, however. Capitol Hill critics charged the administration with driving agriculture into 1930s-type financial disaster. Farmers' financial problems quickly pushed up the costs of their price support programs. Commodity program outlays went from $4 billion in fiscal 1981 — a figure not much higher than historical levels — to $11.9 billion in fiscal 1982 and an unprecedented $18.8 billion in fiscal 1983. The last figure did not include the cost of the PIK program; the outlay figures generally reflect conditions of the preceding crop year.

"Farm Crisis" Legislation

The painful combination of sinking farm income and soaring federal program costs produced a flurry of bailout bills in 1982. Most were considered little more than sympathy gestures. But support for one multi-part "farm crisis" measure was strong enough that the bill just missed winning approval of the House Agriculture Committee.

The crisis legislation was promoted by younger Democrats from Western farm states where production costs were high and farm economic problems the most pressing. The centerpiece of the bill was a series of national referendums for each major crop, empowering farmers to decide whether to adopt mandatory controls on planting. The bill, sponsored by Thomas A. Daschle, D-N.D., provided higher price supports if the mandatory controls were voted in and stiff penalties for noncompliance. The administration vehemently opposed the bill. Agriculture lobbyists divided on its merits.

In mid-June, after a day and a half debate, the House Agriculture Committee rejected the measure on a 21-21 tie vote. Positions of individual members signaled strong objections from cotton, soybean, and sugar growers. The latter feared that House opponents of the controversial sugar program would use the crisis bill as a vehicle to attack the program. The panel later reported a truncated version that did not receive further consideration.

However, congressional sympathy for the farmers' plight did not evaporate. An omnibus budget reconciliation measure passed in August 1982 required the secretary of agriculture to offer farmers payments for taking land out of production in 1983. That bill also boosted commodity loan rates to farmers.

As the magnitude of the 1982 crop — and its attendant program costs — came into focus during the fall months, USDA officials were under stiff pressure from the farm community to take further steps. There were equally strong pressures, from budget director David A. Stockman, against any further farm program expenditures. By mid-November, Block was talking privately with leading agricultural lobbyists in Washington about using the surplus commodities to entice farmers into taking more cropland out of production. On Dec. 9 Block formally proposed the PIK plan, asking Congress for legislation to clear two relatively minor roadblocks.

Block and other USDA officials insisted initially that the PIK program was without new expense because the stocks to be used were under the control of the federal government. The PIK payments were to be made with crops forfeited to the government when farmers decided not to pay the loans they secured and with crops still under loan.

Eventually, the book value of the stocks used for PIK payments was estimated at $9 billion to $12 billion. That was the amount of money the government had lent against the value of the crops — and would not recover. Whether the full amount could, in fact, have been recovered by selling off the crops (instead of using them in PIK) was open to question. Block and others also pointed out that money losses would be offset by savings in storage costs, among other things.

The PIK legislation passed the House but not the Senate, where objections of a few members, and animosity toward Agriculture Committee Chairman Jesse Helms, R-N.C., prevented floor action. Block had asked Congress to exempt the PIK commodity payments from a $50,000 limit on federal farm program payments to an individual farmer. He also wanted an exemption from mandatory limits on prices for which government-owned commodities could be sold. These changes, he believed, would protect PIK from lawsuits. There was little question that he had authority administratively to offer the program itself.

With the 1983 winter wheat already in the ground and spring planting of other crops fast approaching, Block felt compelled to go ahead with the program without waiting for Congress. He announced its terms Jan. 11, 1983.

Under the program, wheat, corn, and other feed grain, cotton, and rice farmers who had joined the previously announced acreage-reduction programs could also receive PIK payments for retiring an additional 10 to 30 percent of their land. Combined with other acreage retirements, that offered farmers a chance to take out as much as half their customary acreage. And individual farmers could even bid to take entire farms out of production in return for PIK payments. The PIK payments were to be made with crops that farmers used as collateral for federal price support or reserve loans, or stocks that had become federal property because of default by farmers on the loans. PIK payments would be made at harvest time but, to prevent immediate dumping of these crops, the pro-

gram also offered subsidies for short-term storage.

How PIK Worked

From the start, the PIK program was controversial. When the administration first revealed it late in 1982, critics predicted failure. As the program began operating, the difficult logistics of making some "in-kind" commodity payments provoked ridicule. By the end of 1983, angry members of Congress were inveighing against million-dollar PIK payments to large, individual corporate farms. A much less ambitious PIK program, for wheat only, was offered in 1984.

Still, farmers' initial response to PIK was dramatic. In March 1983 the Agriculture Department announced that farmers had signed agreements to idle 83 million acres. That was more than a third of the nation's 231 million base acres usually planted in wheat, cotton, feed grains, and rice. The USDA corrected that figure to 75.6 million acres, 57 million acres less than were idled in 1982. Of that total, farmers put 47.3 million acres out of production under PIK and an additional 28.3 million acres under the acreage diversion program.

When harvest-time dates for payment came, it developed that the government did not own enough surplus crops to meet its PIK commitments. For many farmers, payments were in the form of forgiveness of their price support loans. This effectively gave back to farmers full title to the crops used as collateral for the loans. But for some farmers the payment process was more convoluted. They were required, in effect, to grow wheat or cotton in 1983 to be put under loans, which were then forgiven. These farmers grew the crops which they received as payment for not growing more.

These maneuvers did not go unnoticed, and the program was ridiculed by numerous editorial writers and cartoonists. In one of his nationally syndicated columns, humorist Art Buchwald quoted a fictional farmer who said that, to pass the time away, he made daily checks to make sure no one had planted anything on his land. "Then I go down to the coffee shop and sit around with the other boys, talking about what great crops we didn't raise this year."

One skeptical Oklahoma farmer told the House Agriculture Committee in 1984 that he doubted there ever had been a surplus of cotton and wheat. "If we have such an oversupply of everything," he demanded, "how come you have to raise it, you know? Raise your PIK crops?"

The answer appeared to be miscalculation by the Agriculture Department. Early in 1983 USDA cleared out its inventory of surplus wheat with a subsidized sale to Egypt in which bonuses of government-owned wheat were used to sweeten the terms of the deal. Farmers who had retained control of their surplus wheat stocks in the loan programs could be paid by loan forgiveness, but participating farmers without such reserves were required to grow their own payments. In the case of cotton, one USDA official acknowledged later, "We goofed. Early on, we thought we had enough — and found that we didn't."

One dire prediction, that farmers would dump their PIK commodities on markets simultaneously and ruin prices, failed to come true. At the end of 1983, farmers appeared to be treating the PIK commodities as they would crops they had harvested — watching markets and spacing out sales.

Participation figures suggested that the PIK program was popular. Yet, when a devastating drought wiped out crops late in the summer, it was blamed in some regions for amplifying inequities among farmers. The worst drought in 50 years began in July 1983 and devastated corn, soybean, and other crops in at least 28 states across the Southeast, Midwest, and Southwest. Damage was estimated at about $7 billion.

Those in the program were comfortably cushioned because they had their PIK stocks to sell. Non-participants who lost their crops, however, had also lost their claims to federal disaster aid and other assistance. (The PIK payments were only part of a broad acreage reduction strategy; farmers were also paid in cash and in eligibility for federal farm programs.) Producers of livestock and dairy animals also complained bitterly that the combined impact of PIK and the drought had made feed too expensive.

Some participating farms reaped PIK payments worth a million dollars or more. Because compensation for idling crop land was made in the form of surplus crops, USDA lawyers had decided that these "payments" were exempt from a $50,000 statutory limit on cash program payments to farmers. But this interpretation, and the very large PIK payments it permitted, were called into question in Congress.

USDA economist Lesher and others defended the large payments, saying that they were necessary to ensure participation of larger farms. Without such participation, they argued, there would have been little real reduction in output. But in the 1984 wheat PIK program, the payment limitation was back in place.

Aftermath

Block never promised that the PIK program would dramatically and quickly alleviate farmers' financial problems. When he described the plan to members of Congress in December 1983, Block said its major benefit would be to ensure the economic recovery of agriculture two or three years hence, by eliminating the surpluses that "hang over the market like the dark clouds of a summer thunderstorm."

The precise effect of PIK on farm markets could not be quantified because the

1983 drought caused extensive crop damage. This natural "production cut" greatly amplified whatever impact the PIK program may have had. For instance, corn production was cut in half and carryover stocks — those left over at the end of the year — were reduced by about four-fifths, compared with the previous year.

The short supplies abruptly hiked market prices. In mid-September, according to USDA, the farm price of corn was up more than 50 percent, compared with September 1982. Soybeans were up more than 60 percent, cotton prices were up about 15 percent. Wheat did not show such results because because the winter wheat crop for the year was already established when the PIK announcement was made in January, and it was harvested before drought began the following July.

The PIK program appeared to put the United States at a disadvantage in world markets. In October 1983 Block told a congressional committee that the large production cuts at home had stimulated extra production by nations that compete with the United States in agriculture. "While U.S. grain production for 1983-84 is expected to be down by 129 million tons, foreign production is expected to rise by 43 million tons to a new record," Block said.

The program may have had another unintended, negative effect, according to CRS analysts. They pointed out that for more than a decade U.S. farm policies generally had been moving away from protectionist interventions in the agricultural economy, toward a more "market-oriented" approach. But PIK, these analysts suggested, sent American farmers a strong signal that if the realities of the marketplace became too harsh, they could count on the federal government for a bailout.

Nevertheless, critics of the administration's farm policies conceded that PIK helped an unknown number of farmers survive another financially difficult year. They also said that, without it, surplus stocks would have been much larger. But these critics, in Congress and elsewhere, also declared that the conditions leading to PIK — surplus production for sluggish markets — discredited the administration's free-market agricultural philosophy.

Despite their use of PIK, Reagan administration officials renewed their pitch in 1984 for agricultural policies that would reduce federal interventions and leave farmers more at the mercy of market forces. Their opponents, however, insisted that Washington go in the opposite direction and manage agricultural production more directly. Both sides expected these two opposing policies to be at the center of congressional debate in 1985 on four-year, omnibus farm legislation.

3

Soil Erosion: Threat to Food Supply

A list of the most pressing problems confronting modern civilization certainly would include the threat of nuclear war, worsening air and water pollution, over-population in Africa, Asia and Latin America, and the depletion of worldwide supplies of fossil fuels. Agriculture experts add another candidate to that list: the potentially catastrophic consequences of soil erosion.

"[T]he loss of soil is in some ways the most serious of the threats civilization faces...," wrote Lester R. Brown in *Building a Sustainable Society*. "[T]here are no widely usable substitutes for soil in food production. Civilization can survive the exhaustion of oil reserves, but not the continuing wholesale loss of topsoil." Brown, a former administrator of the International Agricultural Development Service in the U.S. Department of Agriculture (USDA), is president of Worldwatch Institute, a non-profit research organization that focuses on natural resources and environmental threats to food production.

"Soil erosion is absolutely a tragedy of mounting proportions in some of the developing world," said R. Neil Sampson, executive vice president of the National Association of Conservation Districts. In the United States, he added, "The soil erosion rates are pretty alarming. There's no amount of rationalization to make them go away. They are pretty serious."

Erosion — the wearing away of earth

— occurs whenever rain and wind come into contact with soil. Some erosion therefore occurs naturally on all types of land. But agricultural practices that take little account of erosion control add greatly to the natural loss of soil throughout the world. *(Types of erosion, p. 27)*

Agricultural scientists say that land with deep topsoil can lose as much as five tons an acre each year and land with thin layers of topsoil as much as three tons an acre annually without adversely affecting crop production potential. But on some 141 million acres of U.S. cropland — about 34 percent of the total — annual erosion averages more than five tons an acre, according to data compiled by the Agriculture Department.

In the "Corn Belt" states of Iowa, Missouri, Illinois, Indiana, and Ohio, soil erosion averages twice that of any other region. Cropland erosion also is particularly serious in Hawaii, western Texas and eastern New Mexico, the Palouse Basin of eastern Washington and the western border of the Idaho panhandle, east-central Texas' Blackland Prairie, and the southern Mississippi Valley Delta.

Altogether, some two billion tons of soil wash away from U.S. croplands each year. Three billion tons of soil vanish from range land, forests and pastures. The yearly erosion from all lands adds up to more than the amount washed away during the "Dust

Bowl" years of the 1930s. What is lost cannot easily be regained. "It takes nature more than 100 years to produce a single inch of topsoil," said William L. Armstrong, R-Colo., in a Senate speech Nov. 18, 1983, "but that inch of soil can blow away in less than an hour if not protected against erosion."

As bleak as the erosion problem is in the United States, the situation in many other parts of the world — especially in developing nations — is exceedingly more serious. The problems of soil conservation in the Third World "are much worse and the difficulties of applying the solutions are much greater" than in the United States, wrote Norman W. Hudson in a journal article. Hudson is vice president of the World Association of Soil and Water Conservation and professor of field engineering at the National College of Agricultural Engineering in Bedford, England.

Although there are no reliable statistics measuring the extent of soil erosion around the world, extremely serious problems exist in Australia, China, Ethiopia, Haiti, India, Indonesia, Nepal, Pakistan, South Africa, the Soviet Union and Zimbabwe. Most soil scientists agree with Lester Brown's assessment that erosion has become epidemic around the world.

A 1977 survey undertaken by the United Nations Conference on Desertification estimated that excessive erosion exists on about one-fifth of the world's cropland. Other experts, including Brown, say that the problem is much worse. "Close to half the world's cropland is losing topsoil at a debilitating rate," Brown said in a Worldwatch Institute study.

A 1980 report commissioned by President Jimmy Carter to assess international environmental problems categorized erosion and other soil deterioration as "perhaps the most serious environmental development" facing the world. The report, prepared by the Council on Environmental Quality and the U.S. State Department, predicted that soil losses from erosion "can be expected to accelerate, especially in North and Central Africa, the humid and high-altitude portions of Latin America and much of South Asia."

This large-scale loss of soil causes two basic environmental problems. First, the washing away of the most fertile topsoil makes eroded cropland much less productive. The soil is unable to supply plants with nutrients; its capacity to retain water is diminished. In short, as another government report put it, "crop production suffers as erosion progresses."

Second, billions of tons of soil — along with residues from chemical fertilizers and pesticides — wash into the world's waterways, lakes and reservoirs, restricting water flow, increasing flood damage, reducing water quality and damaging fish and wildlife habitats.

Experts say that overpopulation and the resultant increased demand for food greatly exacerbate the soil erosion problems around the world. "It's the basic demand pressures pushing farmers into doing things they would not otherwise do," Brown said.

In the United States the pressure to produce more grain to meet demand and mortgage payments has prompted farmers to plow up marginal grass and pasture lands. Brown estimated that the world demand for grain doubled between 1950 and 1973 and could possibly double again by the end of the century.

In developing coutries, the demand for food output has forced farmers "to farm more intensively in some situations where the land doesn't hold up very well under more intensive cultivation," Brown said. More farmers have been "pushed up the hillsides, particularly in much of the Third World. And so a lot of the steeply sloping land is being farmed, and when you see it plowed, you know 15 years from now there won't be any agriculture there."

It is thought that the Soviet Union, which has the most cropland of any country, may also be losing the most topsoil. Again, the cause is the push to expand production — in the Soviet Union's case to grow enough grain for self-sufficiency. Brown blamed the Soviet erosion problem on the government's high grain production quotas. "In trying to meet a production quota you don't want to worry about spending your time and energy building terraces and developing [crop] rotations and whatever else is needed" to fight erosion, he said.

Damage From Deforestation

Adding significantly to erosion problems around the world are two closely related environmental phenomena: deforestation and desertification.

Trees and forests are among nature's most powerful anchors, holding the soil in place. When they are absent there is little to prevent wind and rain from playing freely with the soil and, in the world's arid places, turning the land into desert.

Growing demand for food, fuel and housing — especially in Third World countries — is leading to widespread deforestation. "In a tremendous number of poor countries you have this problem of tree cutting for houses or firewood," said Nicholas Raymond, external relations director for the United Nations Food and Agriculture Organization (FAO). "Since forests are the main block against soil erosion — especially water, but also wind — if you cut down the woods, you're in a mess."

Although accurate statistics are impossible to pin down, the FAO estimates that some 18.5 million acres of closed forest and 9.4 million acres of open tree formations are cleared annually, mainly to extend croplands and supply firewood. Because newly plowed former forest lands generally are marginal and unsuitable for cultivation, however, serious soil erosion often occurs, as

Runoff from spring rains

it has throughout Central America and large portions of Africa, northern India, Thailand, the Philippines, Nepal, Haiti, Brazil, Chile, Venezuela, the Peruvian and Colombian Andes and West Java in Indonesia.

"The situation in West Java is bad," said Emil Alim in a quarterly publication of of the London-based International Planned Parenthood Federation. Alim, Indonesia's minister of state for development supervision and the environment, explained that "It has no plantation history and as long ago as 1918 it was called the 'Dying Land.' To a visitor [today] it looks like the surface of the moon. Nothing can grow."

In Haiti, Nicholas Raymond said, "where you have steep slopes and heavy rains, the people have gone up and cut the trees and tried to plow. When the rains came, the soil went away. And when the soil goes away, it doesn't come back. . . . You can look at any local painting made of Haiti and see those grey, barren hills all over the place. Those used to be covered with forests. It's a disaster down there."

In Ethiopia erosion caused by deforestation and overgrazing — in combination with a lengthy drought — has led to greatly diminished food production and food shortages. Moreover, a guerrilla war in the early 1980s disrupted food supply lines and forced thousands of persons to leave their homelands. Experts believe that as many as 4.5 million Ethiopians — about 14 percent of the population — were facing malnutrition and starvation in 1984.

At one time forests covered nearly all of Ethiopia's mountainous highlands, where more than 70 percent of the nation's population lives. But by the 1960s, according to a report by the United Nations Environmental Program, forest cover had been reduced to some 20 percent. Twenty years later only 3.1 percent of the mountainous land was covered by trees. This drastic depletion of forest cover, along with overgrazing, has led to severe soil erosion. "Enough topsoil has been lost that Ethiopia may never get the food situation straightened out during our lifetimes," said Lester Brown.

Fast-Growing Desertification

Desertification — the spread of deserts and desertlike ecological conditions onto formerly arable land — destroys both vegetation and fertile soil. Once desertification occurs, crops cannot grow on the land until it is somehow reclaimed. Restoration of such land can take years to accomplish and is extremely costly. Some 11.58 million square miles — about 20 percent of the Earth's land surface — is threatened by desertification, according to Jon Tinker, director of the environmental group Earthscan.

Desertification, evident throughout the world, is a serious problem in Africa, the Middle East, Iran, Afghanistan and northwestern India. In the United States, overgrazing of sheep is contributing to desertification on the Navajo Indian reservation in northern Arizona and New Mexico.

Overgrazing, overcultivation and deforestation — all of which stem from overpopulation — are the primary causes of desertification. "With population growth, agricultural people — people who don't know how to do anything else — are going to start moving farther and farther from good, traditional agricultural land onto marginal land," said Nicholas Raymond of the FAO. "Then two things happen. They cause erosion, and when the whole thing breaks down, that adds to the number of people who go hungry."

By far the world's worst case of desertification is in the eight African countries of the Sahel: Chad, Niger, Mali, Upper Volta, Mauritania, Senegal, Gambia and Cape Verde. Desertification in this belt of land, which is situated directly below the Sahara Desert, was one of the causes of a devastating famine that killed hundreds of thousands of Africans in the region in the early 1970s. Only a monumental international relief effort and the return of rains in 1974 eased the suffering.

The same conditions that caused the famine in the early 1970s — a drought, the destruction of vegetative cover, wind erosion on cultivated fields and high population growth — once again are causing severe food shortages in most of the Sahel. Sen. John C. Danforth, R-Mo., returning from a fact-finding tour of the region, described what he saw in Senegal in a *Washington Post* interview. "One drives for miles through a land with no ground cover and scattered scrub trees to the dust-shrouded village of Mafré. No rain has fallen for more than a year. No crop has been produced. Once the villagers owned 300 head of cattle. Now they own six. Of 40 families that lived in Mafré several years ago, only five remain."

Erosion in America

In the United States erosion has been a problem since colonial times. But only a few perceptive soil conservationists and scientific farmers recognized its potential seriousness and sought to control it. Among them were George Washington and Thomas Jefferson. Washington "fought erosion with ... zeal," wrote agricultural historian Edward Jerome Dies in *Titan of the Soil.* "Each year the rains would wash topsoil down into his 'Muddy Hole' farm, and each year he would haul it back to its proper place. . . ."

Jefferson, Dies said, "noted that rainstorms washed both crops and soils down the hillsides of many farms. He attacked the problem and at length introduced horizontal or terraced plowing. Marked benefits resulted."

But few farmers adopted these erosion control methods. One reason was the availability of vast new areas of land. As Dies put it: "Planters simply opened new acreage when the soil of old fields was exhausted, for as Thomas Jefferson observed, it was cheaper to buy a new acre than to fertilize an old one."

One area that appeared to be closed to farming was the Great Plains, a stretch of land that lies between the 100th Meridian and the Rocky Mountains. Atlases published between 1820 and 1850 showed this region as "The Great American Desert," and it was thought at the time that no farm economy could be sustained on these seemingly desolate lands.

Attitudes toward the "Great Desert" changed drastically in the following decades. The new transcontinental railroad companies, land speculators and civic boosters who advertised the region as heaven on earth and the prospect of free land provided

Types of Erosion

Soil erosion is caused by wind and water. Wind erosion occurs when the wind is strong enough to lift particles of unprotected, dry soil into the air. The Great Plains and Western states are most susceptible to wind erosion.

There are four basic types of water erosion; the first two are the most damaging:

● **Sheet erosion** — the removal of a fairly uniform layer of soil from the land surface by the action of rainfall and surface runoff.

● **Rill erosion** — the formation of numerous small channels that occurs primarily on recently cultivated soil.

● **Gully erosion** — an advanced state of rill erosion in which water accumulates in channels and washes away soil to depths ranging from one to two feet to as much as 75 to 100 feet.

● **Streambed erosion** — the widening of streams.

by the Homestead Act of 1862 lured thousands of pioneers to the plains.

Settlement of the plains coincided with development of agricultural equipment — particularly the steel plow in 1839 — which allowed the homesteaders to farm the hard prairie sod. But the plains had comparatively little water even in the best of times, and the periods of drought that beset the region roughly every 20 years from the time the homesteaders arrived drove many of them away.

But by then the damage to the soil had been done. Winds blew the loosened particles away and the rains, when they finally came, washed away more soil.

The farmers persisted, however, slowly turning the land into what would become the world's breadbasket. In the second decade of the 20th century, drought-induced scarcities, together with the food demands of World War I, drove farm prices up, prompting farmers to plow up pasture land to grow more grain. When farm prices fell after the war, farmers returned many of their wheat fields to grazing land.

In the early 1930s, the nation experienced a sustained drought. The damage done by cultivating the former grasslands in the prairie states was compounded by the lack of rain. Beginning in 1934 a series of devastating dust storms smothered crops, buried buildings, destroyed pasture land and forced many farmers to leave their land.

May 1934 brought some of the worst storms to the Great Plains, particularly in western Kansas, Texas, Oklahoma and eastern Colorado. Hugh H. Bennett, the pioneering soil scientist and the first head of the USDA's Soil Conservation Service, described the May 12, 1934, storm as "a disturbance that was completely without precedent in American history." The dust lifted from the prairies, "darkened the sun over the nation's capital, sifted through the screens of tall office buildings in New York City and moved on for hundreds of miles over the Atlantic Ocean," wrote Bennett in *Soil Conservation*.

A presidential commission, directed in 1934 to assess the erosion problem, reported that some 35 million acres of former farm land had been destroyed by gullying and that nearly 140 million acres had been stripped of much of its topsoil. Severe damage occurred not only in the Great Plains but in many parts of the South and Far West as well. The storms and the farmers they forced onto the relief rolls focused national attention on soil conservation for the first time and influenced Congress to institute the first federal erosion control programs.

Federal Commitment

In 1933 Congress took two steps to curb erosion. The first was the creation of the Civilian Conservation Corps (CCC) intended to put jobless men — some of them farmers forced off the land by the dust storms they helped to create — back to work on conservation projects throughout the United States. In its first year, the CCC built 420,000 erosion control dams, planted 100,000 acres of trees and put up 4,000 miles of fence.

The second was creation of the Soil Erosion Service within the Department of the Interior. Using CCC workers, the Soil Erosion Service set up dozens of erosion-control demonstration projects.

After the dust storms of 1934 the federal government undertook a greater commitment to soil conservation and erosion control. On March 25, 1935, the Soil Conservation Service (SCS) was established as a permanent agency within the Department of Agriculture. Its first director was Hugh Bennett, who had run the Soil Erosion Service and worked to bring the problems of erosion to the attention of the government and the American people.

Since 1937 the SCS has worked directly with farmers through soil conservation agencies set up by individual states and local conservation districts. The first local district was set up in August 1937 in Anson County, N.C., Bennett's home. By 1984, according to the National Association of Conservation Districts, there were 2,950 districts covering virtually the entire country.

Most observers agree that this new federal-state-local cooperation made significant progress in controlling soil erosion. "[T]he national goal of soil and water con-

Dust storm, Cimarron County, Oklahoma, 1936

servation was translated into local action programs designed to fit local conditions and guided by locally elected leaders," Neil Sampson wrote in *Farmland or Wasteland.* "Through conservation districts, the SCS could bring a national research and testing effort and the knowledge of skilled technicians to the farmers of America. . . . The federal agent did not have any authority over the landowner; the district provided a local agency to establish a cooperative, voluntary arrangement."

With SCS advice and the help of federal loans and subsidies, many farmers began using conservation and erosion-control methods. Marginal lands were left unplowed and used for pasture. Farmers practiced crop rotation, planting corn or wheat one year followed by cover crops such as hay, grass or soybeans. Fields were plowed in contours rather than straight rows to cut down on rain-induced erosion. Artificial terraces were bulldozed into place on erosive slopes. Fences were built and tree rows planted to ward off wind-borne erosion.

Stepped-Up Production

Progress in the fight against erosion continued until the early 1970s when a new surge in demand led many farmers to sacrifice control measures in their quest to increase production. Three factors contributed to the heightened production. First, crop failures in many parts of the world increased demand for U.S. grains. Second, the dollar was weak compared with other currencies and so American grain was cheaper to import. Third, the Nixon administration in 1972 signed an agreement that sent $1.1 billion worth of U.S.-grown grain to the Soviet Union.

The federal government encouraged the increased production; Agriculture Secretary Earl Butz called on the nation's farmers to plant "fencerow to fencerow." And in 1973 Congress passed a farm bill designed to spur farmers on to higher productivity. Blessed with good weather and ample rain, farmers produced bumper crops. In the process of increasing produc-

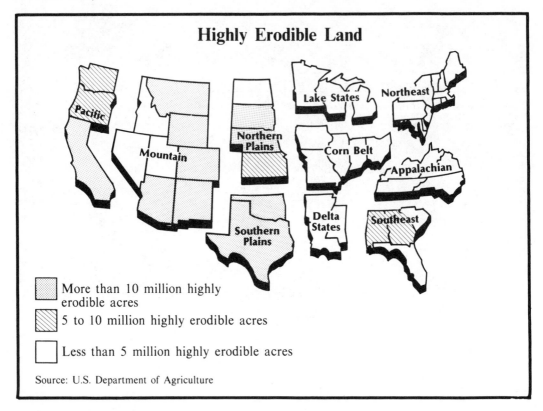

Highly Erodible Land

☐ More than 10 million highly erodible acres

☐ 5 to 10 million highly erodible acres

☐ Less than 5 million highly erodible acres

Source: U.S. Department of Agriculture

---

tion, they also abandoned many longstanding soil conservation practices.

"In the all-out push for production we began to lose some of the old soil conservation practices," said Norman Berg, the former Soil Conservation Service head who now represents the Soil Conservation Society of America in Washington, D.C. By the late 1970s, Neil Sampson said, "We found ourselves ... with a very specialized, very intensive agriculture that had abandoned the age-old techniques for controlling soil damage, such as crop rotations.... Suddenly we were out there with huge new tractors farming land that was a great deal steeper or sandier or rougher just because we had the power and the mobility and the ability and technology to do it."

Even falling farm prices do not necessarily mean that farmers will take some

land out of production. They are just as likely to till even more land in an effort to pay their often staggering production bills and keep their income levels stable. That is what happened after 1976 when bumper crops in the Soviet Union and elsewhere cut demand for American grain and left farmers with huge surpluses and depressed prices.

The amount of U.S. farm land under cultivation in this country hit a post-World War II low of 333 million acres in 1969. But the number of acres under cultivation began rising steadily in 1972 and stood at some 413 million acres by 1984.

Some of that newly plowed land, which had been used for grazing, is highly susceptible to erosion. Soil scientists estimate that about 10 percent of the land under cultivation in this country — about 40 million acres — is subject to average annual erosion rates of from 10-30 tons per acre. Moreover, experts say, about 250 million acres of fragile lands may be plowed in the near future. *(Map, p. 30)*

The federal system of economic incentives designed to allow farmers to make profits while keeping consumer food costs low also had an unintentional effect on the erosion problem. Price supports and other federal farm programs encourage "land speculators to buy and plow up rangelands that should be left alone," said Armstrong on the floor of the Senate.

In some cases, Armstrong noted, the value of land doubles "by the very act of plowing," no matter how potentially erodible the land is. "So when a farmer, an investor, or a speculator can plow such lands with a very limited economic risk to himself, he has a powerful incentive to plow.... If the crop should grow, price supports will roughly cover the cost of production. If not, the farmer can get crop insurance, even disaster payments under some circumstances...."

In Montana, for example, the Soil Conservation Service estimates that between 750,000 and two million acres of range land have been plowed in the last 10 years. At least 250,000 acres of Montana grazing land was plowed out in 1983 alone, according to SCS estimates. "Most of that land is considered highly erodible," said Bill Laycock, a range management specialist with the USDA's Agricultural Research Service in Fort Collins, Colo. "It's grazing land that had never been plowed before."

Traditional plow, left, turns over soil, exposing it to wind, water erosion. Conservation tillage, right, disturbs less earth, leaves crop residue to retain moisture, slow erosion.

Financial pressures often compound the difficulty of rectifying the soil erosion problem. A great many farmers' "options are reduced on the way they use their land" because of pressing financial problems, commented SCS soil scientist Don McCormack. "They have to use it pretty intensively and therefore risk soil erosion in order to make their commitments for the annual production costs, plus any investments they have in land."

The array of federal farm programs can become the deciding factor when such farmers opt to put marginal lands under the plow. "Under such circumstances," Sen. Armstrong said, "a farmer or rancher trying desperately to eke out a living under what are already difficult conditions may be led to conclude he should plow fragile lands even when his best instincts warn against such a move."

On Nov. 18, 1983, the Senate passed a bill sponsored by Armstrong that would prohibit the payment of some government incentives to farmers who plowed up highly erodible land. The measure, informally referred to as the "sodbuster" bill, was endorsed by a long list of farm organizations and conservationist groups — two sectors that do not usually agree on farm policies and programs.

A companion measure, introduced in the House by Ed Jones, D-Tenn., combines the sodbuster plan with much broader financial incentives to get erosion-prone land out of crop production on a long-term basis. The legislation, approved by the House on May 8, 1984, makes farmers who plow fragile land ineligible for farm aid, including federal price support programs, federally subsidized crop insurance, Farmers Home Administration loans and disaster payments.

A compromise version between the two bills sought by the Reagan administration was considered likely to be approved by Congress in 1984.

Search for Solution

Solving the world's erosion problems is going to be, at best, an extremely difficult task. Some fear it may be impossible, especially in some of the Third World countries. But there are some encouraging signs. In the United States new techniques of tilling that reduce erosion are gaining popularity. The moldboard plow that made it possible to bust the sod is giving way, if slowly, to conservation tillage systems that in some cases barely disturb the soil.

There are many types of conservation tillage systems — also known as plowless farming, reduced-tillage, no-till, and eco-till, among other terms. These methods have three things in common: They do not use the moldboard plow; they leave some residue on the soil surface to fight erosion and help retain moisture; and they depend primarily on herbicides for weed control.

The traditional moldboard plow has a series of curved plates that dig into the soil, lift it and turn it over. Disks and harrows are then dragged over the plowed soil to break up clumps of sod. Once seed is planted, a farmer may repeatedly run a cultivator between the rows to destroy weeds. Even on fields that are contour-plowed or otherwise treated to reduce erosion, the exposure of land to wind and rain can still result in high levels of erosion.

The invention of the chisel plow, described by an Office of Technology Assessment (OTA) report as "the primary tool of conservation," has reduced reliance on the traditional tilling methods. Chisel plows typically expose only enough soil to plant each row, leaving crop residue on the surface. This helps the soil retain moisture and thus reduces soil runoff and wind erosion.

Chisel plowing and other types of conservation tillage systems disturb the soil less than conventional tillage methods do, but the amount of disturbance varies widely. Some tillage techniques churn up as much

Soybeans planted in "no-till" wheat straw

as 95 percent of the ground, while no-till planters seed new crops directly into existing crop residues with minimal disruption of the soil.

One of the newest types of conservation tillage, called slit planting, has been developed by soil scientist Charles Elkins of the USDA's Soil and Water Research unit. This method uses blades that cut slits 15 inches deep and only one-sixteenth of an inch wide at the base, into which the seeds are dropped. Slit planting leaves topsoil and crop residues in place and at the same time penetrates the hardpan beneath the topsoil allowing better root development.

Successful tests of this method on soybeans, sunflowers, okra and peanuts have encouraged USDA soil scientists to try to develop a farm implement that could make large-scale slit planting practical.

Soil scientists continue to develop and refine tilling technologies that cut back on erosion and still give farmers high crop yields. "Too often tillage systems are combinations of operations applied in a broad manner without regard for all the needs of the plant or for conservation," said agricultural engineer Robert L. Schafer, director of the USDA's National Tillage Machinery Laboratory in Auburn, Ala. "Future tillage systems must be much more specific than present systems. Specific crops, soil types and environments must receive their own special treatment."

PIK and Erosion

Under the 1983 Payment-in-Kind (PIK) program, the U.S. Department of Agriculture allowed wheat, corn, sorghum and rice farmers to take up to 50 percent of their cropland out of production and receive surplus government crops in return. The idea was to cut back on federal farm program outlays and help stabilize farm prices. Although it was not designed as a conservation measure, the PIK program required farmers to plant clover or alfalfa on the idle acreage to cut down on erosion.

Peter Myers, head of the USDA's Soil Conservation Service, and Everett Rank, head of the agency's Agricultural Stabilization and Conservation Service, in March 1983 estimated "soil savings at around three tons per acre, for a total in excess of 240 million tons of soil which may be kept on farms as a result of the PIK program in 1983."

However, a preliminary USDA report issued in February 1984, estimated that only about 1.6 tons of soil were saved on each of the approximately 82 million acres set aside under PIK and a related program. Environmental and wildlife groups have charged that many farmers disregarded the requirement to plant cover crops on the fallow soil. Instead, millions of PIK acres were left bare and unprotected or covered with the previous year's crop residue and weeds, providing little protection against erosion.

USDA officials say they are generally satisified with the conservation aspects of the PIK program. "I would have been satisfied if we had just held our own," said Wayne Chapman, an SCS soil conservationist. The soil saved, Chapman added, is "a positive showing that [PIK] was really worthwhile from a conservation standpoint."

Prospects for Reduced Tillage

Conservation tillage practices are "taking off faster than any agricultural technology we've ever seen, but it'll take a while to make a full contribution to the problem," Neil Sampson said. In some areas of the country significant numbers of farmers have put erosion-control systems into place.

In Ohio, for example, a 1980 survey of 808 farmers indicated that 43 percent used some type of conservation tillage practice. According to the Maryland conservation service, nearly 85 percent of the corn crop in Howard County (located between Balti-more and Washington, D.C.) is farmed with no-till technology.

On a nationwide basis, however, the percentage of farmers using conservation tillage is much lower than in Ohio or Howard County. A survey released Feb. 8, 1984, by the National Association of Conservation Districts found that nearly 87 million acres of cropland were planted in some form of conservation tillage in 1983, more than 31 percent of the total cropland planted. "That is up from very, very negligible amounts five or six years ago," Sampson said.

Many farmers have turned to conservation tillage primarily because it saves expensive fuel and precious time. In those cases erosion control is a secondary benefit. And some experts believe that conservation tillage must be used with other conservation methods to be most effective.

Norman Berg of the Soil Conservation Society of America, for example, said that conservation tillage systems "are very promising providing they are combined with other erosion-control methods such as contour or terraced planting. They may eventually apply to most of the agricultural soil in America."

Conservation tillage systems also present a major unknown — namely, how their heavy reliance on chemical herbicides affects the environment. "While current evidence suggests that herbicides have relatively minor effects on the environment, the evidence is incomplete," noted Pierre R. Crosson in *The Cropland Crisis.* "As more information becomes available, controls on the use of herbicides may greatly restrict the spread of conservation tillage," added Crosson, a senior fellow at Resources for the Future. *(Pesticide controversies, p. 65)*

One stubborn problem in the fight against soil erosion is that most of those who employ conservation practices are successful farmers who work rich land that is not subject to severe erosion. Unfortunately, the converse also is true: Very few farmers working land that suffers from severe erosion use conservation tillage practices.

Conservation tillage is generally used by farmers with better soils, Sampson said, "because the payoffs are better and also because those farmers are using their financial condition to take the risk, for example, of buying a new piece of machinery or trying an untested technology. The last place these technologies go is on the marginal farms where the risks are already so marginal in terms of both economics and production that taking new risks is hard to do."

The OTA report observed that the suitability of particular soil conservation technologies are "site specific, as are the soil and water savings they will achieve." Nevertheless, the report concluded, if conservation tillage and no-till systems are applied to the worst areas of erosion in this country, and if they are "well designed and adequately funded," they could "significantly reduce the nation's overall erosion problem and protect some of its most fragile lands."

Erosion in Developing Countries

If the United States has not been able to solve its erosion problems "with all the advantages of research, extension, and conservation services, plus wealthy, educated farmers on good land with a gentle climate . . . then what hope is there for struggling countries that have few, or none, of these advantages?" asks Norman Hudson of the World Association of Soil and Water Conservation.

The answer to that question, most agricultural experts say, is that soil conservation problems, particularly erosion, are so intractable in many developing countries that there may not be any near-term solutions.

Nonetheless, several nations have made strong commitments to fight soil erosion and put soil conservation plans into practice. A presidential commission for soil conservation has been set up in Kenya, for example. And Indonesia instituted a "Greening Program" of soil conservation and reforestation in 1983. Peru's National Agrarian University soon will offer its first postgraduate program in forestry science in a cooperative project with the University of Toronto in Canada. Soil scientists in South Africa have been experimenting with conservation tillage methods of corn in the country's Highveld region.

Several international organizations also are involved in the fight against soil erosion. The World Bank, for example, is backing reforestation programs in the Sahel, including an ambitious irrigated plantation of eucalyptus trees in Niger. The FAO's Soil and Water Division has helped design erosion-control programs for specific countries.

A new international organization, the World Association of Soil and Water Conservation, was set up in January 1983 to promote cooperation on soil and water conservation issues among governments, international agencies and private and public groups. The association, which is still in its formative stages, will monitor, assess and support soil and water conservation practices around the world.

Despite these steps, soil erosion, desertification and deforestation remain extremely serious worldwide problems. The only positive factor Lester Brown named when asked to assess the future of the fight against soil erosion was "that awareness of the issue is gradually rising. . . . When you see the news reports now on famine in Africa they often talk about population growth and soil erosion and recognize it's not just a climatic phenomenon. The drought is clearly bringing a deteriorating situation into focus and there is now a wide awareness that there are some very basic problems that have to be dealt with."

4

Migrants: Enduring Farm Problem

"Harvest of Shame," Edward R. Murrow's television documentary exposing the misery of migrant farm workers, made history in 1960. By the 1980s, few subjects had been explored more thoroughly by the news media, by scholars and by the government at all levels. Despite the passage of time, however, it is clear that the issues raised more than two decades ago remain — and others have emerged.

Lawmakers responded in the years that followed Murrow's exposé with an impressive array of legislation to improve the lives of the nation's farm migrants, who according to estimates number 1.5 million. New laws made them eligible for food stamps, provided rural clinics for medical aid, created special school programs for migrant children, and sent federally paid attorneys into the fields and courtrooms to fight migrants' legal battles. Yet serious problems persist, causing some advocates to despair that migrant workers remain outcasts in a land of plenty.

"By and large, all the resources that have gone in have amounted to very little," said Steve Nagler, executive director of the Migrant Legal Action Program, a federally funded program based in Washington, D.C. "Many of the gains made on paper don't translate into reality. Migrants are still on the bottom."

Even more desperate are the uncounted thousands of illegal aliens, mostly Mexicans, who form a large segment of the farm labor force in some of the Sun Belt states — notably California and Texas. Farmers say they hire illegal aliens because not enough Americans are available and willing to work in the fields. Ironically, farmers are breaking no federal law by hiring illegal aliens. It is the aliens who are breaking the law by accepting the jobs.

Migrant-worker advocates argue that farmers prefer illegal aliens because they work longer hours for less money than Americans and are not safeguarded by minimum wage, workers' compensation, or other laws. Labor unions complain that farmers have no excuse for hiring illegal aliens while unemployment levels continue to remain high and millions of Americans are looking for work.

Unemployed Americans are not flocking to the fields because they have an alternative in unemployment compensation, said Perry R. Ellsworth, executive vice president of the Washington-based National Council of Agricultural Employers. Unemployment payments vary from state to state, ranging in duration from 34 to 53 weeks.

Ellsworth said farmers are willing to hire the unemployed American workers but few of them are willing to relocate for jobs that pay less than they are accustomed. Unemployment compensation recipients must look for work, but they are not required to relocate to find it.

Proposals to end farm employment of illegal aliens have generated intense debate in Congress. President Reagan has urged Congress to enact measures "to regain control of our borders." Like-minded members of Congress advocate penalties for all employers who hire illegal aliens. And they favor a "guest-worker" program, modeled on the discarded "bracero" program that would admit thousands of Mexicans to the fields on temporary work permits. *(Legislation, p. 48)*

Critics of the guest-worker idea, including Hispanic groups, point to the difficulty European countries have had in convincing millions of their own guest workers to return home now that Western Europe has more workers than work. *(European 'guest workers,' p. 49)*

Misery in Spite of Reforms

Migrants can toil 12 hours a day and still end up owing the crew leader money for cigarettes, beer, and room and board at the end of the week. The median income for a family of six, with children often working, is $3,900 a year, far below the federally defined poverty line of $12,499.

Despite federal migrant education programs, only 14 of every 100 children graduate from high school, compared with 75 out of a 100 for the general population. Malnutrition and inadequate medical treatment are as routine as the next day's trip to the fields. Diarrhea and parasites are expected; tuberculosis is common. Pesticide poisoning frequently goes undetected and untreated. Life expectancy is 49 years, roughly two-thirds the national average.

The crew-leader system has been blamed for many of the abuses suffered by migrant workers. Most migrants rely on crew leaders to arrange their jobs, transportation, and room and board. Farmers generally deal with crew chiefs, not individual migrants. Sometimes the system works well,

especially when the crew leader is a member of an extended family that travels together from state to state. Leaders provide an essential service by organizing and delivering a work force when and where it is needed. By its nature, the crew-leader system lends itself to abuses by those who would prey on the helpless.

In 1963, three years after Murrow's documentary touched the nation's conscience, Congress passed the Farm Labor Contractor Registration Act to correct abuses in the crew-leader system. The law required crew leaders to obtain a Labor Department license. Obtaining a license required little: absence of a criminal record and proof of liability insurance on vehicles for transporting workers. In addition, it required crew leaders to inform workers in writing of the conditions of their employment and housing.

The law was amended in 1974 after Congress determined it did not deter violators. Stiffer criminal penalties were added and the registration requirement was broadened to include crew leaders who operated solely within one state. The previous law applied only to those who crossed state lines.

Five years passed before new congressional hearings were called. This time the farm lobby complained that the law had "gone wild" because it required corporate agribusinesses, the largest employers of migrants, to register. Spokesmen for farm groups contended Congress never intended for the law to reach into the corporate personnel office.

John F. Ebbott, who was then director of the Migrant Legal Action Program, had a different story to tell a House subcommittee: "Many of the abuses which the Farm Labor Contractor Registration Act was enacted to remedy still occur today. . . . These abuses are perpetrated not only by individual labor contractors, but increasingly by corporate entities."

Migrant Farm Worker Routes

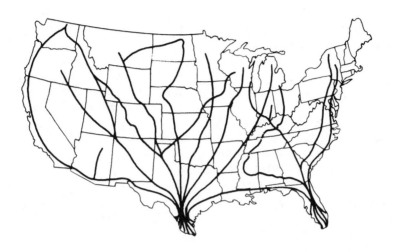

Migrant farm workers have developed many discernible routes in their seasonal search for jobs. The main ones are up the East Coast from winter headquarters in Florida, across the Midwest from a home base in the Rio Grante Valley, and up the Pacific Coast from Southern California. Others branch off and fan out into nearly every state. The Sun Belt states, primarily California, Texas and Florida, specialize in winter vegetables and citrus.

The summertime path northward for East Coast migrants leads through peach orchards in Georgia, tobacco fields in the Carolinas and Virginia, and truck farms on the Maryland Eastern Shore and in New Jersey. Appalachian range apple orchards extend the season into the fall and as far northward as New York.

Texas-based migrants are drawn to the grain harvests in the Plains states as far north as Canada, and to Michigan, where they find as abundance of vegetables and cherries. Vineyards in northern California, strawberries in Oregon and apples in Washington await the seasonal flow of farmhands up the West Coast.

Source: Office of Migrant Health, U.S. Public Health Service.

The hearing also brought out differences over the condition of migrant housing. Perry Ellsworth testified: "Over the past 10 to 15 years, there has been dramatic improvement in housing across the land. . . . Running hot and cold water and inside plumbing are the rule." That assertion was challenged by migrant spokesmen who contended that camp conditions tended to remain "filthy" and "disgusting."

Even with the registration law, Ebbott testified, "Farm workers are routinely not told by recruiters what they will be getting into if they accept a job offer. . . . [They] frequently find they must buy food, cigarettes and other items from the crew leader or the corporate cafeteria. Often the price of these items is hugely inflated. They are soon in debt, and purchases are deducted from their pay, leaving them little or no money. If they try to leave the job, it is not uncommon for the labor contractor, or foreman, to beat them up, threaten to kill them." Ebbott said the Labor Department had failed to enforce the crew-leader law.

New Law's Exclusions

Craig Berrington, a deputy assistant secretary of labor, told the subcommittee that the Carter administration had "given high priority" to improving both the living and working conditions of farm workers. He acknowledged the need for stepped-up enforcement but noted that the department's efforts had suffered, "because we have had substantial resistance to even the basics of the act."

The resistance, he added, came "from the farm owner and the corporate farm community."

It took three more years for a compromise rewrite of the law to clear Congress on Jan. 14, 1983. The new law, entitled the Migrant and Seasonal Agricultural Worker Protection Act, carried over most of the worker protections from the past, with two notable exceptions.

Family farms were excluded from coverage, and a damage ceiling of $500,000 was set on class-action lawsuits brought by farm workers. Farms owned by corporations remained under the act.

In addition, record-keeping requirements were extended to growers who in any way supervise field labor. And responsibility for complying with federal housing standards was broadened to include the person who controls the property — that is, the crew leader — as well as the owner.

The change in housing compliance means an end to confusion over who must comply with Occupational Health and Safety Administration (OSHA) standards. Charles Jeffress, deputy labor commissioner for North Carolina, said, "In the past, there was a lot of confusion over who to cite and who to bring enforcement action against."

Congress created OSHA in 1970 with a mandate to the secretary of labor to prescribe and enforce health and safety standards for the benefit of workers in agriculture and industry. Authorizing legislation stated that OSHA was meant "to assure so far as possible every working man and woman in the nation safe and healthful working conditions."

The states were encouraged to develop their own health and safety programs. As an incentive, the legislation provided that the states would be 50 percent federally funded if their regulations equalled or surpassed federal standards. As of 1984 about half the states had done so.

OSHA's critics took the agency to court as early as 1975 over alleged failure to enforce its migrant housing safety standards. The court ordered the Labor Department — OSHA's parent organization — to improve enforcement and appointed Washington lawyer Ronald L. Goldfarb to oversee the department's efforts.

Goldfarb later recounted in *A Cast of Despair*: "In 1975 when I called upon OSHA officials to do something about the horrible condition in migrant housing sites around the country, they excused their historic inactivity, blaming overwork and lack of funds. Under pressure, they promised to make a concerted effort to inspect 3,500 migrant housing places in that summer, 10 times the number they had inspected the year before. They actually conducted only 1,825 inspections of migrant labor camps, claiming inadequate enforcement staff and inability to locate migrant camps in some states (as if they could be hidden). And this was with a court order and a court-appointed committee focusing attention on their efforts."

Migrant housing for the duration of the harvest season

Health-Safety Enforcement

Congress in 1977 imposed new restrictions on OSHA's authority to inspect labor camps, barring inspectors from camps with fewer than 11 workers. In New Jersey, for example, eight out of every 10 camps were exempt. Regulations also limited OSHA to pre-season camp checks. Inspectors return only to investigate an alleged violation and only if the complaining worker identified himself. Nagler of the Migrant Legal Action Program said a farm worker who complains can expect to be without a job. The Reagan administration has made matters worse, he added, by cutting back on the number of inspectors.

In states that handle their own OSHA inspections, the situation is reported to be no better. A 1978 housing study of licensed labor camps in eight states that perform their own OSHA inspections — California, Colorado, Florida, Michigan, New York, Ohio, Texas, and Washington — found inside running water available in two-thirds of the camps. But two-thirds of the inspected camps were without heat, even though most of them were in areas where indoor heat was a common requirement. One-fourth of the kitchens had no working refrigerators, and one-half were without piped-in water. Bedrooms were crowded, though there were not enough beds for all.

Even if OSHA housing regulations were enforced, "the minimum standards still allow you to live in a slum," said Charles Jeffress. "The regulations are meant to prevent people from being electrocuted or falling through holes in the floor, that's all."

Aside from minimum housing standards, OSHA has issued only two other regulations applying to agriculture. They require rollover protective structures on tractors and set standards for handling anhydrous ammonia, a liquid fertilizer.

The absence of standards for field sanitation has been the subject of debate and legal battles for a decade. When OSHA proposed in 1974 to require portable toilets, drinking water and handwashing facilities in the fields, farmers succeeded in killing the idea. The farmers argued that the proposed requirements were unnecessary and too costly.

Federal courts subsequently have twice ordered OSHA to write such regulations. A ruling issued November 1981 by U.S. District Court Judge June L. Green in Washington, D.C., ordered OSHA to make its "best, good-faith effort" to develop field sanitation regulations within 18 months. She reacted with anger at the agency's claim that it needed another five years to study the matter. "OSHA's actions have been and continue to be irrational and taken in bad faith," she said. "OSHA's timetables belong in Alice in Wonderland's tales: each step forward brings us two steps backward."

Farm Pesticide Poisoning

In August 1980, seven physicians in Kerns County, Calif., were fined $250 each by the state Occupational Safety and Health Administration for failure to report they had treated 54 farm workers for apparent pesticide poisoning. In no other state, however, could there have been made a similar ruling, for no other state requires doctors to report pesticide poisoning.

Yet pesticides have become a prime health concern of America's farm workers and the focus of a political battle in Congress. Opposing sides came to a draw at the end of the 1982 session over proposed changes in the law governing pesticides —

the 1947 Federal Insecticide, Fungicide and Rodenticide Act (FIFRA).

Putting aside the controversial policy issues that had kept Congress from enacting a pesticide bill in 1982, a simple one-year authorization of the pesticide control program was approved the following year. The measure also extended through September 1987 the authority for a scientific advisory panel on pesticides. Further legislation was expected in 1984.

The dispute began in 1978 when Congress amended the pesticide law to require chemical manufacturers to make public their previously secret pesticide health and safety studies. The chemical makers responded with a lawsuit that blocked enforcement of disclosure for three years. They argued that divulging the data would amount to giving away trade secrets. When a federal court ruled in favor of disclosure in the summer of 1981, the chemical industry began to lobby Congress for changes in the law. There the industry ran into a coalition of labor and environmental groups that lobbied just as hard for strengthening worker protections.

After much debate, the House Agriculture Committee approved in 1982 a number of industry-sought changes: to limit public disclosure of health and safety data and to keep states from requiring more information than the federal government does in registering a pesticide for in-state use. The American Farm Bureau Federation backed both changes.

Environmentalist, farm-worker, and labor groups argued that eliminating state control over pesticide registration was unwarranted. They viewed the move as an attack on California's tough registration law, which has slowed the introduction of new pesticides in that state.

Manufacturers feared other states might follow California's example. Farm-worker advocates also pushed in vain for a proposal to allow farm workers to sue farmers for damages in case of injury from pesticide poisoning. Farm workers are covered only by workers' compensation, and only in those states providing such coverage.

When the committee-approved bill reached the House floor, it was rewritten by a series of amendments that eliminated the key measures sought by the farm and chemical industry lobbyists. The House bill, however, died at the end of the 97th Congress for lack of Senate action.

No one knows how many farm workers and their children are treated for pesticide exposure each year. Even in California, which has the nation's only mandatory reporting law, many doctors are not aware of the requirement, and some who are do not make the reports.

A 1977 study by a California farmworker group concluded that only 1 percent of the state's pesticide poisonings were reported. Rural America, a non-profit organization concerned with low-income people in rural areas, held three regional hearings on pesticide poisoning in 1980. At all three sites — Pharr, Texas; Ocoee, Fla.; and Salinas, Calif. — farm workers complained of rashes, vomiting, stomach cramps, burns, skin peeling, blurred and spotted vision, and dizziness associated with pesticide exposure.

In addition, most of the farm workers said they had no idea what chemicals had been used, nor could they obtain any information on the health effects. One worker at the Texas hearing said farmers have used aerial spraying to break up union picketing.

Pesticide poisoning is difficult to diagnose, the report stated, because such clinical symptoms as respiratory problems, dizziness and gastro-intestinal disturbances are attributed to flu or other ailments. Few doctors are trained to recognize and treat pesticide poisoning.

The risks associated with pesticide poisoning are even greater for children. Yet the existing federal standards for re-entering fields sprayed with pesticides, set by the Environmental Protection Agency, are based on estimated adult tolerance to pesticide exposure. Of all the chemicals available on the market, EPA has developed re-entry times on only 12, according to the Migrant Legal Action Program. There are no separate standards for children for any pesticides.

The absence of such standards triggered a round of lawsuits after Congress amended the Fair Labor Standards Act in 1977. The amendment allowed growers to obtain permission from the secretary of labor to employ 10- and 11-year-olds, provided the growers can prove no harmful effects to the children.

Migrant-worker advocates filed suit, charging no studies existed for making such a determination. In March 1981, a federal appeals court ordered the Labor Department to develop safety standards before allowing children to enter pesticide-treated fields. At about the same time, the department and EPA announced a joint, five-year study to determine effects of pesticide exposure on children under 16. *(Pesticide controversies, p. 65)*

Migrants and Social Policy

The first migrant farm laborers who trekked into the fields may have been white hobos hired in the mid-1800s by a California grower and cattle baron named Henry Miller. They worked for food, not wages, according to a latter-day account written by Richard S. Johnson, setting an enduring tone for the treatment of migrant help. Miller instructed his cooks to serve the workers last on dirty plates — to discourage any who otherwise might feel at home and wish to settle.

California got a second source of cheap labor after the Union Pacific built its railroad across the nation in 1869. Thousands

Foreign Temporary Workers
Admitted for Farm Employment

1958	433,704	1970	47,483
1959	464,128	1971	42,142
1960	447,207	1972	38,752
1961	312,991	1973	37,294
1962	303,638	1974	33,908
1963	243,120	1975	25,434
1964	237,700	1976	22,124
1965	155,671	1977	21,671
1966	64,881	1978	18,679
1967	57,720	1979	18,213
1968	50,782	1980	16,548
1969	43,527	1981	16,190

Source: U.S. Immigration and Naturalization Service

of Chinese coolies who had been imported to lay the railway suddenly had to find other jobs. It is estimated that by 1880, 100,000 Chinese were at work in California fields holding 90 percent of the farm jobs. Their population increase alarmed trade unionists and small manufacturers who engineered the state's Chinese Exclusion Act of 1882, banning further Chinese immigration.

The next wave of cheap labor came from Japan. By 1910, the state had 72,000 Japanese farm workers. But the federal government slammed the door on virtually all immigrants from Asia in 1924. By this time it was clear that Mexico would supply future farm labor.

Thousands of Mexicans fled that country's revolution, which broke out in 1911. The American government welcomed their arrival during World War I, at a time when domestic labor was in short supply.

The labor shortage, however, became a labor glut during the Depression, and the Mexicans were no longer welcome. America's own economic refugees fled the central plains Dust Bowl for California's verdant fields, as portrayed in John Steinbeck's 1939 novel *Grapes of Wrath*.

Mexicans re-entered the farm labor market in the early 1940s after America's entry into World War II. Farmers again needed a source of cheap labor to replace the farm hands who were drafted or went to work in factories. Legally or illegally, Mexican field hands have remained on the scene ever since. During the war years, upwards of 200,000 Mexican "braceros" — literally strong-armed men — entered the country on temporary work permits to toil in the fields.

Congress extended the "wartime" bracero program until 1964 when civil rights groups prevailed in their fight to end what they considered exploitation of foreign workers at the expense of unemployed Americans. But laws prohibiting employment of aliens have been too weak and too poorly enforced to prevent what since has become a flood of Mexican illegal immigrants.

On the East Coast, the history of migrant labor is simpler. Following the Civil War, the sharecropper system replaced slavery. But there was not enough work to go around. Desperation sent ex-slaves and some poor whites on a seasonal surge northward for work.

The East Coast stream took a more definite shape in the 1920s when vast amounts of rich muckland came under the plow in Florida. The state became the winter haven for workers who traveled as far north as New York and Michigan on their cyclical search for jobs.

Mexicans joined the stream after cotton harvest mechanization in the early 1950s left thousands without jobs, primarily in Texas. Since 1980, Haitian immigrants have joined the stream and now make up an estimated 10 percent of the migrant work force.

Wage, Welfare Protection

The social history of the past 50 years is replete with examples of government intervention on behalf of the poor, the uneducated, the sick, and the young, beginning with the New Deal. But much of it never extended to the fields. While the Social Security Act of 1935 made history, agricultural workers were not covered until 15 years later.

The minimum wage law of 1938, the Fair Labor Standards Act, championed the rights of workers to earn a decent wage without excessive labor. It put a floor under wages at 25 cents an hour, limited the work week to 40 hours, required overtime pay for more than the normal work week and restricted child labor. Agricultural workers were excluded.

Twenty-eight years later, in 1966, Congress amended the act to include workers on large farms, thus covering about 30 percent

of all farm workers. An additional 10 percent came under the law's coverage with passage of a 1974 amendment. Farm workers still are not eligible for overtime pay.

Enforcing the wage law is difficult. Migrants in 1982 testified during a legislative commission hearing in North Carolina that crew leaders keep two sets of books, one for the state Labor Department inspector and one with the real balance sheet. "I've been at this for five years, and I haven't met a farm worker yet who has made the minimum wage for the entire season," said Chuck Eppinette, community education coordinator with North Carolina Farm Worker Legal Services.

Since the 1938 wage law excluded farm workers, their children were not covered by its child-labor provisions. Congress provided some coverage in 1949 by prohibiting children from working in the fields during school hours. But migrant parents usually ignored the law, knowing enforcement was lax or non-existent.

The Senate Labor Committee in 1974 issued a report favoring tougher child labor laws: "Thirty-five years ago, Congress reacted to a national outcry by banning industrial child labor. However, since 1938 the nation has permitted in the fields what it has prohibited in the factories — oppressive and scandalous child labor. The committee once again urges that this shameful double standard no longer be tolerated." Congress did not act then, nor has it acted since. The child labor provisions remain unchanged.

Today, all children may work in the fields if they are 14 or older. Children 12 and 13 may do so with parental consent, and those under 12 may do so on a parent's farm or with parental consent on farms not large enough to be covered by minimum-wage provisions.

A 1977 report for the Department of Health, Education and Welfare (now Health and Human Services) concluded: "Child labor is an economic necessity for the migrant family due to the low level of income. . . . Many children begin to do some work in the fields by age four, and by age 10 are expected to carry their own weight and usually drop out of school by age 12 to work full time."

Workers' compensation laws also arose during the New Deal era to assure workers of insurance coverage for job-related injuries regardless of who was at fault. The laws were enacted by the states, which tailored them to meet their individual needs.

Today, farm workers remain exempt in nearly half the states. In 13 states — Arizona, California, Colorado, Connecticut, Hawaii, Massachusetts, Montana, New Hampshire, New Jersey, Ohio, Oregon, Pennsylvania, and Washington — and Puerto Rico, migrants are covered on the same basis as other workers. Another 13 states — Alaska, Florida, Illinois, Iowa, Maryland, Michigan, Minnesota, New York, Utah, Vermont, Virginia, West Virginia, and Wisconsin — provide partial coverage with numerous exemptions. The remaining 24 states provide no coverage at all.

Farm workers also were excluded from federal unemployment compensation benefits from the time the first bill passed in 1935 until 1976. At that time, migrants and other farm laborers hired by large employers, usually corporate farms, became eligible for unemployment benefits. Those hired by family farms remain outside the system.

Farm Unions: Success in California

Migrant farm workers have not accepted their second-class status without complaint. Chinese laborers organized the first recorded farm strike in 1884 in the hop fields of Kern County, Calif. It failed. So did sporadic strikes by Mexican and Japanese workers in the early 1900s. The Depression brought on a new round of farm work stoppages, 140 by one count. But

growers aligned themselves with powerful political and economic forces that broke the resistance.

Farm worker organizers often carried the banner of groups considered to be a threat to the government: the Industrial Workers of the World (Wobblies), the Communist Party, or the Socialist Party. For example, the Southern Tenant Farmers Union was set up in the 1930s with funds from the Socialist Party. It eventually claimed 25,000 members in five states. But it made no headway.

Spontaneous non-union farm strikes took placed in numerous states during the Depression. Labor historians have counted 275 such strikes in 28 states joined by an estimated 178,000 workers.

No doubt Congress was aware of agitation on the farm when it excluded farm workers from coverage of the 1935 National Labor Relations Act. The act recognized the right of industrial workers to organize and bargain collectively, but it has never been amended to include farm workers.

"The National Labor Relations Board [created to administer the act] requires employers to bargain in good faith with a union," said Steve Nagler of the Migrant Legal Action Program. "But if that [union organizing] happens in the fields, the crew leader can say, 'I'm sorry, there is no protection for these people. They are fired.' "

Arguments for exempting agricultural workers from collective bargaining have remained unchanged. Farm spokesmen contend that agriculture is uniquely vulnerable to work stoppages. The crops cannot wait for a strike to be settled. A farmer facing a strike is at the mercy of the workers and would be compelled to give in to demands no matter how unreasonable or arbitrary. Collective bargaining would not equalize the bargaining power of farmers and workers; it would make farmers subservient to labor union leaders.

Against this backdrop of resistance,

the United Farm Workers union, led by Cesar Chavez, overcame the odds and established its presence in California in the mid-1960s. Chavez, a second-generation Mexican-American, emerged as a national figure during a 1965 strike against Delano, Calif., grape growers. Growers and agribusiness fought unionization while Chavez appealed for a nationwide boycott of California grapes and wine.

The UFW's major breakthrough came in 1975 when California's newly elected governor, Edmund G. "Jerry" Brown Jr., personally directed negotiations that produced the state's landmark Agricultural Labor Relations Act, patterned after the National Labor Relations Act.

For the first time, California farm workers were given the right to organize and bargain collectively. The act created an Agricultural Labor Relations Board to supervise union elections, hear complaints and develop regulations. Since passage of the act, agricultural employers estimate that in the Monterey-Salinas area 80 to 90 percent of the workers in fresh vegetables are under labor contract. In other vegetable areas, approximately 40 percent are under contract. Fewer than 20 percent of the workers in vineyards, orchards, and citrus groves are unionized.

Unionization has brought farm workers higher wages and an array of educational and social service programs funded by union dues. The programs include medical clinics, a pension fund, an economic development fund for workers' centers, and language training programs.

From the time of the Delano grape strike, Chavez allied his union with the AFL-CIO. Together they fought a bitter jurisdictional battle with the powerful Teamsters Union over the next decade. The two rivals ended the feud in 1975 by signing an agreement giving the United Farm Workers exclusive rights to organize field hands and the Teamsters the right to orga-

North Carolina: A Question of Slavery

Some migrants find working conditions so unpleasant they try to flee, only to be rounded up by crew leaders or foremen. By definition, that amounts to slavery, a federal crime since 1865. The North Carolina constitution also outlaws slavery, but there are no penalties in state law for enslavement. Thus the U.S. Justice Department's Civil Rights Division must be called on to prosecute all such cases.

From 1978 to 1983, 10 such convictions had been obtained in North Carolina, more than in any other state. An antislavery bill imposing penalties was passed by the state legislature in 1983. The original bill allowed the state bureau of investigation to look into charges of migrant slavery, but the final legislation gave that authority to the local sheriff's office.

nize farm workers in transportation jobs.

Chavez has made repeated pledges to lead union drives in other agricultural states, such as Texas and Florida. To date, the UFW's magic has worked only in California. And Chavez's critics say the union is floundering at home because its charismatic leader cannot make the transition from strike organizer to effective manager.

Immigration and the Economy

Problems faced by domestic migrants are multiplied for thousands of illegal aliens who live in what has been described as an economic underworld that demands their silence and obedience in return for a job. It operates outside the control and protection of the law. The Census Bureau estimates there are three to six million illegal aliens working in the United States, many of them in the fields. Nearly two out of every three come from Mexico.

The number of aliens caught crossing the border illegally has mounted steadily since the bracero program ended in 1964. The Immigration and Naturalization Service (INS) deported 1.3 million Mexicans between 1965 and 1970. In 1980 alone more than one million aliens entered the country illegally, most of them Mexican.

INS Commissioner Alan Nelson in 1983 told a Senate committee that Border Patrol apprehensions of illegals are at their highest levels in 30 years. In January of that year 86,811 aliens were caught at the border, a 46 percent increase over the same time a year earlier. But the Border Patrol estimates that only every third person trying to enter is caught. Many keep trying until they cross undetected.

President Jimmy Carter sent Congress a comprehensive set of immigration law reforms in 1977 to curb the flow of illegal aliens, but the legislation never came to a vote. The Reagan administration renewed the reform effort and backed a number of changes, including an amnesty program to allow many illegal aliens already in the country to become permanent residents, and imposing sanctions against employers who knowingly hire them.

The Reagan administration's proposals were contained in the Immigration Reform and Control Act, popularly known as the Simpson-Mazzoli bill for its sponsors, Rep. Romano L. Mazzoli, D-Ky., and Sen. Alan K. Simpson, R-Wyo. The Senate passed the bill in 1982, but it died in the House.

Reintroduced in the 98th Congress, the bill was approved by the Senate May 18, 1983. After seven days of often heated debate, the measure finally was passed by the House June 20, 1984, and sent to conference.

If enacted, the legislation would be the first wholesale revision of immigration laws since 1952, when Congress enacted a law to restrict and apportion immigration into the United States. Both the House and Senate versions of the 1980s bill have the same basic goals — curbing the flow of illegal aliens into the United States and granting legal status, or amnesty, to millions of illegal aliens already in the country.

However, there are important differences between the two versions. Both would penalize employers who knowingly hire illegal aliens, but the Senate version authorizes criminal penalties for repeat violators, while the House bill provides only civil fines.

While both proposals include amnesty programs, the House version is far more generous than the Senate's. It would allow illegal aliens who could prove they entered the United States before Jan. 1, 1982, to apply for temporary resident status within one year after enactment of the bill. After two years, they could seek permanent resident status provided they have no serious criminal record and have accquired a "minimal understanding of ordinary English" and of U.S. history and government.

The Senate bill allows illegal workers who were in the country before Jan. 1, 1977, to qualify for legal resident status, but makes them ineligible for such public benefits as unemployment compensation and food stamps for three years. Workers in the United States before Jan. 1, 1980, would qualify for temporary-resident status but would have no access to public benefits for six years.

There is a signficant difference between the two bills in another major area — the extent to which foreign workers should be allowed in the country for temporary agricultural work. Both bills revise the existing temporary worker program, known as

European 'Guest Workers'

As many as 15 million "guest workers" and their dependents have migrated from Southern Europe, Turkey, and North Africa to Northern and Western Europe since 1960 to find jobs, most of them menial. The host governments encouraged them to come in a time of prosperity and labor shortages — but supposedly on a temporary basis. Though times have changed and far fewer guest workers are needed, only one of every three has returned home.

With the 1973 Arab oil embargo and the ensuing worldwide recession, the labor-importing countries moved to halt or severely restrict further recruitment of aliens. But no country attempted massive expulsions. The belief that guest workers would not settle in the host countries proved false for a number of reasons. The need for foreign labor turned out not to be temporary. Native workers have tended to shun the lowliest jobs, even in times of rising unemployment.

The economic and social consequences of the programs have caused alarm in Europe. It is argued that the social and political costs outweighed the economic benefits. As workers were joined by their families, government expenditures rose for schools, housing, medical care, and other social services. In Switzerland, opponents of the guest-worker program waged four unsuccessful referendums to restrict their numbers. Racial problems arose in several countries. Tension between aliens and residents occasionally erupted into violence. Backers of the programs contend that Europe's economy would not have prospered and grown as it did without imported labor.

the "H-2 program," to make it easier for employers to obtain foreign workers when federal officials determine there is insufficient domestic labor.

But the House bill also includes a new "guest-worker" program for growers of perishable crops that could allow around 500,000 foreign workers into the country every year. It also permits farmers more flexibility in obtaining workers under emergency conditions.

Both the Senate- and House-approved bills include a compromise amendment giving agricultural employers three years to phase out their use of illegal aliens. In the fourth year, farmers either would have to employ American workers or obtain foreign laborers through a revised guest-worker program.

Hispanic, civil rights, and lawyers' groups opposed the immigration reform bill, estimating the cutoff date would leave half of the illegal aliens ineligible for citizenship. A number of liberal Democrats in Congress also opposed the bill, siding with Hispanic members who led a futile crusade against the measure because of the employer penalties.

The Hispanics argued repeatedly that the provisions would result in discrimination because employers, anxious to avoid the sanctions, would not hire anyone who looked foreign, spoke with an accent, or had a foreign-sounding name.

'Guest-Worker' Concept

The guest-worker program considered in both bills is based upon the 30-year-old "H-2" temporary worker program, named for the section of the 1952 immigration law authorizing importation of foreign laborers. The H-2 program was designed to allow temporary employment for workers performing services for which domestic workers could not be found. The secretary of labor must certify the absence of American labor before H-2 workers may be hired.

The program operates under much stricter controls than the old bracero program and therefore has remained far smaller, averaging fewer than 20,000 workers a year. The program now operates primarily for the benefit of East Coast apple growers, who import about 5,000 Jamaicans each fall, and Florida sugar cane growers, who bring in about 8,500 Jamaican cane cutters during the winter harvest.

Southwestern farmers contend that the H-2 program is too rigid to accommodate their need for thousands of workers on short notice. They acknowledge widespread use of illegal aliens but blame H-2 red tape for forcing them to hire aliens. Farmers have lobbied for a guest-worker program far more flexible than the H-2 program. Hispanic groups strongly oppose the guest-worker plan and have called it "a backdoor bracero program" to exploit immigrant workers.

Some economists and politicians suggest that a solution to the illegal immigration problem does not require exclusionary laws. They argue that the only effective approach is economic development in the countries spawning the immigrant stream.

This was at least part of President Reagan's rationale — other than security reasons — for proposing a "Caribbean Basin Initiative" to Congress in 1982. He asked for legislation opening U.S. markets more fully to most Caribbean nations to stimulate their economic growth.

There is another project that seeks a similar objective. It is much more modest in size and does not require new laws or public funding. The small, independent Arizona Farm Workers Union has started a fund to channel money into job-development projects in Mexico. One project is taking shape in La Caja, a small village 185 miles north of Mexico City, where an irrigation project will supply water to 4,000 acres of arid farm land. The villagers' only obligation to the union is to help neighboring villages.

The plan may seem impossible, but so did the union's chances of obtaining its first, and only, contract in 1978 when 300 citrus workers went on strike at Arrowhead Ranch in Arizona. Several years later, the workers have a union contract, live in a $250,000 camp with showers, laundry, a courtyard, and communal kitchen. Their wages have doubled and they receive three hot meals a day for only $5. More than two decades after "Harvest of Shame," such accommodations remain the exception, not the rule, for the nation's migrant farm workers.

5

Advances in Agricultural Research

The United States is the No. 1 agricultural nation in the world. America's farms produce more than enough food to feed this nation's population, and U.S. agriculture also dominates the international food market. But as the world's population soars, the amount of arable land decreases, and the rate of crop production levels off, will this country be able to continue feeding the world? A close look at the situation reveals some disturbing trends. *(U.S. farm exports, p. 89)*

First, both in the United States and around the world, population pressures and environmental factors are causing millions of acres of farm land to be lost each year. The United States alone lost some 16 million acres to urban development and soil erosion from 1975 to 1980, according to Agriculture Department (USDA) calculations.

Second, the world's population, which stands at approximately 4.5 billion, will be at least 6 billion by the year 2000, according to demographic projections. Third, U.S. agriculture, though still producing record amounts of crops, has experienced lowered gains in productivity since the mid-1970s. "Yields are increasing at decreasing rates," said Norman Berg, director of USDA's soil conservation service, in a magazine interview. "Pure technology may have reached the point of diminishing returns."

Furthermore, the high-yielding varieties of wheat, corn, and rice developed by U.S. agricultural scientists since the 1920s were chosen especially for their adaptability to fertilizers, pesticides, and highly mechanized farming methods. This method of cultivation uses large amounts of energy, and the cost of fuel for agricultural machinery and of petrochemical feed stocks for the production of fertilizer has shot out of sight since the mid-1970s.

In addition to the monetary factor, heavy dependence on petroleum-based pesticides and fertilizers has had another unwanted consequences: soil erosion and pesticide pollution. According to the Agriculture Department more than 140 million acres of U.S. cropland are threatened by high erosion rates. And although the widespread use of fertilizers and pesticides has raised crop yields dramatically, pollution problems have resulted "when these materials or their breakdown products are washed or blown from the fields," concluded the Council on Environmental Quality in a 1980 report. *(Soil erosion, p. 23; pesticide controversies, p. 65)*

To complicate matters further, American farmers use only a few high-yielding varieties of most crops. This practice makes these crops vulnerable to epidemics such as the Southern corn leaf blight that wiped out 15 percent of the U.S. corn crop in 1970.

Moreover, the expanding worldwide population has caused the irrevocable loss of hundreds of plant species and thousands of indigenous crop varieties. These wild strains are important because, even though they are not needed now, plant breeders in the future may need these plants' characteristics to breed with existing varieties to ward off a new insect pest or plant disease. Preservation of wild species' seed "is what stands between us and serious genetic vulnerability or crop losses," said Quentin Jones, USDA's national coordinator for germ plasm.

Shrinking agricultural acreage. Increasing population. Decreasing productivity gains in most crops. Heavy dependence on petroleum-based pesticides and fertilizers. Genetic vulnerability. Together these factors could have disastrous consequences for the world's food supply. According to Lester R. Brown, president of Worldwatch Institute, and a former USDA official, "these trends ... suggest that the world's ever-growing dependence on the North American export surplus is risky."

Search for Answers

Many observers say the solution to these potentially grave problems lies in expanding agricultural research with the specific aim of increasing U.S. agricultural productivity. Applied scientific and technological innovation is what accounted in large part for the rapid rise of U.S. agriculture beginning in the 1930s, and many see the fruits of today's research as providing the answers to the world's future food needs.

The American agricultural research network — which includes various branches of USDA, state agricultural extension agencies, private and state universities, and American industry — is engaged in a multibillion-dollar effort to come up with solutions to these problems. The research is focusing on offshoots of age-old plant breeding techniques. In conventional plant breeding, scientists essentially take characteristics from two different varieties of the same species and inbreed them to form a third type containing the best features of the two.

The newest experimental plant breeding technology, genetic engineering, could some day allow biologists to design actual new genetic material rather than just manipulate genetic material already present in crops. Genetic engineering, also called recombinant DNA technology, is a gene-splicing technique that enables scientists to combine the genetic material DNA (deoxyribonucleic acid) of different species and create new or drastically altered forms of life.

Since this is done on the molecular level, it "offers a wholly new concept in genetic manipulation," said Raymond C. Valentine, who heads a 15-member genetic engineering research team at the University of California at Davis. "A gene from corn could be theoretically introduced into soybean or potato; a microbial gene could be introduced into a plant. We now have the ability to move any gene from any organism. Any particular strain that we're interested in could be moved from one organism to another."

Most scientists foresee few imminent breakthroughs with recombinant DNA technology and plant breeding. The research taking place centers on learning exactly what is involved in this extremely complex process. There may be no practical applications in agriculture for decades. "I think the short-term contribution of genetic engineering will be to help our understanding of the plants we are working with," said G. W. Schaeffer, chief of USDA's Cell Culture and Nitrogen Fixation Laboratory. "When you are talking about a gene being inserted into a plant cell and being expressed, the problems are ... great. It's very difficult to design an experiment at the cell level that will be meaningful in the agronomic sense and in the setting of the farmer's field. You really can't make that quantum jump in one step. It has to evolve." There may be "dramatic findings in specific areas" Schaeffer said, in the near future, but he warned that "there is a lot of what I call 'biology' to be worked out before a recipient plant can tolerate external DNA and express it.... There are very large problems, and it will take time to ferret them out."

How much time? "I think we are 20-50 years away from being able to manipulate [recombinant DNA] to our advantage in an agricultural way — maybe longer than that," said Quentin Jones of the USDA. "Someone may come along and open up some new avenues and make it happen faster, but it's a very complicated and involved process."

Jones explained some of the problems blocking successful application of recombinant DNA technology to plant breeding: "When you look at the enormous complexity of all the things that go into what we call environment — temperature, light, moisture, heat, other biological systems other than plants that we're trying to grow — for us to get to the point where we can say, 'What we need is a gene that controls this reaction by this plant' and then design it by putting together DNA from wherever our knowledge tells us it should come from, this I think ... most of us probably won't live to see."

Thomas N. Urban, president and chief executive officer of Pioneer Hi-Bred International Inc., the world's largest producer and marketer of hybrid seed corn, also expressed pessimism about the near-term potential of recombinant DNA technology. "Genetic engineering techniques cannot simultaneously work with large numbers of genes, which is a prerequisite for most hybrids and variety improvement," Urban told *The New York Times* in a 1981 interview. "Plants have some 10,000 genes and very few of their characteristics are con-

trolled by a single gene. The new techniques will be helpful in speeding up our work; for example, in identifying and releasing varieties with improved disease resistance. But they won't change conventional breeding methods."

Genetic Engineering

Despite these problems, agricultural researchers in government, university, and corporate laboratories are working on a number of genetic engineering applications. One of the most promising areas is nitrogen fixation. Certain bacterium on the roots of soybeans, peanuts, clover, and other plants are able to take nitrogen from the air and transform it into nitrates. This means that these plants, in effect, fertilize themselves.

The process does not occur in cereal crops such as wheat, corn, or rice, which therefore must be fertilized. Most farmers use heavy concentrations of chemically produced nitrogen fertilizer. Scientists are studying the possibility of transferring to wheat and corn the genes that are responsible for nitrogen fixation in crops such as soybeans. The hope is that new strains of wheat and corn bred in this fashion then can be grown without using expensive fertilizers.

Another goal is improving the nitrogen fixation ability of soybeans. Some scientists predict that soybean plants with improved nitrogen fixation efficiency could yield 10-15 percent more than varieties without that ability.

Researchers at USDA laboratories, schools such as the University of Wisconsin and the University of California at Davis, and private corporations such as Allied Chemical Corp., Dow Chemical Co., E.I. Du Pont deNemours & Co., and Monsanto Co., have been working for years on this technology. Yet many questions remain unanswered, and there is only the slightest possibility that this technology will come

Corporate Investment in Agricultural Research

Company	Area of Long-term Agricultural Research	Estimated R & D Funds Spent on Agriculture *(millions)*	Percentage of Total R & D Budget
Allied Chemical	nitrogen fixation	$30	43%
American Cyanamid	plant growth regulants	73	59
Dow Chemical	photosynthesis	40	15
Du Pont	nitrogen fixation	42	10
Eli Lilly	recombinant DNA	63	36
Merck	plant genetics	24	13
Monsanto	plant growth regulants	84	49
Pfizer	plant genetics	22	16
Upjohn	soybean hybrids	26	20
Union Carbide	plant growth regulants	46	26

Source: *Forbes,* March 2, 1981.

into general use before the turn of the 21st century.

Photosynthesis is the process by which plants convert the sun's energy into plant sugars. But most plants convert only about 1 percent of the energy contained in the light rays falling on them into chemical energy. Scientists therefore are trying to find ways to increase photosynthesis efficiency. "Think of what it would mean if we could raise that to 2 percent," commented Charles E. Hess, dean of the University of California at Davis's College of Agricultural and Environmental Sciences, in a newspaper interview. "That could mean a doubling of plant growth rates, and that might be reflected in massive food production increases."

Finding genes to splice into plants to increase photosynthesis efficiency is compli-

cated by the fact that molecular knowledge of most of the world's 300,000 species of higher plants is quite limited. This slows all genetic engineering research significantly, as scientists first must learn much more about the molecular structure of thousands of plants before they can undertake complex gene-splicing experiments.

Another area of genetic engineering research concentrates on transferring disease-resistant genes from one species to another. The object is to eliminate the need for pesticides. Conventional breeding techniques already have been developed in this area. Several disease-resistant strains of sorghum from Africa, for example, have been bred into American-grown sorghum. And some materials from African and South American corn have been bred into American corn to fight certain types of leaf blight.

Among the other genetic engineering techniques under scrutiny is plant growth regulant technology, which would allow scientists to breed major crops for specialized uses. These include varieties bred for specific animals or for specific shapes, textures, and sizes to mesh with processing equipment.

Hydroponic Technology

While most applications of genetic engineering in agriculture probably will not be in widespread use for decades, there is a new type of crop production already in use, and another on the drawing board, that allows the growth of crops in media other than conventional farm soil.

Hydroponics is a technique in which crops are grown not in soil, but in water fed with chemical nutrients in what is called a "controlled environment" — in other words, indoors. One indication that hydroponics has a promising future is that some large corporations have entered the field in recent years. Whittaker Corp., a Los Angeles-based conglomerate; Control Data Corp., the Minneapolis computer and financial services company; and General Mills, the food producer also located in Minneapolis, all own so-called "lettuce factories."

These computer-run indoor operations have the advantage of controlling all the environmental factors involved in lettuce growing, including the exact chemical composition of fertilizers and other nutrients, temperature, humidity, and light. These automated facilities produce as much as 100 times more lettuce per acre than conventional outdoor agriculture.

Whittaker's Agri-Systems Division's lettuce factory in Somis, Calif., is the first such structure to grow plants solely with natural light, thus saving the enormous expense of artificial light. The 1.8-acre, plastic-greenhouse-type facility also produces cucumbers and tomatoes. Harvesting and packaging is done mechanically inside the factory, saving additional labor costs.

Plant scientists also hope to develop crops that can survive in salty soil. For example, heavy irrigation has left significant salt deposits in the San Joaquin Valley, the heart of California's agribusiness. Researchers at the Bodega Marine Laboratory at the University of California at Davis are experimenting with special types of barley, wheat, and tomatoes that are being irrigated with seawater.

"In the future, it may even become possible to use seawater to produce crops along sandy coasts and coastal deserts," said Emanual Epstein, in a newspaper interview. Epstein, a scientist at the Davis campus, added that "[I]mproving the salt tolerance of crops for conventional irrigation agriculture on salt-affected soils also is an important goal."

Advances in Plant Breeding

Plant breeding dates from the time before recorded history when primitive humans first moved from hunting, fishing, and food gathering to the domestication of animals and the deliberate cultivation of wild plants. The earliest plant breeding came about when man learned the differences between plant species and then selected and sowed the seeds of the plants that produced the largest and tastiest fruits. The earliest farmers used a combination of wild strains and those produced by chance as a result of mutations.

In time, thousands of varieties of plant species came to be used throughout the world. And those varieties not used for breeding remained in nature, growing wild. "Clearly all of the horticultural plants, domesticated animals and useful strains of microorganisms upon which we now depend are the product of a very rapid and recent evolution under human selection from wild relatives found in natural ecosystems around the world," concluded a 1979 report prepared by the National Academy of Sciences.

Migrating tribes and adventurous explorers took seeds throughout the world. For example, the Indian tribes that moved from what is now Mexico into what is now the Western United States brought along corn, beans, and squash. Indians from Central and South America introduced the tomato to North America. Columbus brought wheat, barley, sugar cane, and grapes to the Americas in 1493. The Spanish introduced alfalfa, oats, lemons, oranges, walnuts, cabbage, lettuce, and peas.

Nearly all the food grown in the United States is descended from plants and seeds that were brought to this country from other lands. The only crops native to the United States are sunflower seeds, cranberries, blueberries, strawberries, pecans, and Jerusalem artichokes.

Thomas Jefferson and Benjamin Franklin were among the many early Americans who imported varieties of crops into the colonies two centuries ago. Franklin is credited with bringing rhubarb and kale from Europe, and Jefferson with illegally taking upland rice from Italy and introducing it in South Carolina.

"Each wave of immigrants came with seeds from their homeland, enriching and diversifying American agriculture," wrote Cary Fowler in *The Graham Center Seed Directory.* Fowler is co-director of the Resource Center at the Frank Porter Graham Demonstration Farm, a project of the National Sharecroppers Union in Wadesboro, N.C.

The U.S. government began to take an interest in imported seeds early in the 19th century. American embassy personnel were asked by the federal government to collect seeds they thought would be useful in this country and to ship them here.

From 1836 until the Agriculture Department was established in 1862, the U.S.

Patent Commissioner supervised the introduction of plants from abroad. Hard red-winter wheat, for example, which now is grown extensively in Kansas, Nebraska, Oklahoma, Montana, Texas, and Colorado, was brought to this country for the first time in August 1874 by a group of German-speaking Mennonite immigrants from Southern Russia. Durum wheat, grown primarily in the Dakotas and in Minnesota, was brought here in the late 19th century by Mark Alfred Carleton, a USDA cerealist.

Plant Breeding

The start of modern plant breeding technology came at the beginning of the 20th century when plant breeders discovered the concept of hybridization. The rediscovery of the genetic laws of Gregor Mendel aided immeasurably in this work.

Mendel, a 19th-century Austrian monk, had demonstrated the fundamental laws of genetic inheritance while experimenting with pea plants. He showed that for each physical trait every individual possessed two "factors," or what later came to be known as "genes." Mendel's findings, first published in an obscure journal, aroused little interest until they were rediscovered in 1900.

Around this time, too, came the development of the chromosome theory of heredity in which biologists discovered that genes were arranged in linear sequence along chromosomes that are present in the nucleus of every living cell. By applying Mendel's laws and the chromosome theory, breeders were able to develop new crop varieties that were uniform in quality and yield and adaptable to specific environments.

The best-known American plant breeder was Luther Burbank, who died in 1926. Working primarily in his Santa Rosa, Calif., laboratory, Burbank experimented

The work of George Washington Carver helped increase the production and use of peanuts.

with thousands of different plant types. He developed new varieties of many fruits, berries, and vegetables, including prunes, plums, apples, peaches, nectarines, raspberries, blackberries, potatoes, tomatoes, corn, squash, peas, and asparagus.

Agricultural chemist George Washington Carver, who was born a slave in the 1860s, discovered hundreds of uses for peanuts, sweet potatoes, and soybeans. Carver's work at Tuskegee Institute in Alabama stimulated the wide cultivation of these three popular American crops.

During the first five decades of this century plant breeders refined their work. Their discoveries led to significant increases in agricultural productivity. In the mid-1960s, farmers in traditionally food-short countries such as India, Pakistan, and the Philippines began to cultivate new "miracle grains" — wheat, corn, and rice, and to a

lesser extent, sorghum, millet, and soybeans — on a broad scale.

The cultivation of these new varieties, which required heavy use of chemical fertilizers and pesticides, was termed the "green revolution." American agronomist Norman E. Borlaug, considered the "father" of the green revolution, was awarded the Nobel Peace Prize in 1970 for his work in helping ease world food problems.

Genetic Vulnerability

As breeding techniques improved and higher-yielding varieties were produced on a wide scale, older "folk" varieties of plants were virtually abandoned, leading to increased concern about the shrinking genetic base. "In some areas there is a clear danger that plantings of the new crops will completely replace plantings of indigenous folk varieties," the National Academy of Sciences said in a 1979 report. "Should this happen, important reservoirs of genes needed under less-favorable conditions will be irretrievably lost unless adequate provisions are made to guarantee their preservation."

Bernard Finkle, a biochemist at the USDA Western Regional Research Laboratory, described the problem in a magazine article. "The more I work, the more I realize what an important problem this is. We are losing the thousands of ancestral strains — handed down from generation to generation — as well as the wild strains often intermingled with them at precipitous rates. This complex, poorly controlled, dynamic system just cannot resist the onslaught of modern, organized agricultural methods. Disasters are staring us in the face."

A shrinking genetic base leads to what biologists call genetic vulnerability. This is when major food crops are left vulnerable to insects and disease. Quentin Jones has described the extent of this vulnerability: "Environmental factors keep changing," he said. "They are not totally predictable. And we can get new insect pests, new disease pests. We can get changes in climate or even weather within the climatic regimen. And so we would have to modify our plants so that they could successfully react to these changes and continue to yield well."

But if biologists do not have access to wild strains with which to modify the plants, he added, "then if you do get a breakout of a new disease or insect, it can build rapidly into epidemic proportions leading to economic catastrophe. . . . It ranges all the way from extremely serious problems like starvation, to losses to the individual farmer. . . ."

What Lester Brown termed the "classic example" of genetic vulnerability came in 1845 in Ireland when that nation suffered through one of the greatest natural disasters in history: the Great Potato Famine. Ireland's staple food crop, the potato, which had been introduced from South America, was hit by a blight for four consecutive years.

Hundreds of thousands died of starvation, and by 1854 some 1.6 million people had emigrated to the United States. The nation's population fell from 8.5 million in 1845 to 6.5 million six years later. The Republic of Ireland's population was only 3.4 million by the early 1980s.

"The potato does not readily contract blight," Brown wrote in *Seeds of Change*. "The temperature and humidity, among other factors, have to be exactly right — or rather, wrong. But when these very specific conditions occur, the crop failure can be total. The same is true of wheat rust and some other diseases attacking cereals."

Several wheat rust epidemics have struck the United States this century. One such disaster in 1916 destroyed 3 million bushels of wheat in the United States and Canada. Two other less extensive wheat rust epidemics hit in 1935 and 1953.

The term "genetic vulnerability" was coined to explain the main cause of the blight that struck the U.S. corn crop in 1970. The blight, caused by the fungus Bipolaris maydis, hit especially hard in the Southern states where some areas lost 50 percent of the corn crop. Overall, about 15 percent of the nation's corn crop was lost to the disease.

Experts say the corn blight came about primarily because U.S. farmers had planted too much of several corn varieties that were vulnerable to the Bipolaris maydis infestation. The main effect of the blight in this country was an increase in food prices. But as agricultural specialist Noel D. Vietmeyer wrote in a magazine article, "in countries such as Guatemala and Kenya, where half of the diet is corn, such a crop failure would have brought disastrous starvation."

The uncomfortable news is that a similar blight could occur in this country at any time. A 1972 study commissioned by the National Academy of Sciences pointed out that "vulnerability stems from genetic uniformity." On this basis, it concluded, "some American crops are . . . highly vulnerable."

Storage Facilities

One way agricultural scientists are working to preserve the genetic base is to collect germ plasm — the living material used to generate new plants that usually is in the form of seeds or cuttings of living plants — and preserve it so it will be available for future use.

There are large storage systems in the Soviet Union, the United States, and Mexico. Mexico's International Maize and Wheat Improvement Center was set up by that nation's Ministry of Agriculture in Mexico City in the early 1950s. It has the largest collection of corn germ plasm and seeds in the world — some 13,000 different items stored in refrigerated concrete vaults.

The American system of seed storage is coordinated by the USDA's Germ Plasm Resources Laboratory in Beltsville, Md. The main facility for long-term storage is the National Seed Storage Laboratory located on the campus of Colorado State University in Fort Collins. Other regional facilities, which are joint ventures run by USDA and various state agricultural agencies, are located in Pullman, Wash.; Ames, Iowa; Geneva, N.Y.; and Experiment, Ga. In addition, several large corporations engaged in agricultural research have their own germ plasm storage facilities.

The material stored in the facilities is gathered from all over the world. The germ plasm is sent first to one of the four regional centers where it is multiplied and made available to research scientists. The seeds are also evaluated before they are sent to Fort Collins for long-term storage.

The regional centers maintain working

stocks to distribute to scientists engaged in breeding research. At Fort Collins the seeds are dried to a point where their moisture content is suited for storage — between 5-7 percent moisture. They are then sealed in moisture-proof polyethylene bags and placed in cold storage. The seeds are tested for germinating ability about once every five years. If there is danger that they are losing potency, the seeds are taken out of storage and grown to produce more seeds.

There has been some criticism of the adequacy of the U.S. system of germ plasm storage. According to a 1981 study by the U.S. General Accounting Office (GAO), "the small grain storage facility at Beltsville, Md. — the principal facility for cereal germ plasm storage in the United States — is considered totally inadequate by many members of the germ plasm community."

The GAO report said the Maryland facility's "humidity and temperature control equipment was not only obsolete, but barely operable, seriously jeopardizing the collections. The building itself was not well designed for the needed temperature and humidity control." The report also cited problems of inadequate personnel and funds.

The National Seed Storage Laboratory in Fort Collins also has come in for criticism. Lobbyist Jack Doyle of the Environmental Policy Center, a public interest organization specializing in energy and natural resource policy, said that the facility is not equipped to handle some sensitive varieties of seeds that do not store well. "There has been some criticism . . . that some of the seeds are not in fact viable for reproduction and for breeding purposes," Doyle said.

Louis Bass, director of the Fort Collins facility, said in an interview that the only thing about the National Seed Storage Laboratory that is "inadequate" is the USDA-allocated budget. The 1981 fiscal-year budget for Fort Collins was some $437,000, the same as in 1977. Bass said the facility has a

Seed germination tests at the National Seed Storage Laboratory

staff of 19 and handles 4,000-6,000 accessions (varieties, cultivars, and other highly developed breeding lines) a year.

There are 120,000 accessions stored at Fort Collins, representing more than 1,200 species. Bass said the facility needs a larger budget because of inflation. One of the biggest costs, he said, is seed propagation. "As the laboratory gets older and older [it was built in 1957], this will increase because more and more seeds will have to be multiplied," Bass said. "What we really need is a budget that has built into it an escalating factor for increasing accessions, increasing costs of operations and increasing amounts of seeds that need to be multiplied."

Fort Collins is about 65 miles north of Denver and about 40 miles from the Fort Saint Vrain nuclear generating plant and about 60 miles from the Energy Department's Rocky Flats Plutonium Fabrication Plant in Golden, Co., which manufactures plutonium triggers used in hydrogen bombs. Bass contends that neither nuclear facility poses any threat to the seeds stored at Fort Collins "because our prevailing winds blow in that direction and not from that direction this way.... They are all downwind from us, so to speak."

Future of Research Effort

If corporate involvement is an indication of the future of agricultural research, the picture would seem quite rosy. Some of the biggest corporations in the nation, including Atlantic Richfield Co., International Telephone & Telegraph Corp., Occidental Petroleum Corp., and Union Carbide

Corp., have acquired seed companies in the last decade. Other large corporations, led by chemical and pharmaceutical firms, are spending tens of millions of dollars a year researching the applications of genetic engineering to agriculture. *(Corporate acquisitions, p. 63; corporate investment, p. 54)*

Bob Tamarkin of *Forbes* magazine labeled genetic engineering in agriculture the leading "growth industry" of the 1980s. "Amid all the unrelieved bad news about food supplies ... there is good news, too," he wrote. "It comes from what is going on in agricultural research, most importantly in the laboratories of American universities and of major U.S. companies positioning themselves for a great growth market."

A significant difference of opinion exists as to what this growing corporate involvement in agricultural research portends. There are those, including many USDA officials, who welcome the recent infusion of corporate money. They believe industry involvement will stimulate discoveries and other breakthroughs in agricultural research.

"The companies can make real contributions," said G. W. Schaeffer of USDA's Cell Culture and Nitrogen Fixation Laboratory. "Some of these companies are bringing 10, 20, 30 Ph.D.s to work on some of these problems. And if you put those kinds of resources into it, there's no question in my mind that they can make some real progress on some things that we don't know now or understand very well."

Other observers question the benefits of this corporate involvement. They maintain that the corporations will have little incentive to produce a wide range of different crop varieties because the biggest profits will come in the development of a few high-yielding varieties. If corporate seed companies and agricultural research laboratories turn out still more uniform crops, they say, the world's food supply will be even more vulnerable to disease and pest damage.

"Over time, the largest of America's farms could come under contract to the laboratory-based corporations, using corporate-bred plants, chemicals and hormones," said Jack Doyle of the Environmental Policy Center in a *New York Times* article. "Food crops might one day be ordered and formulated in the lab, especially when large international trading companies want a certain kind of grain in supertanker proportions. . . . Food quality and genetic diversity might not fare well under the corporate mantle."

Plant Patent Amendments

The debate over corporate involvement in agricultural research surfaced in 1980 as Congress considered two amendments to the 1970 Plant Variety Protection Act (PVPA), which set rules for patenting new plants.

Since 1930, American developers creating new plant varieties by grafting and other "asexual" techniques have been able to patent plants under a process called "certification." The 1970 law brought new plant types developed by other means into the system.

One of the 1980 amendments excluded six vegetables — carrots, celery, cucumbers, okra, peppers, and tomatoes — from the original act eligible for patents. The other amendment extended the period of exclusive control by a breeder from 17 years to 18, making the act more compatible with international law.

A number of groups — including the National Sharecroppers Union (a tenant farmers and migrant workers group), the Consumer Federation of America, the National Farmers Union, and the Environmental Policy Center — objected to the amendments for several reasons.

One of their chief concerns was that

the amendments would hasten the takeover of seed companies by petrochemical and pharmaceutical companies, a trend they believe is leading to the production of fewer varieties of plants and to higher food costs.

"We were suggesting to Congress that they should take a careful look at what patenting has done in the last 10 years — since the enactment of the Plant Variety Protection Act," Jack Doyle told a reporter. "Has the [law] contributed to [the development of] more varieties that are genetically better? Has our seed pool been enhanced in the process? Have we introduced strength in varieties? Is our genetic position strengthened?" he questioned.

Proponents of the amendments, principally the American Seed Trade Association, said that plant certification procedures mandated by the 1970 law actually encouraged plant diversity and also helped small seed companies. Harold D. Loden, executive vice president of the association, testified that since the early 1970s plant breeders have developed an unprecedented number of seed varieties.

Former senator Frank Church, D-Idaho, one of the amendments' sponsors, agreed. "What must be remembered is that plant variety protection has worked to protect the new varieties developed by small companies against exploitation by larger seed companies. It has proven effective in the last nine years for those plants already on the protection list. All I am doing now is extending that same protection to six vegetable types. . . ."

Supporters of the legislation conceded that large corporations have been acquiring seed companies. But they maintained that the 1970 law was not the reason. It was, they said, more a part of a general takeover movement by large firms through all sectors of the economy. In the end, Congress passed the amendments and, on Dec. 22, 1980, President Carter signed the bill into law.

The Office of Technology Assessment summed up the outcome of the bill and the debate this way: ". . . although no conclusive connection has been demonstrated between the two plant protection laws and the loss of genetic diversity, the use of uniform varieties, or the claims of increasing concentration in the plant breeding industry, the question is still controversial and these complex problems are still unresolved."

Approaches to Crop Diversity

Nearly everyone on both sides of the plant patenting issue is concerned about the shrinking genetic base. All concerned have called for more effective collection and storage of germ plasm. But there is disagreement over the exact way to solve the genetic diversity problem.

Those in industry say the best way to end genetic vulnerability is to continue supporting agricultural research. They are counting on a scientific breakthrough in university, USDA, or corporate laboratories. Others say preserving seed is the answer.

The 1979 National Academy of Sciences report on germ plasm resource conservation said that the "only reliable method" of preserving endangered plant species is "in the natural habitat." But the report went on to say that "when preservation in nature is not possible, intelligent zoo or garden maintenance, with encouragement of breeding potentiality, offers a possible alternative."

Jack Doyle said the best way to ensure the survival of threatened varieties is to encourage farmers to plant more varieties and different crops. "If you look at a good business, it's diversified. You have a lot of things scattered across a lot of areas," Doyle said. "The farm community, I think, needs to make that same kind of diversified investment strategy."

Quentin Jones of the USDA agreed with Doyle's main point. Jones told a re-

Corporate Acquisitions of North American Seed Companies

Corporate Owner	Seed Company
Agrigenetics Corp.	Agricultural Laboratories
	Arkansas Valley Seeds
	Jacques Seeds
	R. C. Young Seeds
	Seed Research Inc.
	Sun Seeds
	Taylor-Evans
	V. R. Seeds
Amfac	American Garden Products
	Gurney Seeds
	Western Seed Co.
	Henry Field Seed & Nursery
Atlantic-Richfield	Dessert Seed Co.
Celanese	CelPril Inc.
	Joseph Harris Seed Co.
	Moran Seeds
	Niagara Seeds
ITT	Burpee Seeds
	O. M. Scott
Occidental Petroleum	Ring Around Products
	Excel Hydrid Seeds
	Missouri Seed Co.
	Moss Seed Co.
	Payne Bros. Seed Co.
	Stull Seeds
	West Texas Seed Co.
	East Texas Seed Co.
Olin and Royal Dutch Shell	North American Plant Breeders
	Agripro Inc.
	Midwest Seed Growers
	Tekseed Hybrid Co.
	Rudy-Patrick
Purex	Advanced Seeds
	Hulting Hybrids
Sandoz (Swiss)	National-NK (Canada)
	Northrup, King & Co.
	McNair Seed
	Woodside Seed Growers
	Rogers Brothers
Union Carbide	Keystone Seed Co.
Upjohn	Asgrow Seeds
	Associated Seeds
	Farmers' Hybrid Co.

Source: Environmental Policy Institute, partial list.

porter, "We tend to go for monocultures to begin with — growing wheat and nothing but wheat over large areas and corn sometimes rotated with soybeans. There are a few crops growing over huge areas and few varieties of those crops."

Jones said the "only hope for the forseeable future if we're going to continue to improve production ... is to do more collecting of germ plasm before it disappears. And we have to do a lot better job of maintaining it in our system once we get in gear. And we have to do a lot more in the way of evaluating it so that this diversity can be identified and related to the needs of the breeders."

6

Pesticide Controversies

Since men first tilled the earth, farmers have fought endless battles with pests that prey on crops and livestock. For nearly half a century, the agricultural industry has waged all-out war on insects, disease, worms, and weeds with modern-day chemical weapons. But powerful pesticides, once hailed as miracles of science, have spread mixed blessings on the fields.

Agricultural pests still consume at least one-third of the food crops that the world grows each year. Synthetic chemical pesticides, while helping farmers double crop yields, also have bred resistant insects and set new pests loose by killing their natural enemies. Sprayed indiscriminately across the fields by helicopters or low-flying "crop dusters," lethal compounds have killed wildlife, contaminated soil and streams, and built up in human tissues.

Americans first became aware of the possible hazards of widespread pesticide use with the publication in 1962 of *Silent Spring* by Rachel Carson. In the book, which became a national best seller, Carson argued that many pesticides in use on farms and timberlands had unknown and cumulative toxic effects. Because so little was known about the effects of these chemicals, Carson said, their use should be curtailed.

The federal government in the 1970s banned most uses of DDT (dichlorodiphenyl trichloroethane) and other potent chemicals that threatened human health and environmental safety. Despite stricter government regulations, however, pesticide spraying has doubled since the early sixties as farmers turned to new chemical compounds to protect their harvests and make their fields more productive. U.S. farmers apply about 700 million pounds of insecticides, herbicides, and fungicides a year, at a cost of around $2 billion.

Despite such weapons, pests still plague the world's most productive agricultural country. In developing lands, where the specter of famine still looms, the fight against pests may be more desperate. "Neither the hungry nor the affluent can continue to pay this price, which is to receive only part of their daily bread," wrote William R. Furtick, former chief of the United Nations Food and Agriculture Organization, in *Pesticides and Human Welfare*.

From the Biblical locust plagues to California's "Medfly" invasion of the early 1980s, which threatened that state's vital fruit and vegetable crops, agricultural pests have posed threats to food supplies. In agrarian and industrial societies alike, on peasants' plots and mechanized agribusiness farms, huge amounts of food are lost before ever reaching the table. A 1977 National Academy of Sciences study estimated that pests cost the world about 35 percent of its potential food production.

Pests afflict all the world's major crops, infest forests, and attack horses, sheep, and cattle. Along with the celebrated Medfly, common pests go by such colorful names as the gypsy moth, boll weevil, grasshopper, Hessian fly, blights and rusts, wild oats, and wild buckwheat. They include insects, weeds, worms, bacteria, fungi, rodents, and larger mammals that nibble crops or prey on domestic livestock.

Since World War II, farmers have relied on synthetic chemical pesticides as their principal defense against pest losses. Pesticide spraying has grown tenfold since 1945 — and more than doubled since *Silent Spring* was published in 1962.

More than 1,200 basic ingredients now are labeled for pesticide use, and 35,000 formulations have been registered. According to government figures, however, farmers use a relatively small number, depending on 20 insecticides to combat insects, 17 herbicides to keep down weeds, and six fungicides to prevent plant diseases.

Pesticides have helped farmers around the world harvest larger crops and send more food to market. Norman E. Borlaug, a crop researcher who was awarded the 1970 Nobel Peace Prize for his work in launching the "green revolution" in Asia, contended in 1972 that banning chemical pesticides would cut crop yields in half and raise food prices four or five times. The congressional Office of Technology Assessment (OTA) in 1979 concluded that without pesticides — or equally effective alternative measures — grain prices would jump 60 percent and commercial producers of lettuce, apples, potatoes, and strawberries would suffer intolerable losses.

Pest losses remain high, however, even with widespread spraying. Insect damage has nearly doubled since 1945, and herbicides at best have slightly curtailed weed problems. At the same time, many people worry that campaigns to curb a few unwanted species could endanger the entire fabric of life on earth. Environmentalists now demand, in Rachel Carson's words,

that "the methods employed [to control pests] must be such that they do not destroy us along with the insects."

Since 1970, when regulation was transferred from the U.S. Agriculture Department to the newly created Environmental Protection Agency (EPA), the federal government has tightened controls over the manufacturing, distribution, and use of pesticides. Even so, fears persist that pesticides now being sprayed eventually will turn out to be damaging to wildlife and humans. "In the past we willingly accepted claims that pesticides had no long-term effect on humans," Douglas M. Costle, EPA administrator under President Carter, commented in a magazine article devoted to the pesticide dilemma. "Neither EPA nor the industry is in a position to make such reassurances honestly."

Medfly Spraying

Such doubts were apparent in several pest control controversies of the early 1980s. In California, farmers, and state officials have been watching carefully for any reinvasion by Mediterranean fruit flies, which threatened the state's fruit and vegetable crops in 1980 and 1981. Over vehement local objections, California governor Edmund G. "Jerry" Brown Jr. authorized aerial spraying over heavily populated suburbs in 1981 to keep the hardy insects from spreading from backyard fruit trees into the state's rich agricultural Central Valley.

Although Medflies had not been sighted in the state since Nov. 20, 1981, California officials continued to be cautious. In 1982 they resumed weekly sprayings of the pesticide malathion over 166.6 square miles, primarily in the northern part of the state.

To avoid aerial spraying when the Medfly infestation was first discovered, Brown had ordered residents in the infected areas to destroy all fruits and vegetables and to apply the pesticide malathion on the ground. But the U.S. Secretary of Agriculture, John Block, threatened to impose a quarantine on all California produce to keep the Medfly from spreading.

Brown gave in despite public fears that malathion, a non-persistent but highly toxic organic phosphate, would endanger residents of the 1,486-square-mile area where aerial spraying was conducted in 1981. The justification for the spraying was two-fold: to prevent the spread of the flies to other parts of the country and to save California's $14 billion agriculture industry.

The dispute sparked the sharpest pest control conflict yet between urban and agricultural interests. Some critics, including Stanford University biologist Paul Ehrlich, said that other methods could have kept the Medflies under control without aerial spraying. But Dick Jackson, deputy director of a joint state and federal Medfly project, argued in *Science* magazine that the spraying "opened the door to a sensible use of pesticides." In California, Jackson insisted, "we've proven that we haven't even made anybody sick and have done a hell of a lot for our credibility."

Medflies again were sighted in 1984. The pests, however, were found in urban Miami, Fla., where residents willingly submitted to a localized quarantine of fruits and vegetables and aerial spraying over a nine-square-mile area. One reason for the difference in public reaction between California and Florida was that Miami, a large port city, had dealt with Medfly outbreaks in the past. In addition, none of the state's agricultural areas appeared to be threatened by the outbreak.

Pest eradication programs in other parts of the country, however, have caused alarm among local populations. The use of chemicals to fight the gypsy moth in New England and New York metropolitan areas has raised strong public objections. In New England, neighbors argued bitterly in town

Former governor Edmund G. "Jerry" Brown

meetings about whether to allow chemical sprayings to protect vegetation. In 1981, gypsy moth caterpillars attacked more than 500 species of plants.

Edward J. Markey, D-Mass., who represents the Medford area, where the gypsy moth first appeared in the United States late in the 19th century, cautioned against massive applications of pesticides. "We can't forget that what may seem like a prudent and expedient action now can have drastic implications for the general public far into the future."

In 1981 state and federal wildlife officials in the West debated canceling hunting seasons after dangerous levels of the acutely toxic pesticide endrin were found in ducks, geese, and other game birds in Montana. The birds, which apparently had fed on wheat and other grains sprayed with the pesticide, contained endrin traces that were potentially hazardous for persons who shot and ate the fowl.

Environmentalists from Massachusetts to Oregon have blamed increasing cancer rates and other health problems on picloram, a herbicide that the U.S. Forest Service and timber companies use to clear hardwoods from pine forests and that railroads and power companies spray to keep rights-of-way free of weeds.

President Nixon, responding to environmentalists' outcries, in 1972 banned use of those poisons, including Compound 1080 (sodium monofluoroacetate), in predator control programs on federally owned lands. EPA subsequently clamped severe limits on state and private use of Compound 1080, strychnine, and other toxicants as baits to kill coyotes.

Environmentalists argued that the toxicants killed other wildlife, including endangered species, that ate the baits or fed on the carcasses of coyotes. The Reagan administration rekindled this debate in 1982 by moving to allow use of chemical toxicants to control coyotes on federal rangelands in Western states. *(Predator losses, p. 76)*

Government Regulations

U.S. pesticide regulation dates from early in the 20th century. Responding to pressure from farm organizations and the U.S. Department of Agriculture (USDA), Congress in 1910 set standards for ingredients in Paris green, lead arsenate, and other pesticides then being used.

In 1947, with new synthetic chemical pesticides coming on the market, Congress enacted the Federal Insecticide, Fungicide, and Rodenticide Act (FIFRA) requiring for the first time that all pesticides be registered before going on the market and that packages be labeled with their contents. USDA administered the law, concentrating on making sure that pesticides worked as claimed. Few chemicals were barred from the market.

Responsibility for regulation of pesticides was transferred from the Agriculture Department to the Environmental Protection Agency when it was created in 1970. The EPA's regulation and enforcement powers were enlarged with the passage of the Federal Environmental Pesticide Control Act of 1972. The legislation required that all pesticides be registered with the EPA and empowered the agency to control the manufacture, distribution, and use of pesticides. It also freed the EPA to ban hazardous chemicals and imposed penalties for their improper use.

Pesticides were divided into two categories: general and restricted use by qualified applicators, depending on the hazards involved. Under the law, pesticide manufacturers or retailers were entitled to federal indemnity payments if their products were declared an imminent hazard by the EPA and removed from the market. No payments would be made, however, if the pesticide owners knew in advance that their products were hazardous but continued to use or produce them.

The controversial indemnity provision in the original House-passed version of the bill was deleted by the Senate. It was reinserted in response to pressure from the pesticide industry and agriculture interests.

Congress in 1978 adopted legislation to simplify pesticide registration and marketing procedures, allowing EPA to classify and register pesticides by chemical composition rather than product name. In 1969 the departments of Agriculture, Interior, and Health, Education and Welfare joined forces to impose limitations on the use of DDT. The EPA enlarged the prohibition in 1973, announcing a ban on almost all remaining uses of the chemical. EPA banned the pesticides aldrin, dieldrin, chlordane, and heptachlor in 1975; the following year, manufacturers voluntarily ceased production of four other chemicals — mirex, Kepone, stibane, and BHC.

The EPA's efforts to regulate pesticides have left the agency open to criticism from farmers and the pesticide industry on one side and from environmentalists on the other side. Farm and chemical industry spokesmen have charged that environmentalists have exaggerated the pesticide threat and argued that the nation relied on pesticides to provide its abundant supply of food and fiber. Chemical producers contend that stringent federal and state standards and time-consuming registration procedures discourage development of new insecticides targeted on specific pests.

One EPA opponent charged that "The Environmental Protection Agency has started a trend that will turn our farms back to the insects, weeds, and fungi ... reduce output and quality ... and accelerate food shortages." Environmental groups, on the

---

Defining Pesticides

Pesticide is a general term for any substance or mixture of substances intended for preventing, destroying, repelling, or mitigating any pest, including insects, rodents, fungi, or weeds. This includes any substance intended for use as a plant regulator, defoliant, or dessicant.

Between 35,000 to 40,000 pesticides products are registered with the Environmental Protection Agency (EPA). They are made from one of more of approximately 600 basic chemical compounds. There are also approximately 1,200 active ingredients registered with the EPA.

Farmers use by far the largest volume of pesticides produced in this country, but a little less than half of registered pesticide products are intended for home, institutional, or industrial use. All sterilizing, disinfecting, sanitizing, germicidal, and bacteria killing chemicals (if they make pesticidal claims and are not sold exclusively for use in or on the living bodies of men or animals) are classified as pesticides and must be registered.

The three major families of pesticides are:

- Chlorinated hydrocarbons, or organochlorines — "Hard" pesticides, which break down chemically quite slowly and can remain in the environment for long periods of time. Pesticides of this type include: DDT, DDD, DDE, dieldrin, chlordane, toxaphene, aldrin, endrin, helptachlor, and lindane.

- Organic phosphates, or organophosphates — Not persistent in the environment, but highly toxic to humans. They include: parathion, malathion, chlarethion, thimet, phosdrin, methylparathion, and trichlorphone.

- Carbamates compounds — Of low toxicity to humans.

The three major functions of pesticides are as:

- Herbicides — killing weeds
- Insecticides — killing insects
- Fungicides — killing fungus

Source: Congressional Quarterly Inc., *Environ*̇ *ient and Health* (1981), p. 82.

other hand, have demanded that the EPA's regulations of potentially dangerous pesticides be strengthened.

Congress was unable in 1982 to reconcile conflicts surrounding a rewrite of the Federal Insecticide, Fungicide, and Rodenticide Act despite nearly a year of negotiations. However, a simple one-year authorization cleared Congress the following year. The measure extended through September 1987 the authority for a scientific advisory panel on pesticides. The bill's sponsors decided to pass a simple funding measure and put aside, for the time being, controversial policy issues surrounding federal regulation.

Pesticide producers were urging the House Agriculture Committee's Subcommittee on Department Operations, Research and Foreign Agriculture to limit public access to industry studies on how various chemical compounds affect human health and the environment. The companies contended that the toxicity studies contain trade secrets. Industry officials also have asked Congress to pre-empt state laws, which sometimes — as in California — are more restrictive than federal regulations. Environmentalists, fearful that pesticide controls will be watered down, want FIFRA extended without change. Further legislative action was expected in 1984.

Worldwide Pest Problems

Farmers have contended with pests ever since men first cultivated crops 10,000 or more years ago. The Bible describes several crop and livestock infestations, including the locust plague on Egypt that "covered the face of the whole earth, so that the land was darkened. . . ."

Early civilizations lived in fear of plagues that could bring famine upon the land, and more recent infestations at times have changed the course of history. After a blight destroyed Ireland's potato crop in 1845, a million Irish died and a million and a half more emigrated to America. In 1916-17, U.S. grain farmers lost at least a third of their harvest to wheat rust disease, and the resulting food crisis may have delayed the nation's entrance into World War I.

Developing lands, especially in tropical climates, still are threatened with calamity. But even in industrial countries, where farming has been mechanized, men compete for food with a host of organisms. In many cases, modern agricultural practices have created more problems for farmers and ranchers by encouraging the spread of new pests.

Specialized monocultural farms, growing vast stretches of a single cash crop, have given some pests free rein to spread unchecked from field to neighboring field. The Western corn rootworm, for instance, has been expanding its range by 140 miles a year as it moves through North America's Midwest Corn Belt. Some once-harmless organisms, like the Colorado potato beetle, spread quickly across the continent when farmers began planting new crops that the pests thrived on. Some exotic species, such as the Medfly, gypsy moth, and Japanese beetle, have prospered in North America after being inadvertently brought from overseas.

Insects and related anthropods — from the housefly to the grasshopper — are perhaps the most common and prolific pests. Throughout the world, about 10,000 species of insect are considered important pests for crops, livestock, stored foods, and people. The United States has 150 to 200 insect species that pose serious pest problems.

Weeds are simply unwanted plants that compete with crops for sunlight, water, and soil nutrients. More than 30,000 plant species are classified as weeds, and more than 1,800 cause economic losses to agriculture. Plant diseases caused by fungi, worm-like

More than half of a pesticide sprayed from the air drifts off target.

nematodes, viruses, and bacteria also take large tolls from crop production. And livestock diseases, parasites, and predators kill, maim, and weaken sheep and cattle.

A National Academy of Sciences study team reported in 1977 that insects, weeds, and plant diseases posed serious threats to all the world's major crops. Pests consume 20 percent of all important harvests, their report concluded, and ruin 46.4 percent of yearly rice crops, which provide the staple for many nations' diets. Post-harvest losses of stored foods to rodents, insects, fungi, and bacteria lift the total toll on the world's food supplies to more than 40 percent.

Modern Reliance on Chemicals

Early farmers developed a number of measures through trial and error to limit losses to pests. Around 2,500 B.C., Sumerians used sulfur compounds to control mites and insects. Centuries before Christ, the Chinese developed plant-derived insecticides, adjusted planting times, and used natural enemies to keep pests in check. And through the centuries farmers cultivated the soil by hand, with hoes and eventually horse-drawn plows, to rid the soil of weeds before planting.

During the late 19th and early 20th centuries, public agricultural experiment stations in farming states developed techniques to suppress pests through resistant crop varieties, cultivation practices, and biological control through natural enemies. After the boll weevil spread into Southern cotton fields from Mexico in the late 1800s, farmers fought back by planting varieties that matured earlier in the year, before

Agent Orange . . .

During the Vietnam War, the U.S. Army used Agent Orange — a combination of two herbicides, 2,4,5-T and 2,4-D — to defoliate dense jungles concealing enemy forces. Many U.S. veterans later blamed exposure to Agent Orange for a variety of health disorders, including cancer, liver damage, psychological and neurological symptoms, miscarriages, stillbirths, and birth defects in their children.

The component in Agent Orange that is suspected of causing health problems, TCDD, is a contaminant of 2,4,5-T — that is, a substance inadvertently created in varying amounts in the manufacturing process. TCDD is the most toxic of approximately 75 chemical compounds known as dioxins.

The Defense Department ended its Agent Orange spraying in Vietnam in 1970. In May 1970 the Agriculture Department moved to end the use of 2,4,5-T products on food crops and near homes, recreation sites, and other areas. In 1972 the ban on 2,4,5-T products was successfully challenged in court by Dow Chemical Co.

The Environmental Protection Agency, which had taken over most of the Agriculture Department's regulatory responsibilities for agricultural chemicals, resumed ban proceedings again the following year but abandoned the process and turned to studies instead. In 1979 EPA suspended the use of 2,4,5-T on forests, rights of way and pastures on the basis of a study prompted by complaints from women in Alsea, Ore., that they suffered miscarriages shortly after the herbicide was sprayed near their homes.

Also in 1979 Agent Orange victims formed an organization and launched a class action suit against the manufacturers of the substance. The lawsuit against seven chemical

---

weevils became numerous. They also destroyed post-harvest crop residues and adjusted harvesting schedules to hold down damage from weevils that bored into cotton plant bolls.

As early as 1865, however, American farmers began using an arsenic compound called Paris green to control the Colorado potato beetle. Kansas farmers applied common salt to kill bindweed in the late 1800s, and wheat farmers introduced copper sulfate to control weeds around the turn of the century.

Farmers started spraying orchards with lead arsenate in 1892 and dusting crops with calcium arsenate in 1907. After 1886, California citrus trees were fumigated un-

der tarpaulin tents with hydrogen cyanide. Aerial spraying from aircraft expanded pesticide use in the 1920s.

After World War II the chemical industry marketed more effective synthetic organic pesticides, including the insecticide DDT and the herbicide 2,4-D, which had been developed during wartime. DDT, a synthetic organochlorine, was first formulated in 1874, but its power to kill insects was not discovered until 1939. The U.S. Army classified DDT "top secret" during World War II, and the Allies used it to protect their troops against insect-borne diseases that inflicted widespread casualties among German forces.

During postwar years, German indus-

...The Continuing Debate

companies — Dow Chemical, Monsanto, Diamond Shamrock, Uniroyal, T. H. Agriculture and Nutrition, Hercules, and Thompson Chemical — was settled out of court May 7, 1984, the day it was scheduled to go to trial.

Under the agreement worked out in cooperation with Judge Jack B. Weinstein of the U.S. District Court in Brooklyn, N.Y., the chemical companies put $180 million in a fund to pay claims for damages to veterans and their offspring who believed they had health problems caused by Agent Orange. It was considered to be the largest monetary award ever won in a product liability case.

Veterans' groups had been trying for years to get medical care for veterans exposed to Agent Orange in Vietnam, but the Veterans Administration claimed there was not sufficient proof that the chemical was the cause of the veterans' problems.

Legislation passed in 1981 over VA objections made veterans who served in Vietnam eligible for VA medical, hospital, or nursing home care for problems linked to exposure to any toxic herbicide. By 1984 more than 20,000 veterans who believed they were suffering from Agent Orange-related problems had been treated in VA health care facilities and hundreds of thousands of vets had received care on an outpatient basis.

The agency, however, still had not awarded benefits (or survivor benefits for their families) as of July 1984 to veterans who claimed their disabilities were caused by Agent Orange. Both the Senate and House of Representatives approved bills in 1984 setting up mechanisms for the VA to compensate victims. Compromise legislation was expected later that year.

try modified chemical warfare agents to produce organic phosphate compounds, including parathion and malathion, for use as pesticides. At first, synthetic pesticides brought spectacular results in controlling insects in productive farming regions. Herbicides replaced costly hand labor and machine cultivation for controlling weeds in fields, forests, and along highways.

Pesticides offered improved pest control to protect the high-yielding wheat, rice, maize, and other food grains that Borlaug and other researchers developed for the "green revolution" in developing lands. DDT improved human health in entire countries by controlling pests such as the malaria-carrying mosquito.

Consequences and Hazards

In the United States, a major industry grew up in postwar decades to develop and sell synthetic pesticides. More than 80 U.S. companies produce active ingredients for pesticides, and as many as 1,800 firms manufacture and package pesticide dusts, powders, concentrates, and aerosols.

U.S. production climbed from around 464,000 pounds in 1946 to 1.4 billion pounds in 1977 as pesticides were applied in agriculture, forests, industry, and households. But by 1962, when *Silent Spring* sounded a public alarm, unexpected consequences were already tarnishing the once-bright promise of effective pest control.

After prolonged exposure to particular

pesticides, pest populations began to develop genetic resistance. As susceptible insects were killed off, hardier survivors mated to produce offspring that inherited immunity. Over the 30 years after synthetic chemicals were introduced, more than 300 species of insects, mites, and ticks evolved strains that were resistant to one or more pesticides. The corn rootworm, tobacco budworm, and the common housefly now survive pesticides that once were fatal.

Heavy pesticide use inadvertently created new pest problems for farmers. Some insecticides killed indiscriminately, sometimes disrupting natural controls on potential pest populations. Along with target pests, unselective pesticides may destroy beneficial insects, unleashing new pests that they had preyed on.

In response, farmers sometimes have stepped up spraying, applying heavier doses at frequent intervals. "Over the long term, however, this treadmill chemical approach has proved to be self-defeating, only engendering such serious problems as insecticide resistance, human poisonings, and environmental pollution," a 1979 report by the president's Council on Environmental Quality noted.

Human and Animal Life

Most ominous of all, some persistent pesticides have spread through the worldwide ecosystem. More than half of a pesticide sprayed from the air drifts off target and may be carried miles away from the fields. DDT residues have been found in Antarctic penguins and seals, far from the world's farming regions.

Research has revealed that some pesticides move up the food chain through biological magnification, a process by which minute quantities of chemicals stored in the body fat and tissues of creatures low in the food chain — plankton, for example — are transferred in constantly growing amounts

to predators higher in the food chain, inevitably affecting humans.

Since the early 1960s researchers have documented harmful concentrations of DDT and other chemicals in bald eagles, peregrine falcons, fish, and other wildlife. DDT and dieldrin, another long-lasting organochlorine, slowed reproduction in some threatened bird species by thinning the shells of their eggs. *(Pesticide definitions, box, p. 69)*

The rising use of pesticides is proving to have numerous effects. Pesticide pollution of Lake Ontario and the Chesapeake Bay forced a suspension of commercial fishing in those waters during the 1970s. The U.S. Department of Agriculture in 1976 paid $3.4 million through a special federal program to compensate honey bee owners whose colonies were poisoned by pesticides. Butterfly collectors and other naturalists contend that specimens have been harder to find since widespread insecticide spraying began.

Scientists also began examining the accumulation of pesticides in human beings. They found that Americans carried in their bodies an average of 12 parts per million of pesticide residues, nearly twice the level allowed for most foods in interstate commerce.

Evidence presented in 1970 showed than even very small quantities of DDT could affect human metabolism. The National Cancer Institute reported in 1969 that 11 of 123 pesticides tested caused increased incidence of malignant tumors in laboratory animals.

More than 100,000 Americans a year suffer direct pesticide poisoning, most of them farm workers or workers who handle the chemicals. The accidental death rate has fallen, however, to 52 people in 1974 from 111 persons in 1961. But the long-term dangers from steady low-level exposure continues to be a major subject of scientific research. *(Migrant workers, p. 42)*

Alternative Control Methods

Farmers and chemical industry officials insist that pesticides, properly handled and applied, are both safe and effective. Not all pesticides have been shown to cause harmful side effects, and continued spraying may be essential if farmers are to continue producing the variety of foods that Americans have grown to like. But doubts about pesticides have sent researchers back to their laboratories and experiment station fields to search for alternative pest management strategies.

Instead of relying on heavy pesticide spraying, some farmers now are experimenting with a combination of pest control methods. Those steps include natural biological controls, cultivation practices, crop rotation, pest-resistant plants, weed-burning, release of sterile insects — along with judicious use of chemical compounds targeted on specific pest species.

Since the early 1970s, the Agriculture Department and land grant universities have been encouraging adoption of such integrated pest management (IPM) programs. Some farmers are reluctant to give up pesticides. But a 1979 study of pest management strategies conducted by the U.S. Office of Technology Assessment found surprisingly wide use of IPM practices, particularly by Great Plains wheat farmers. The report estimated that IPM programs for major U.S. crops could cut pesticide use by up to 75 percent, reduce total pest control costs and still cut pest-caused losses to crops in the field by half.

Some IPM practices amount to what old-timers would call "common sense farming." Other procedures, involving sophisticated use of natural control agents, have been proven by demonstration projects and successful pest management programs. For instance, release of sterile blowflies has helped suppress screwworm outbreaks in Florida and Southwestern ranching country. Screwworms and blowfly larvae infect livestock wounds and feed on living tissue. Sterile flies, by mating with fertile populations, reduce the ability of blowflies to reproduce themselves.

Organic Farming

A few farmers, perhaps 20,000 or so around the nation, avoid using any pesticides at all and follow organic farming methods. Alarmed by environmental pollution, declining soil fertility, and rising costs for energy and petroleum-based fertilizers and pesticides, organic farmers rely entirely on natural materials to fertilize the soil and keep pests in check.

As a 1980 Agriculture Department study defined them, "to the maximum extent feasible, organic farming systems rely upon crop rotations, crop residues, animal manures, legumes, green manures, off-farm organic wastes, mechanical cultivation, mineral-bearing rocks, and aspects of biological pest control to maintain soil productivity and tilth, to supply plant nutrients, and to control insects, weeds and other pests."

Many experts dismiss organic agriculture as fine for gardens but impractical for large-scale farming operations. The Office of Technology Assessment study of pest management strategies for seven major U.S. crops concluded that organic methods offered too little protection against pests.

Commercial productions of some field crops, including alfalfa and field corn, was possible without synthetic pesticides, the report said, but heavy fruit and vegetable losses would make organic production of those crops impossible, while the labor costs of weeding by hand would be prohibitive for most large-scale ventures. The Agriculture Department study found a significant number of large farms, even up to 1,500 acres, being farmed organically in the West and

Midwest. The survey reported that organic farmers believe they attain yields that match other farms using chemical pesticides in their regions. "Contrary to popular belief," the study added, "most organic farmers have not regresssed to agriculture as it was practiced in the 1930s . . . . Organic farmers still use modern farm machinery, recommended crop varieties, certified seed, sound methods of organic waste management, and recommended soil and water conservation practices."

Curbing Predator Losses

In Western ranching states, sheep ranchers have been pressing for years for more effective ways to control coyotes that prey on sheep and lambs. Ever since the Nixon administration ended predator toxicant use on public range lands, sheepmen all over the West have blamed coyotes for livestock losses that have thrown the industry into economic trouble. President Reagan reversed Nixon's 1972 executive order, and the Interior Department's Fish and Wildlife Service in November 1981 asked EPA to approve experimental use of Compound 1080 toxicants in collars attached to sheep that were potential coyote victims.

The Fish and Wildlife Service, which runs predator trapping programs and other animal damage control efforts, also wants to resume testing of Compound 1080 in small baits that would be less likely to harm other species. Environmentalists have vehemently opposed resumed use of toxicants. But ranchers and predator researchers maintain that the 1972 ban was ordered without sufficient data to prove, one way or the other, whether Compound 1080 was unduly

hazardous to eagles and other wildlife.

Since Compound 1080 and other toxicants, including strychnine, were outlawed, ranchers and Fish and Wildlife Service trappers have continued hunting and trapping coyotes. Fish and Wildlife Service marksmen sometimes hunt coyotes from the air if ranchers in an area start suffering serious losses.

In 1979 Secretary of the Interior Cecil D. Andrus suspended a practice, known as denning, that burned, gassed, or clubbed coyote pups to death in their dens. The Fish and Wildlife Service in 1981 resumed denning on a restricted basis.

In the meantime, government and university researchers in Western states have been experimenting with alternative methods, both lethal and non-lethal, for curbing predator losses. Among the measures being studied are training large dogs to guard sheep pastures, installing electrified fences to keep coyotes out, setting off strobe lights and sirens to frighten coyotes off at night, and treating sheep with non-lethal chemicals that produce smells or tastes that repel coyotes.

While each of these measures has shown promising results, none has been proven to keep coyotes from killing sheep in all kinds of ranching operations. "There is no one way out there to control livestock losses," Samuel B. Linhart, a biologist at the Fish and Wildlife Service's Denver research center, said in a 1981 interview.

There are no easy answers to the problems of predator and pest control. In order to protect human health and environmental safety, farmers and consumers will continue to pay a price in crop and lifestock losses that add billions of dollars to the cost of food.

7

Lobbying: Regional and Ideological Rifts

"Farm bills satisfy everyone but those who live in the cities, those who live in the small towns and those who live in the country."

—Sen. Robert Dole, R-Kan.

Farm politics in Washington has much in common with Br'er Rabbit's briar patch. Outsiders see only complicated fights over arcane issues that elude understanding. But insiders — farm lobbyists and their allies in Congress — scamper through this thicket year after year, occasionally yelping about the pain of it all. Even as they bemoan their problems, which are significant, farm lobbyists also have managed to protect a multi-billion-dollar array of farm programs that is unlike anything provided for other industries.

Nevertheless, agriculture was approaching a political and fiscal crisis that would severely test the skills of the Washington farm establishment. The federal government's payments for farm price supports had soared to unprecedented levels. Editorial writers were attacking million-dollar federal subsidies to corporate farms. A drought caused widespread crop losses for smaller farms already struggling against bankruptcy. "Nobody really knows what to do about farm programs," Dan Glickman, D-Kan., told the House gloomily in August 1983.

Congressional agriculture debates were routinely punctuated with complaints that farmers were a neglected minority, taken for granted by Washington and hobbled by internal bickering. "We've had bipartisan benign neglect for the past decade," said Mark Andrews, R-N.D., a member of both the Senate Agriculture Committee and the Appropriations Subcommittee on Agriculture.

"We're weak. We're split. The only time we *ever* get anything is when we have righteousness on our side," said a commodity lobbyist whose record of success belied his words. The lobbyist insisted that he and his brethren "pursue righteousness" daily.

The pursuit of "righteousness" has taken the form of frequent chats with key members and staff, regular appearances at congressional fund raisers and timely comments on policy and budget decisions that affect farm incomes. The lobbyists regularly produce crowds of back-home farmers in Washington and reams of statistics and projections to support desired changes in law — or to hold off unwanted alterations.

Members who deal with them call the farm lobbyists shrewd, persistent, and effective. "These guys are some of the most experienced in the business. They know where the buttons are and when to push them," said Rep. Leon E. Panetta, D-Calif., who as a member of the Budget Committee has dealt with a wide range of issues and lobbyists. Panetta also chairs a House Agriculture subcommittee.

Agriculture's Troubles

The biggest problem for agriculture is the extraordinary cost of price support programs. The programs amounted to $18.8 billion in 1983. That was about six times the average $3 billion annual cost of these programs, although 1982 produced a record high of $11.9 billion.

Budget director David A. Stockman complained in May 1983 to the congressional Joint Economic Committee, "We are giving away more money to the farmers of this country than anyone ever conceived of giving away before. . . ." Stockman also observed, "We are spending more for farm subsidies than we are for welfare for the entire poverty population of this country."

The high cost of keeping a very small part of the nation — 2.4 percent of the population — down on the farm might be easier to defend if federal farm programs appeared to be working well. But the stability they were intended to achieve has proven elusive. By the early 1980s the industry had been swamped with overproduction and crushed with high debt loads on individual farms. Net farm income plunged to lows not seen for decades. And the 1983 summer's dry spell, the worst in 50 years, affected production in at least 28 states across the Southeast, Midwest, and Southwest. Drought damage was estimated at about $7 billion. Heavy spring rains in 1984 promised further to hinder production. The American Farm Bureau estimated flood damage at $1 billion. Moreover, the appealing image of farming as "forty acres and a mule" was being overtaken by stories of multimillion-dollar "agricultural factories" whose owners received annual federal benefits that exceeded many Americans' lifetime earnings. Former senator Herman E. Talmadge, D-Ga. (1957-81), once told an

aide that the only time he had seen a Georgia farm neighbor in denim coveralls instead of a business suit was when he showed up in Talmadge's Washington office to protest inadequate federal price support levels. Talmadge chaired the Senate Agriculture Committee. The changing image has eroded sympathies for farmers, as when Rep. Barney Frank, D-Mass., observed, "Squeeze the budget and you may well victimize poor children, while wealthy farmers remain unscathed."

Farm lobbyists were looking ahead with considerable fear to 1985 when the 1981 omnibus farm law was to expire. "It's going to be the longest, hardest go-around we've had," predicted Don Wallace, a Washington consultant who represents sugar and cotton interests and the Alabama Farm Bureau.

Who's Who

The historic political base of the agriculture lobby is general-interest farm groups, such as the American Farm Bureau Federation, which began not as Washington representatives but as service organizations. An exception was the American Agriculture Movement (AAM), which began in 1978 when tractor-riding farmers descended on Washington, protesting federal farm programs and complaining of poor representation.

More typically, the National Farmers Organization began and has continued as a bargaining agent for farmers, enabling them to contract directly with commodity buyers. County farm bureaus were once the conduits for federal extension service information, and present-day critics of the national organization said the Farm Bureau could claim the largest membership because people joined to take advantage of good prices on farm bureau insurance, tires, and other farm-related goods and services.

The old generalist organizations have

Angry farmers descended on Washington in 1978 to protest farm programs.

begun to be jostled by newer groups specializing in a single commodity, such as wheat, and hybrid organizations, such as cooperatives or the National Cotton Council of America, representing both growers and the middlemen that process and sell commodities. There also are swarms of Washington-based lawyers and consultants who occasionally involve themselves in specific issues, such as agricultural trade. Industries associated with agriculture — pesticide and farm machinery makers, for example — also invest much time and effort in agriculture policies.

Memberships in the lobby often overlap: It is not unusual for a leading spokesman for a specific commodity also to be a prominent member of a local or state farm bureau. The Alabama Farm Bureau, which

broke away from the national group, subsequently forged an unusual alliance with state AAM members.

Disagreement among farm groups is never far from the surface because the different segments of the increasingly specialized industry have conflicting needs and philosophies. The National Cattlemen's Association, for example, was unhappy over legislation passed in 1983 to pay dairymen for cutting back on production. Reduced production was expected to be achieved by slaughtering dairy cows, dumping extra beef onto the market in competition with the cattlemen.

High market prices sought by feed grain farmers were anathema to poultry and livestock producers who must buy the grain. Southern dairymen operated under less favorable climate and feed conditions than their counterparts in the upper Midwest and California, and the Southerners favored a far different legislative cure for the high costs of the dairy program.

In general, Southern farmers were more likely to be comfortable with New Deal-style farm programs, such as those covering tobacco and peanuts, which offered high price supports and strictly limited the amount of a commodity that could be produced or sold by each farmer. Midwesterners more often saw such federal controls as a liability, and their prime crops, corn and wheat, were eligible for considerably less federal support and were subject only to voluntary controls.

Such divisions appeared among both specialized commodity groups and within umbrella groups like the Farm Bureau. Nationally, the bureau was identified with Midwestern disdain for federal farm programs, but it also backed the strict regulatory program for tobacco favored by its Southeastern members. And certain state farm bureaus, such as Wisconsin's, strongly disagreed with the national organization on dairy policy.

Dissent Within the Ranks

There have been highly visible episodes of dissension in recent years; of these the 1978-79 AAM invasions of Washington received the most public attention. In 1981 budget pressures created such bitter conflicts among commodity groups involved in omnibus farm legislation that Congress came close to killing target prices — a major crop price support — and the federal tobacco and peanut programs. The legislation finally passed the House by a scant two-vote margin, with a significant number of farm-state members voting against it.

Bill Alexander, D-Ark., christened it "the last farm bill" and declared that the open warfare among commodity groups was "definitive proof that the New Deal coalition is dead." Two years later, Rep. Charlie Rose, D-N.C., was still warning that "agriculture is not strong enough on the floor of the House to have regional splits."

Although many farm bills were considered by Congress every year, the major event occurred every four years when Congress wrote "omnibus" farm legislation, reauthorizing and revising most major farm programs. Until 1981 writing this omnibus bill was largely an additive process. Each group decided what it needed and supported other farm interests against outside attack. But in 1981 the budget resolution, for the first time, put a ceiling on the total amount of money to be divided up, and fights flared over certain commodities, such as peanuts or tobacco or sugar, which appeared to receive a disproportionate share of the total.

The uneasy sense of rivalry has continued. One congressional Agriculture Committee aide likened the situation to a pond in which "the water level is going down and the fish are all flopping around and sticking each other and biting." But Wayne Boutwell, a former aide to Sen. Thad Cochran, R-Miss., and president of the National Council of Farmer Cooperatives, predicted that "adversity is probably going to bring them together. As long as things are good, people can go their separate ways."

There have been efforts to close ranks. In 1983 Washington representatives of dairy cooperatives resisted administration demands that they lobby for a freeze on one of the main price supports, target prices, in return for administration support for their compromise dairy legislation. Rep. Dick Durbin, D-Ill., said that Stockman's reported plan to splinter the farm lobby had become a "real rallying point" in House Agriculture Committee sessions.

According to a 1981 *Atlantic* magazine article based on extensive interviews with Stockman, the budget director believed "that victories over farm lobbies could be won ... if he kept the issues separate — attacking each commodity program in turn and undermining urban support by cutting food and nutrition programs." Said Durbin, "Stockman is alluded to every time we get into a tough political decision."

"The farm groups are so split up that they do more to confuse than convince Congress of what ought to be done," said a frustrated Andrews. "I can't imagine it getting any worse," said Mississippi's Cochran, chairman of the Senate Appropriations Subcommittee on Agriculture.

"... there is never a day that the farmer, too, doesn't get his share ... no session [of Congress] comes to an end without a huge grist of new laws to save him...."
— **H. L. Mencken**

Still Harvesting Dollars

Despite their claims of being a splintered, misunderstood minority, farmers held their own in Washington. As federal programs were being cut drastically in the early 1980s, the farm lobby managed to maintain their slice of the federal pie, as the following phenomena suggested:

● The Reagan administration, in a startling reversal of its free-market philosophy, was paying farmers in cash and surplus commodities for not growing wheat, corn, cotton, and rice in 1983. It was even buying up surplus commodities from farmers — to give back to them as payment for not planting part of their customary acreage. The commodity exchanges were known as the Payment-in-Kind, or PIK, payments.

U.S. corn crop also is used to feed livestock.

Dairy Lobbyist: . . .

Frank Vacca reckons the population of congressional districts in dairy cows. He easily ticks off the numbers: A mere 44 districts produce well over half the milk counsumed by Americans. Some 30 percent of the House districts have "not a cow, not a drop of milk." The rest yield milk in relatively moderate amounts.

Those numbers mean that dairymen make up a minority whose needs require much explaining to an indifferent majority in Congress, according to Vacca, who represents the major Midwestern dairy cooperative, Mid-America Dairymen, in Washington. These days, he acknowledges, dairymen are in trouble. Their federal price support program is badly managed and badly misunderstood, in his view.

And Vacca believes that the Reagan administration had deliberately focused its fire on dairymen because the industry is exceptionally well organized. "They look at us as the head pin in a bowling alley. If they knock us down," Vacca warns, "the rest of agriculture will go down with us."

The Education Process. As the director of government relations for Mid-America, Vacca works on legislative, regulatory, and political strategy. "Our most difficult chore, as farm lobbyists," he says, is educating House members "so they don't reinvent the wheel."

The acreage reduction program, larger than anything envisioned in the heyday of New Deal farm programs, was meant to throttle the excessive production that had depressed farm prices for several years. The program was extended into 1984 for wheat producers. *(Payment-in-Kind program, p. 15)*

The federal government did not generally pay industries to maintain what appeared to be surplus capacity, Rep. John Hiler, R-Ind., noted during debate on a farm-credit measure early in 1983. In the 1970s, Hiler said, when "25 percent of the metal casting industry went out of business . . . there was no one standing on the floor of the House saying that we should provide extra assistance."

● President Reagan Nov. 29, 1983, signed into law landmark changes in federal dairy policy despite his strong objections to the new program. The legislation authorized payments to dairymen, partly financed by dairy farmers themselves, for producing less milk. The bill, which also lowered federal dairy price supports, was meant to reduce surplus dairy production, which had been running about 10 percent more than demand. The federal dairy program had to buy surplus dairy goods at the established support price, and federal expenditures on the program were nearing $3 billion annually.

● The Reagan administration spent much of 1983 trying, without success, to persuade Congress to block scheduled increases in target prices, a major price support program for wheat the other crops. The target price program made "deficiency payments" to eligible producers of wheat, corn, cotton, and rice whenever the market prices for crops dropped below targets set by law. Secretary of Agriculture John R. Block

... Counting Cows and Votes

Education also means explaining to non-farm members that the dairy program has guaranteed their constituents a reliable supply of perishable food at what the industry regards as a reasonable price. Education also means explaining that mammoth milk "factories" of thousands of cows are exceptional, and that most "corporate" farms are run by hard-working families whose members earn little more than the federal minimum wage. "It's not a lifestyle that many people want," Vacca remarks.

Organizational Strengths. Dairymen must recognize that, because they are so few in number, "It's *all* politics," he says forcefully. His organization encourages contributions, which average about $65 per member a year, to its PAC.

Like other dairy co-ops, Mid-America provides an essential service: It collects, processes, and finds buyers for members' milk. It is the agent that pays dairymen for their product. The network of district and division organizations established to do the business of the co-op is also a natural conduit for the business of politics.

Vacca insists it is not dairy PAC money but this organizational strength — unique among farm groups — that accounts for the lobby's successes. "We've *had* the dairy program since 1949, and we didn't go into PACs, none of us, until 1969," he says. Now, he adds, "all we're doing is protecting what we can, as best we can."

---

unsuccessfully sought an end to the program in 1981. The Reagan administration in 1983 wanted Congress to hold target prices at 1983 levels, instead of allowing them to rise automatically over the next two years.

● When growers of "upland" cotton — the bulk of American cotton — asked Congress in mid-1983 to reverse a PIK policy, the desired language showed up in five separate pieces of legislation. It was signed into law July 30 as part of the fiscal 1983 supplemental appropriations bill. Farm lobbyists argued that the PIK policy meant huge financial losses for cotton growers, yet *The Washington Post* was headlining million-dollar PIK payments to conglomerate farms in California as Congress completed the appropriations bill. More importantly, Stockman had objected strenuously to the cotton-PIK provision and administration of-

ficials had vowed that no farm legislation would emerge from the White House as long as the target price freeze was stalled.

● The magnitude of farm exports, $36.1 billion in 1983, suggested that the export-promoting Foreign Agricultural Service (FAS) should be included in the administration's proposed Department of Trade. But the farm community liked FAS just where it was, in the Agriculture Department, and the prospect of farm lobby objections apparently scotched any thought of moving FAS.

"Over at the White House, they just didn't want to take that on," said Robert J. Mullins, director of legislative services in Washington for the National Farmers Union.

● The farm community continued to benefit from a permanent, multibillion-dollar infrastructure created in past decades when farms were mostly small, hand-to-mouth operations. Of the nation's 2.3 million farms in 1983, about 500,000 were defined by the Agriculture Department as "large farms" with gross annual sales exceeding $100,000. But just half that number, some 250,000 farms, produced about two-thirds of the nation's food and reaped about 70 percent of farm program benefits. For two years running, presidential budgets suggested that low-cost federal loans and such fixtures of the rural countryside as the Rural Electrification Administration were inappropriate in an era of massive, corporate farming. But Congress has been cool to proposed cutbacks.

Commenting on the agriculture lobby, Panetta observed: "Some years, their deals fall apart. You don't know who's on first. But over the long haul, they haven't done too badly."

Farm Lobby Strengths

Farm lobbyists insist that they have fallen on very hard times. "Years ago, we had a coalition that looked after agriculture as a whole," said Frank Vacca, the representative of Mid-America Dairymen. Those were halcyon days, veteran lobbyists said, when congressional committees were closed, chairmen were powerful, and farm bills were written by the likes of Talmadge, Sen. James O. Eastland, D-Miss. (1941-78), and Rep. W. R. Poage, D-Texas (1937-78), and passed without much question. Those were also times — the 1950s and 1960s — when farm incomes were depressed by huge surpluses and many families were forced out of farming by the bleak economics of the industry.

Both Congress and agriculture have changed markedly since then. "You can't go in and talk to a chairman and two other people and write a bill today," said Mullins of the National Farmers Union. "You've lost all the strong, Southern chairman for all practical purposes, except for Whitten,"

he added, referring to House Appropriations Committee chairman Jamie L. Whitten, D-Miss. (As yearly confrontations over agriculture appropriations measures showed, Whitten effectively fended off proposed reductions in federally financed agricultural research, extension, conservation, credit, and other programs.)

The dispersion of power to subcommittee chairmen in recent years and the proliferation of staffs and agencies whose work impinged on farmers meant that "you do have to get around to so many more places now," according to Macon Edwards of the National Cotton Council of America.

Agriculture groups have grown, too. Washington-based lobbyists such as Wallace said that they could not exactly describe the growth, but in 1983 they ran into many more people working on agriculture issues than 10 years earlier. The National Association of Wheatgrowers' budget has grown tenfold since 1970-71, according to Carl Schwensen, its executive vice president.

The cadre of seasoned Washington representatives has been bolstered by the farmers themselves, who often appear in substantial numbers to defend their interests. "They do bring the crowds to town. They're good for the hotel business," said Deputy Agriculture Secretary Richard E. Lyng.

"They are not the least bit hesitant to put groups of people on airplanes to come and see us. That's very effective," reported Durbin, a member of the House Agriculture Committee. Durbin added that farm groups also could quickly generate constituent letters — "real" letters that left a lasting impression rather than formula letters and post cards cranked out in volume by banking and other lobbies. And Panetta indicated that farmers who contacted congressional members generally were listened to, because they most often were influential community leaders who ran large, established farms.

Quality vs. Quantity

As congressional power was being dispersed to subcommittee chairmen and agencies proliferated in the 1970s, agriculture itself was going through a feverish expansion to meet rapidly growing export demands. With the expansion came "specialization, industrialization, and, with that, the development of some very, very strong viewpoints," according to J. Steven Gabbert, executive vice president of the Rice Millers Association.

Members of Congress and their aides said that they were turning more readily to the specialized commodity groups for data and policy proposals than to general farm groups such as the National Farmers Organization. "When it comes time to decide what the dairy support price will be, the Farm Bureau probably ends up having less to say about that than Dairymen, Inc.," said Cochran, referring to the dominant Southeastern dairy cooperative.

Meanwhile, however, agriculture had dramatically contracted — in number of farmers and in congressional representation. Rapid gains in productivity, particularly after World War II, meant that fewer people were needed to grow the nation's food and fiber. In 1930 nearly 23 percent of the U.S. population was engaged in agriculture; in 1940 the number was 20 percent; in 1950 it was down to 12.2 percent; in 1970, 4.4 percent; and by 1982 it stood at 2.4 percent.

Rep. Edward R. Madigan, R-Ill., suggested that what farmers lacked in quantity, they made up in congressional quality. "I think the agriculture lobby derives its strength today from being able to key in on well-placed members, rather than relying on a broad base," Madigan remarked. Madigan, ranking minority member of the House Agriculture Committee, had pushed the administration's target-price legislation without success in 1983.

Harvesting wheat in Washington State

In the House, members with active interests in agricultural issues included Whitten, also known as "the permanent secretary of agriculture"; Majority Whip Thomas S. Foley, D-Wash., former chairman of the House Agriculture Committee; Alexander, chief deputy majority whip; Panetta, a respected member of the Budget Committee; and Tony Coelho, D-Calif., chairman of the Democratic Congressional Campaign Committee.

When the conservative American Farm Bureau Federation sought sponsors for its dairy proposal in 1983, it won the backing of influential House Republicans such as Minority Leader Robert H. Michel, Ill., Minority Whip Trent Lott, Miss., and Barber B. Conable Jr., N.Y., the ranking minority member of the powerful Ways and

Means Committee. In the Senate, Robert Dole, R-Kan., chairman of the Finance Committee and head of an Agriculture subcommittee, took an aggressive role in shaping farm policies, although his notions of thrift discomfited wheat and dairy producers.

A key asset of the farm establishment was its aggregate experience. Many farm lobbyists, such as Edwards of the National Cotton Council and Schwensen of the National Wheatgrowers, had been working on farm politics for 10 to 20 years. The basic price support programs began in the 1930s, and two generations of politicians and technicians had invested lifetimes in defending, readjusting, and operating them.

Allies such as Whitten and Foley had been in Congress since 1941 and 1965, respectively. "There are some very able, experienced legislators and that gives [us] continuity that maybe some of the other industries do not have," Edwards said. Its familiarity with Congress also gave the agriculture establishment a grasp of strategy that occasionally left opponents shaking their heads; the inclusion of cotton-PIK language in five different bills, including the "must-sign" supplemental appropriations measure, was a striking example of fancy legislative footwork.

In 1983 the House Agriculture Committee, seeking to block floor amendments to freeze target prices, slash dairy price supports, or kill the tobacco program, sent out farm legislation in the form of single-subject bills and under closed procedures such as the suspension calendar. In early August an exasperated Michel, confronted with a minor bill, later vetoed by Reagan, to postpone an unpopular federal assessment on dairymen, demanded that the panel "quit nickel-and-diming us with these agriculture bills ... on a piecemeal basis." Michel was objecting to the committee's refusal to permit House votes on the target price freeze and his dairy plan. "It kind of

burns me that the whole process is being sidetracked," he said.

Even with their feuds, the farm groups had a long history of circling their wagons to fend off hostile attacks from outsiders. Rose and other members knew how to pleasantly remind urban members of farm-state members' votes for food stamps and other nutrition programs administered by the Agriculture Department.

And the farm establishment knew from experience that internal splits must — and could — be patched over. Sugar producers, for instance, lost their 40-year-old federal program in 1974 in part because internal dissension left them exposed to outside attacks. Sugar partially recovered, however, and by 1981 there was a new federal price support program included in the final version of the omnibus bill, despite a 213-190 House vote against the program.

Panetta and Edwards suggested that the crosscurrents within the farm lobby in 1983-84 could be typical of the period between the four-year reauthorizations of omnibus farm bills. But, "every time you see a farm bill, you can see the coalition in its most vivid colors," Panetta said.

For Panetta, a major factor in the agriculture lobby's coalition building was the inclusion of food stamps, special food programs designed to help the elderly and schoolchildren, and other federal food assistance programs in omnibus farm bills. The broad reach of these programs meant substantial benefits for the constituents of urban and suburban members who might otherwise find little to interest them in agriculture programs.

Another intangible asset of farming was its image, rooted in the nation's history, as special and different from other industries. Thomas Jefferson, for instance, wrote that "those who labor in the earth are the chosen people of God ... His peculiar deposit for substantial and genuine virtue."

Farm advocates frequently cited the

very basic fact that, as Agriculture Department historian Wayne Rasmussen said, "farmers are the only people to produce what everybody else has to have — food." And farmers reminded members that they operated under an overriding risk from which manufacturing and other industries were comparatively insulated: weather. "Production — the volume of production — is between the farmer and the banker and God, and the farmer and the banker don't have much to do with it," Edwards said.

'Hard Row to Hoe'

Even with these advantages, Deputy Agriculture Secretary Lyng believed, the lobbyists had "a hard row to hoe, because of the deep differences in the agriculture community over the philosophy of what role the government was to play." At one end of the spectrum, he noted, was the Farm Bureau with its hands-off, free-market philosophy, and at the other was the National Farmers Organization, with other organizations ranged between these two poles.

Lyng also suggested that farm-based political action committees (PACs), such as the wealthy fund-raising units in the dairy cooperatives, "had some impact for a while, but less so now as more people do it." Lyng noted that the dairy lobby in particular had been unable to secure the Treasury-financed paid production cut program that some elements of the industry wanted. The

PACs, Lyng said, "are not nearly as influential as you'd think from their size. You can't buy votes. I just don't believe you can buy votes."

The farm lobby also had to overcome congressional impatience with farm problems that never seemed to be resolved. Years ago, H. L. Mencken was heaping abuse on farmers for continually asking that Congress to rescue them from bankruptcy. In the 1980s, Andrews thought, farm groups mistakenly continued to stress farm income as an overriding factor in agriculture policy decisions. Said Andrews, "Guys from the cities say, 'So what else is new?' "

The underlying difficulty, however, was that agriculture was so volatile that it could baffle creation of permanent federal policies. It was worldwide crop failures during the 1970s that pushed U.S. agriculture into a major expansion and diverted attention from an array of farm programs that were not much different from those in effect in the 1980s.

Edwards believed that writing comprehensive farm law was as delicate an enterprise as drafting tax legislation, because the interests to be balanced could each be devastated — or elevated above the others — by even apparently minor changes in program terms. Burton Eller, vice president for government affairs of the National Cattlemen's Association, said, "There's no popular farm program in the long run. You just fix it temporarily, but then things go awry."

8

Farm Exports: Subsidies and Barriers

Agriculture long has relied for its economic well being significantly more on exports than have most other sectors of the U.S. economy. About 20 percent of industrial production depends on foreign markets for its existence, whereas one out of every three acres of farmland is planted for export. Each billion dollars in agricultural export sales creates at least 26,000 American jobs, according to Thad Cochran, R-Miss., a member of the Senate Agriculture Committee. It was little wonder that efforts to find foreign outlets for the food surplus had become a priority matter for members of Congress as well as Ronald Reagan's administration.

For nearly a decade, the U.S. government had counted on exports of farm commodities to siphon off excess production while boosting farm income. Between 1970 and 1981 farm exports grew sixfold, from $7.3 billion in 1970 to $43.3 billion 11 years later, comprising 18.9 percent of all U.S. exports and 19.5 percent of total world agricultural trade. By 1982, however, U.S. agricultural shipments abroad had fallen to $36.6 billion, or 17.7 percent of total exports. According to the U.S. Department of Agriculture (USDA), they continued to slide to $36.1 billion in calendar year 1983.

Dawson Ahalt, USDA deputy assistant secretary for economics, blamed the drop in trade on a "simultaneous recession around the world and a strong dollar. . . ." Both

trends meant that foreign customers could not afford to buy as much from the United States. Moreover, other nations had become more efficient at growing their own food and more aggressive about exporting their surpluses.

From Optimism to Eroding Markets

The first of several massive grain sales to the Soviet Union, negotiated in 1972, injected strong expectations of prosperity into the farm community. That optimism was borne out during the early and mid-1970s, as net farm income and land values rose steadily.

During that period grain production rose from 205 million metric tons annually to 303 million metric tons, nearly a 50 percent increase. (A metric ton is 2,200 pounds.) But even as American farmers were beginning to rely more and more on foreign markets, those markets were eroding.

The protective, highly subsidized common agricultural policy (CAP) of the 10-nation European Community (EC), adopted to stabilize markets and ensure domestic food supplies, had become more effective during the 1970s. Western Europe reduced its need for other nations' food and became an aggressive exporter of its own surplus grain, livestock products, and dairy goods.

During this period, developing nations

borrowed heavily to finance their own industrialization efforts, energy needs, and food imports. The resulting debts meant that by the 1980s many could not finance additional U.S. food purchases.

Agricultural competitors of the United States, such as Canada, Australia, and Brazil, stepped up their production, crowding the United States in world markets. And foreign customers found American food more expensive when the dollar rose in value compared with other currencies. "Even though the price of U.S. wheat was declining, the price to foreign buyers in their currencies increased by 160 percent over the last two years," Block told a group of U.S. exporters in late 1982.

Surpluses and Exports

As late as 1980, the encouraging level of agricultural exports had President Jimmy Carter's secretary of agriculture, Bob Bergland, noting that payments to farmers to reduce their crop production were not needed. The valuable export market was absorbing one-third of the U.S. grain production.

The condition of agriculture had altered dramatically by the mid-1980s. The bumper crops of 1981 and 1982, the strength of U.S. currency on the foreign exchange, and increased export competition created costly surpluses for farmers and the government.

During 1981 and 1982 market prices for wheat, corn, and other important grains dipped by one-third. Cotton prices dropped 25 percent. Net farm income nose-dived, too, from a historic high of $32.7 billion in 1979 to an estimated $16 billion in 1983. That was less than the interest payments on outstanding farm debt of $215 billion — a figure that had nearly doubled since 1977 and quadrupled since 1972, according to USDA. Adjusted for inflation, farmers' income in 1983 was the lowest since 1933.

As market prices sank in response to the surplus, the cost of government farm assistance programs soared to a record level of $11.9 billion in fiscal year 1982 — $7 billion in commodity loans, $2.6 billion for purchases primarily of dairy products, $1.5 billion largely for "deficiency" and disaster payments and $700 million mostly for grain storage. Farm programs hit a new high in 1983 of $18.8 billion. Costs were rising because the grain surplus depressed market prices and made selling less attractive to farmers than borrowing from federal price support programs.

The dilemma facing U.S. agriculture in the 1980s had not been experienced for two decades. The last time that American farmers and the government were left holding comparable quantities of grain was at the end of the 1950s. High demand and price supports had encouraged farmers to grow more grain than the United States could use. The supports discouraged export sales by pricing American grain above world markets.

To rid itself of the surplus, the government resorted to export subsidies, paying farmers the difference between the world market price and what they would receive in the higher-priced U.S. market. Additionally, Congress in 1954 enacted Food for Peace (PL 480), a billion-dollar-a-year program authorizing gifts of U.S. commodities to help overcome world hunger and reduce domestic surpluses.

Farm bills after 1965 set relatively low crop price supports. The supports were sensitive to world markets, with supplementary income payments made to farmers in years of very low prices. The major assumption was that even when world prices were low, U.S. farmers would profit from the sheer volume of exports because they could produce more grain, more cheaply, than anyone else. Acreage controls limiting planting, a feature of Depression-era farm programs, were to be used sparingly or not at all.

Soft white wheat is loaded on barges for overseas.

That thinking had changed by 1982, even though a free-market Republican administration controlled the White House. In November, Agriculture Secretary John R. Block unveiled a plan to pay farmers to reduce production. Under the "Payment-in-Kind" (PIK) program, some of the surplus grain was returned to farmers as a way of compensating them for reducing the amount they grew. Block estimated that PIK would take 23 million acres out of production in 1983, but the actual amount far exceeded expectations. Farmers left 75.6 million acres unplanted in 1983 — about 47.3 million acres under PIK and 28.3 million acres under acreage diversion programs. *(PIK, p. 15)*

In addition to those programs, USDA officials also considered increasing food donations abroad. But no combination of government actions could make the surplus vanish quickly. "There's no magic solution," said Ahalt. The Reagan administration asserted that only drastic measures, such as PIK and increased exports, could reduce the American stockpile of surplus commodities. However, both domestic and foreign giveaway programs were expensive. The U.S. government spent $557 million on international food charity in 1982 and increased that amount to $770 million in 1984. The projected figure for 1985 donations was $680 million.

Impact of Embargoes

There was general agreement in the mid-1980s among farmers, members of Congress, and administration officials that agricultural trade suffered not only from unfavorable economic conditions but from a decade of government trade restrictions, imposed both for domestic and foreign policy reasons. Those restrictions had jeopardized future export markets and created doubts in the minds of some potential foreign buyers as to the United States' reliability as a supplier.

1973 Soybean Export Restrictions. Trade experts said that 1973 restrictions on U.S. soybean exports, for example, sent an exceptionally damaging signal abroad: that even America's friends, such as Japan, could not count on contracted food deliveries. The soybean embargo was imposed on foreign markets in the belief that domestic supplies were too low to permit exports. Contracts were briefly suspended, then partially restored, as farmers were given permission to export only half the contracted-for quantity of soybeans.

The cutback had a particularly significant impact on Japan; the price of tofu, the soybean curd common in Japanese meals, rose 50 percent. Before the embargo Japan bought 98 percent of its soybeans from U.S. suppliers; afterwards, it began to buy large quantities from Brazil and invested in major expansions of soybean production there.

According to Bruce Hawley, assistant director of the American Farm Bureau Federation, the U.S. share of the world soybean market had dropped to 59 percent by 1981, compared with 95 percent in 1970. Hawley blamed the decrease on America's trade reputation, which he characterized as "somewhat beneath that of an unreliable used-car dealer."

John Baize, who represented soybean growers in Washington, said the embargo even might have contributed to Japan's persistence in retaining its trade barriers on American farm goods and its reluctance to remain dependent on U.S. agricultural exports. One result of the 1973 soybean restrictions, Baize said, was that the Japanese "were shown how vulnerable they could be to their own lack of self-sufficiency in food."

Soviet Grain Embargo. More damaging by far was the Carter administration's Jan.

4, 1980, decision to halt previously negotiated grain sales to the Soviet Union in retaliation for its invasion of Afghanistan. The embargo, imposed for foreign policy reasons, cost the U.S. economy an estimated $11.4 billion and triggered vociferous criticism from farmers. By the time it was lifted by President Reagan on April 24, 1981, the U.S. share of Soviet grain imports had dropped from 70 percent to 27 percent.

American grain found other foreign markets, however, and the U.S. share of the Soviet market by the end of fiscal year 1982 had climbed to 35 percent, representing 13.9 million metric tons, just shy of the record 15 million metric tons shipped in 1979. Nonetheless, American farm prices did not recover after the embargo was lifted. Members of Congress charged that U.S. sellers and communist buyers were reluctant to trade because of fears that a new embargo against the U.S.S.R. would be instituted by the administration in reaction to Moscow's role in the unsettled political situation in Poland. They insisted that only a new multi-year grain agreement could quell market jitters.

In fact, Reagan did break off negotiations for a new, long-term, U.S.-U.S.S.R. grain agreement in December 1981 to protest the imposition of martial law in Poland. In the meantime, he extended the existing contract twice, each time for a year. In July 1983 U.S. and Soviet officials completed negotiations on a new five-year grain agreement, but not before the sales for fiscal year 1983 had dropped to 6.2 million metric tons.

The pact, which took effect Oct. 1, 1983, committed the United States to sell — and the Soviet Union to buy — at least 9 million metric tons and up to 12 million metric tons of wheat and corn each year. Agriculture Secretary Block said the pact generally followed the terms of the previous U.S.-Soviet agreement, guaranteeing delivery of the specified minimums and permitting either side to opt out under certain conditions, such as short supply in the United States.

Phil St. Clair, vice president of Agri-Products Division of A. E. Staley Mfg. Co., had commented in 1982 that the Soviets needed the predictability of multi-year U.S. commitments to persuade them to rely again on the United States. After Carter's embargo, the Soviet Union sought other suppliers — as had Japan in 1973 — and negotiated major long-term grain trade agreements with Canada and Argentina, a barter agreement with India, and informal grain agreements with Thailand and France.

U.S. Trade Policies Criticized

The cumulative effect of the grain embargo was to burden America with a tarnished reputation as a dependable trader, farm interests said. They noted that when the members of the EC agreed to comply with Great Britain's trade sanctions against Argentina during the 1982 Falkland Islands crisis, the decision affected only new contracts, not existing agreements. Even Britain permitted delivery of goods to Argentina under agreements already negotiated.

Honoring existing contracts had been standard behavior for every nation except the United States, according to Joseph Halow, executive director of the North American Export Grain Association. "I find it unbelievable that a country built on free enterprise and business should be the first to cancel contracts. Nobody else does it."

Other nations occasionally found excuses to back out of contracts if subsequent price changes made the agreement considerably less favorable to them, according to Jules Katz, who served in the Carter State Department as assistant secretary for economic and business affairs and later chaired a commodities brokerage subsidiary of Acli International Inc. But he stressed that the offending nations generally were the less developed countries. "If you ask what is the experience with Europe and the developed countries? No contest. We're the worst. We are certainly unique as a major developed trading country in using export policy as an instrument of other policies," Katz said.

Competing exporters, he added, "largely divorce their trade interests from political considerations, except in the most egregious circumstances." Katz suggested that other governments, faced with political pressures such as those following the Afghanistan invasion that prompted Carter's embargo, "would say, 'The Soviets have committed a dastardly act. They will be condemned for all time.' Period. Business continues."

'Contract-Sanctity' Guarantee

Although the embargo tarnished America's reputation as a reliable supplier, there was little agreement on what should be done to remedy that lack of confidence. Some members of Congress and farm lobbyists wanted to enact legislation guaranteeing that export contracts would be honored despite any embargoes or other foreign policy actions. "The farm economy has a continuing problem [because] there is no guarantee that we will not have a similar embargo at any moment," Sen. Richard G. Lugar, R-Ind., told a hearing of the Senate Banking, Housing, and Urban Affairs Committee early in 1982.

Donald E. Henderson, of the Indiana Farm Bureau, testified that "as long as there is the slightest indication in foreign countries that we will use food as a foreign policy weapon, we will continue to be the world's storage bins," with foreign customers buying from America only as a last resort.

On the last day before adjourning for the 1982 election recess, the Senate with little debate approved a "contract-sanctity"

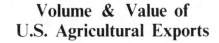

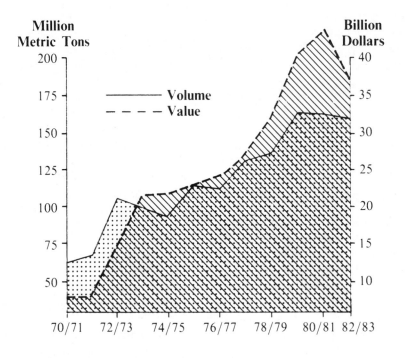

Source: Department of Agriculture

proposal intended to improve the U.S. trade image abroad by guaranteeing that trade contracts would be honored. The proposal, offered by David Durenberger, R-Minn., required that, except in time of war or national emergency, delivery be made on agricultural export contracts in effect at the time an embargo or other restraint on U.S. trade was imposed. "A strategy of market development can never succeed with the specter of the federal government hovering over the market every time it believes food can be used to achieve foreign policy objectives," Durenberger said.

The contract-sanctity proposal was added to a bill reauthorizing the Commodity Futures Trading Commission. The House-passed version had no such provision, but the House accepted the proposal, and it was included in the final bill that cleared Congress in December. The bill's guarantee on delivery of agricultural exports, with an exception only for national emergency or war, drew objections from the State Department that it restricted the president's freedom to act. But because the trade guarantee had wide support within the financially troubled farm community, administration officials avoided objecting to it publicly.

Sen. Robert Dole, R-Kan., told House-Senate conferees on the measure Dec. 9 that he and other supporters of the provision had offered to soften the language in conference if the State Department would agree to negotiate a long-term grain sale agreement with the Soviet Union. But "to try to reason with the State Department is, as in any administration, impossible," Dole said. Although department officials did not respond to his offer, Dole added, "now, at the last minute, they're calling frantically and saying, 'you've got to change this.'"

Administration officials sought, without success, to convince farm lobbyists and their congressional allies that they did not need the statutory guarantee because Reagan repeatedly had pledged to avoid trade embargoes, except in extreme circumstances. (However, he did impose sanctions in 1981 and 1982 on U.S. exports for use in construction of a Soviet gas pipeline to Western Europe.)

Export Subsidies

Most analysts contended that two years of worldwide recession and a strengthened dollar accounted for the decline in farm exports by 1982. Others pointed to an additional factor — export subsidies offered by the EC (whose members are Belgium, Britain, Denmark, France, Greece, West Germany, Ireland, Italy, Luxembourg, and the Netherlands), as well as a handful of other nations, that enabled their farmers to undercut American food prices in world markets.

U.S. farmers decried Common Market food export subsidies as unfair and pressed Congress to retaliate. A number of subsidy bills were introduced in the 98th Congress, raising the possibility that a trade war could break out unless the United States and the EC arrived at a negotiated settlement.

Common Market representatives de-fended their export subsidy practices at a November 1982 meeting in Geneva of the 90 nations subscribing to the General Agreement on Tariffs and Trade (GATT), an international trade forum for negotiating trade issues. Shortly before the meeting, a Nov. 8 EC news release stated that the Common Market "does not see the need for any new negotiations on agriculture trade." The EC contended its food export subsidies did not violate a GATT agreement that permitted such subsidies if they did not result in the takeover of traditional markets of other GATT nations. The United States claimed that Common Market wheat exporters violated that agreement. But a special GATT judicial panel announced in 1983 it could find no evidence to support the U.S. charge.

Reagan Administration Views

The administration shelved its aversion to export subsidies when it concluded that other nations would continue to refuse U.S. requests to alter their practices unless the United States fought back in kind. But Reagan officials clearly were reluctant to declare an all-out trade war. Testifying before the Senate Foreign Relations Committee on Feb. 15, 1983, Secretary of State George P. Shultz warned members that if subsidies were commonly used to market agricultural products, "the net result will not be good, and we will be in effect giving products away."

Yet the purpose of the subsidies, Agriculture Committee Chairman Jesse Helms, R-N.C., told the Senate, was to convince other nations "that the United States is serious when it said that their right to swing their export subsidy fist ends at Uncle Sam's nose."

Block and his colleagues likened the subsidies to warning shots to make foreign subsidizers reconsider their trade practices. But Glenn Tussey, assistant director of the

American Farm Bureau Federation's national affairs division, wondered whether the administration would spend enough on export subsidy programs to be taken seriously. And if it did, farm lobbyists agreed, American agriculture would not easily return to life without subsidies.

The last time the United States began to directly subsidize farm exports, the procedure continued for more than 20 years. Between 1949 and 1972, the government paid commodity exporters the difference between high, federally supported domestic prices and lower world prices. The payments were suspended in September 1972, when the U.S.-Soviet grain sale agreement pushed world prices well above domestic prices, and they were never reinstituted. However, some foreign observers contended that such policies as the favorable credit provided to needy nations for PL 480 purchases of U.S. food and other programs constituted de facto subsidies.

In October 1982 the administration began to underwrite farm export sales with a $1.5 billion, three-year "blended credit" program. The program offered foreign importers of U.S. farm products loans with interest rates 2 percentage points below market rates. The lower rates were achieved by combining interest-free loans by the Agriculture Department's Commodity Credit Corporation with federally guaranteed commercial loans. In January 1983 Reagan announced the program would receive an additional $1.25 billion for loans. Block said USDA estimates of exporting financing for 1983 was $5.1 billion. All but $350 million of that was in federal guarantees for private loans, which rarely cost the federal government substantial sums because of the low default rate.

Also in October 1982 the administration announced the sale of one million tons of subsidized flour to Egypt. By providing U.S. millers with enough surplus wheat, the government succeeded in reducing the net price per ton to the Egyptians by $100, far below the prevailing U.S. price of $255 per ton. The net cost to the government was estimated to be about $130 million. The sale was viewed by an unidentified Common Market official (quoted in the Jan. 21, 1983, *New York Times*) as "a brutal takeover of one of our major markets."

Subsidy Legislation

Meanwhile, as disagreements over the subsidy issue persisted, the Senate Agriculture Committee in March 1983 approved a bill requiring the secretary of agriculture to sell at least 150,000 metric tons of federally owned surplus dairy products abroad annually for the next three years at prices substantially below U.S. market prices. The panel's bill also would authorize an export payment-in-kind program in which federally owned commodities would be given to buyers as bonuses, thereby lowering the overall purchase price. In addition, federal funds would be used to subsidize exports of eggs, raisins, and canned fruit. Contrary to President Reagan's wishes, the bill contained a provision exempting export-PIK and commodities financed by the blended credit program from the federal cargo preference law. The law required roughly half of the goods exported under federal programs to be carried on U.S.-flag ships. Farm interests disliked the requirement because U.S. shipping was more expensive, raising the cost of the exports to foreigners.

The committee members were almost unanimous in laying a large share of the blame for sagging U.S. farm exports on what they viewed as predatory trade practices by the EC and others. Acknowledging that the legislation could invite international retaliation, Sen. Pete Wilson, R-Calif., said, "I don't think that's much of a risk because we're already suffering." The trade bill, he said, "will send a message that we're willing, however reluctantly, to escalate the arms race" in agricultural trade.

Only Lugar opposed the thrust of the legislation. He warned that such actions as actively promoting foreign sales of heavily subsidized U.S. butter, cheese and dry milk were "likely to be disruptive of our agriculture policy and our foreign policy." Further action was expected in 1984.

Farm Response

Farm leaders generally agreed that export subsidies were unwise in the long term. But many of them added that subsidies were increasingly necessary if the United States was to compete effectively in the commodity markets of the 1980s.

The American Farm Bureau Federation welcomed the subsidy proposals, albeit reluctantly. "The one group that might have philosophically come out against it is us," said Tussey. He said the organization disliked the economic distortions caused by subsidies but decided that the United States

had to fight for foreign markets. The $6 billion a year that it would take to match EC subsidies, or "rebates" as European officials termed them, seemed cheap, compared with $18.8 billion in outlays for fiscal 1983 for domestic price support loans and payments to farmers who could not sell their crops.

The National Farmers Union was even more skeptical about the impact of the export aid programs, holding that the subsidies would not put cash in farmers' pockets in the near future. The NFU feared that subsidies would drive world prices dangerously low and keep them there, according to an NFU spokesman. "We're still exporting for less than it costs to produce. This destabilization could come back to haunt us," he said.

"I'm concerned about this move to trade barriers. I don't think it's the best way to go," said Baize of the American Soybean Association. He warned that indiscriminate use of export subsidies would stimulate

One out of every three acres of farmland is planted for export.

retaliatory trade barriers. Yet the soybean group had asked the Reagan administration to put together a subsidized export sales program for soybean oil. Baize contended that Brazilian export subsidies had severely damaged American sales of soybean oil to India. In 1977-79 India bought $155 million worth of American oil a year; at the end of 1980 those purchases had dropped to $22.1 million. The time had come, Baize said, for the United States aggressively to assert itself in subsidized markets.

Poultry, egg, and rice producers also were seeking export-PIK sales, and Rep. Charlie Rose, D-N.C., told Block that his tobacco and peanut growers wanted help for their products as well. The National Cotton Council sought legislation to permit U.S. textile manufacturers to use free surplus cotton to lower their export prices for finished cotton clothing. That way, according to the council's Macon Edwards, "we could ship our cotton out in blue jeans" and combat subsidized foreign clothing manufacturers.

Some administration officials warned the U.S. farm subsidies could prove costly, ineffective, and difficult to turn off. They suggested that competing nations were unlikely to retrench on subsidies unless they felt the United States would spend as much or more than they did, for many years. That level of spending, they added, could draw American farmers and related industries into an unhealthy dependence on subsidies. And even without approaching European expenditures, the United States could create "chaos" in world markets, according to Deputy Agriculture Secretary Richard E. Lyng. Asked whether he worried about weaning U.S. agriculture and related industries from subsidies, Lyng said, "Yes. We all worry about that potential. And over time, government involvement [in trade] gets greater and greater, and a lot of us don't like that."

Gary Hufbauer, a specialist in trade subsidies at the Institute for International Economics (a Washington, D.C., research organization), suggested that American beneficiaries could become so dependent on subsidies that they would lobby against international negotiations to end them. "Once the government starts giving subsidies, you see a buildup of powerful internal groups that oppose international agreements. They will hire very good lawyers. They will hire very good lobbyists," he warned.

The GATT talks in Geneva in November 1982 illustrated Hufbauer's warning about dependency on subsidies, according to one high-ranking trade expert. The agriculture ministers of the Common Market nations took the unusual step of accompanying their spokesmen to Geneva. Like lobbyists in a congressional committee session, the official said, the ministers watched closely as the negotiators flatly told the American team they would not discuss the U.S. proposals. The United States had gone to the talks hoping to persuade other members to freeze and then reduce their agricultural export subsidies.

Lyng, who also took part in the November talks, said that it was the European resistance there that finally persuaded the Reagan administration to increase the limited U.S. export subsidy programs. Lyng told reporters shortly after the talks that the subsidies would be applied to commodities that were the subject of unresolved complaints to GATT — wheat, flour, poultry, pasta, and raisins, among others.

In spite of those actions, it was far from certain that an expansion of U.S. subsidies would influence the larger political and economic concerns underlying foreign trade practices. For instance, Brazil, which was selling in markets once considered to be American, was under stiff pressure in the mid-1980s from international and U.S. banks to increase its export earnings to pay off its massive debts and was likely to continue marketing subsidized exports despite opposition from Washington.

Additionally, the EC-initiated agricultural rebates were part of a protective internal farm policy grounded in memories of hunger and food shortages, according to Ulrich Knueppel, first secretary for agriculture with the EC's Washington, D.C., delegation. Knueppel added that the European community was taking steps toward making its farmers pay some of the costs of their surplus production. The long-term goal was to reduce the need for subsidies by bring European prices closer to world levels.

Part II:

Development of Federal Policy

Origin of Farm Community

Nature endowed the United States with cropland of unusual quantity and fertility. Enlightened agricultural policies and the ingenuity of the American farmer have enhanced this endowment to the point where U.S. agriculture is the envy of the world. Developing countries barely manage to feed themselves despite the fact that 50 percent or more of the population is engaged in agriculture. In the United States, according to the 1980 census, only 2.7 percent of the population was so engaged, tilling less land than a decade earlier. Even so, steady increases in productivity have kept harvests at a high level.

Tradition of Independent Farmers

Formulation of farm policy was one of the federal government's major concerns in the early years of the republic. Murray R. Benedict, the author of a survey of farm policies from 1790 to 1950, has pointed out that "Possibly never in the world's history has a new government, representing so few people, had so free a hand in deciding what kind of an agricultural economy it wanted to develop on so large an area of rich and reasonably accessibly lands." The choice lay between the old European system of landlordship and peasantry or a democratic society of shirt-sleeved farmers who owned the land they tilled.

Thomas Jefferson and Alexander Hamilton differed sharply on the farm question, as they did on many other matters. Hamilton, seeking funds for an empty national treasury, wanted to sell land in the public domain to the highest bidder, even if doing so led to creation of manorial estates farmed by sharecroppers. Jefferson envisioned a nation of small, independent farmers, for he believed that "Those who labor in the earth are the chosen people of God, if ever He had a chosen people, whose breasts He has made His peculiar deposit for substantial and genuine virtue."

Jefferson's view eventually prevailed. Land-hungry settlers, pressing westward in advance of government surveyors, insisted ever more belligerently on easy access to the public domain. Some but not all of the settlers' demands were met by an 1820 law authorizing the sale at auction of public land in half-sections (320 acres) and quarter-sections (160 acres). The minimum price was set at $1.25 an acre to be paid in cash. The national census taken in 1820 was the first to include occupational data; it showed that almost three-fourths of all Americans were engaged in agriculture.

The chief defect of the Land Act of 1820 was that it made no provision for the rights of "squatters" — persons who had occupied and improved public land prior to the time of sale. It was not unusual for squatters to hold such land for years and to make improvements worth hundreds of dollars, only to find themselves in danger of losing everything to a speculator at public auction. Finally in 1841 Congress passed the Pre-emption Act, which gave squatters the right to obtain improved land at the minimum price without competition from other bidders.

Two laws approved in 1862 — the Homestead Act and the Morrill Act — were probably the most important pieces of farm legislation of the 19th century. The Homestead Act gave to "any person who is the head of a family, or who has arrived at the age of 21 years, and is a citizen of the United States, or who shall have filed his declaration of intention to become such," the privilege of obtaining a quarter-section of land without payment (except for a small filing fee) by living on the land for five years and meeting certain conditions of cultivation.

Under the Morrill Act, each state was offered 30,000 acres of public land for each of its members in Congress as an endowment for an agricultural and mechanical arts college. In some states the lands were deeded to existing institutions, as in Wisconsin where the state university was the beneficiary; elsewhere they were conveyed to newly established colleges such as Purdue University or the Illinois Industrial University, now the University of Illinois.

Rise of Agricultural Exports

Settlement of public lands and creation of a network of agricultural colleges were accompanied by a mechanical revolution on the farm. The first patent for a mowing machine was granted to John Manning in 1831. The steel moldboard plow appeared two years later and was soon in general use. Obed Hussey and Cyrus McCormick obtained patents on the reaper in 1833 and 1834. Seed drills were introduced in the 1840s, and the threshing machine came on the scene in 1850. These machines and their

successors were to make the American farmer pre-eminent in the world for economy of manpower in agricultural production.

Farm output soared between the Civil War and the turn of the century. Wheat production, for example, rose from 236 million bushels in 1870 to 522 million bushels in 1900. Over the same period, corn output increased from 1,094 million to 2,105 million bushels and cotton output from 1,451 million to 4,757 million pounds.

The United States became the principal overseas food supplier of Western Europe in the latter part of the 19th century. European countries were then concentrating on industrialization, and their populations were outstripping domestic food sources. Thus, U.S. exports of wheat and flour rose from about $68 million in 1870 to more than $200 million in the banner year of 1898. In the same period, exports of meat and meat products climbed from $21 million to more than $175 million, an increase in excess of 700 percent.

The spectacular growth of farm production and exports toward the end of the century was made possible by this country's position as a debtor nation. The United States was still short of industrial goods and was importing them in quantity from Europe. At the same time, European investment capital was flowing into the country in large volume. Interest payments on these investments supplied European countries with the dollars they needed to buy American food. *(Farm exports, p. 89)*

American farm production continued to grow from 1900 to 1915, but at a slower pace than before. Total output rose from an index figure of 87.3 in 1900 to 95.4 in 1910, and by 1915 had reached 107.8 (1910-14 = 100). Of more importance was the steady advance of prices paid for American farm products. In 1900 the price index stood at 69.0; an almost uninterrupted rise brought it up to 105.0 in 1910. This represented a

More than 250 million acres were granted to citizens under 19th century homesteading laws designed to turn plots over to settlers who cultivated them.

gain of 52 percent in 10 years, a rate of increase seldom duplicated in peacetime.

The years from 1910 to 1914 are often described as the golden age of American agriculture. Farm prices were relatively high and stable, and land prices were rising. The gap between farm prices and the prices of goods bought by farmers had narrowed sharply. For these reasons, 1910-14 has long been used as the base period for determining parity — the price calculated to give the farmer a fair return in relation to the things he must buy.

The Postwar Depression

Despite heavy European demand for American food during World War I, pro-duction increased only moderately because of a series of poor crop years and a shortage of farm labor. As a result, farm prices more than doubled between 1914 and 1918. But instead of plummeting after the November 1918 Armistice, as had been expected, they remained abnormally high through 1920. Farmers thus were led to believe that a new and permanent higher price level had been established, and that there would be no return to the levels that prevailed before the war.

A disastrous farm slump, perhaps the worst in the country's history, began in 1921. The farm price index for that year dropped 87 points, to 124. The primary reason for this catastrophic decline was that the war had transformed the United States from a debtor nation into the world's leading creditor nation. If the country were to continue exporting on the prewar scale, it would have had to import more goods or extend additional loans to foreign debtors. Washington did not wish to do either. Thus, cessation of wartime credits to Allied countries in June 1919 brought on a sudden drop in European demand for American farm products. The resulting farm depression was to last until World War II.

McNary-Haugen Remedy. Various proposals for improving the condition of American agriculture were put forward in the 1920s. Among these, the McNary-Haugen plan, named for its sponsors, Sen. Charles L. McNary, R-Ore., and Rep. Gilbert N. Haugen, R-Iowa, aroused the most interest. Based on an earlier proposal of George N. Peek and Hugh S. Johnson, both of Moline Plow Co., the McNary-Haugen plan sought to equalize supply and demand at parity on the domestic market, and to dispose of surplus commodities overseas.

Sen. McNary and Rep. Haugen first introduced bills embodying their plan in 1924. The plan called for creation of a government export corporation with a capitalization of $200 million. The corporation would buy specified agricultural commodities in amounts sufficient to bring the domestic price up to the ratio or parity price. The parity price was to bear the same relation to the general price level as the price of the supported commodity had borne to the general price level in the period immediately prior to World War I.

To maintain farm prices at parity, the corporation would have to buy more than could be absorbed by the domestic market. The excess would be sold on the world market, the corporation absorbing the difference between the prices it paid and the prices it received in foreign countries. Tariffs at least equal to the difference would have to be imposed to prevent imports of cheaper foreign commodities.

The McNary-Haugen bill underwent numerous changes in its five-year sojourn in Congress. The original version went down to defeat after opponents had charged that it was unconstitutional, unworkable, and sectional. Similar bills introduced in 1925 and 1926 also got nowhere, but the fourth version was approved by both houses of Congress early in 1927. President Calvin Coolidge vetoed the bill on the ground that it would benefit only "certain groups of farmers in certain sections of the country." The fifth and last McNary-Haugen bill swept through Congress in the spring of 1928. Coolidge again returned the bill unsigned, and a motion in the Senate to override the veto fell four votes short of the required two-thirds.

Production Controls in 1930s. Although the McNary-Haugen plan failed to be enacted, it helped to win acceptance of the principle of government intervention in agriculture. The Agriculture Adjustment Act of 1933, one of the first major pieces of New Deal legislation, sought to help farmers by cutting supplies of basic commodities, thus to raise prices and change the agricultural pattern from overproduction of staple crops to more diversified farming. Farmers were offered contracts providing benefit payments in return for limiting acreage planted to staple crops. Penalty taxes on cotton and tobacco produced in excess of contract allotments forced producers to curtail marketing of those crops in 1934 and 1935. This curtailment, along with severe droughts, helped to boost the farm price index from 70 in 1933 to 109 in 1935.

When the Supreme Court struck down key sections of the Agricultural Adjustment Act in 1936, Congress responded by passing the Soil Conservation and Domestic Allotment Act. That law encouraged conservation by paying benefits for planting soil-building crops in place of staple crops. The principal objective of A A A was thereby perpetuated.

The farm price index, which had begun an uninterrupted five-year climb in 1932, tumbled from 122 to 97 between 1937 and 1938. Congress thereupon approved the Agricultural Adjustment Act of 1938, which established the "ever-normal granary." The Agricultural Adjustment Administration was empowered in years of abundant harvests to extend loans to farmers on staple crops, to store the surpluses, and to release them in years of poor harvest. The act also enabled farmers to adopt compulsory marketing quotas by two-thirds vote; this was done in the cases of cotton and tobacco. By 1941 the federal government had made direct payments of around $5.3 billion to farmers under the various agricultural programs set up in the previous eight years.

Surpluses After World War II

Entry of the United States into World War II brought an about-face in farm policy; expansion rather than restriction of food and fiber output was encouraged. However, a severe shortage of farm labor threatened to restrict production. The farm population, which had numbered about 30.5 million in the decade before the war, began a precipitous decline after 1940. It has been estimated that between April 1940 and April 1944 nearly 5.2 million farm people of working age (14 years and over) left agriculture for military service or industrial jobs.

The farm labor shortage was more than offset by mechanization. As farm income rose, commercial farmers were able to buy labor-saving equipment that they had not been able to afford in earlier years. Intensive use of fertilizers, sprays, and improved seed, together with generally favorable weather, also helped to produce a series of bountiful harvests through the war years.

Reconstruction programs for war-torn countries, notably the Marshall Plan, kept American farm production, prices, and exports at high levels after V-J Day. Accord-

ingly, Congress did not get around to re-examining farm policy until 1948-49, when demand was beginning to ebb and the Korean War was unforeseen. Two approaches were hotly debated — a free market system for farm products or strict federal management.

In a free market, it was argued, surpluses would drive down prices and thus force inefficient producers to leave farming. At the same time, efficient farmers presumably would cut back on capital investment. In the long run, supply would fall to the level of demand. The great advantage of a free market, supporters contended, was that it would cost the government nothing and at the same time benefit consumers.

Advocates of government controls maintained, on the other hand, that farm prices would decline so drastically in a free market as to inflict economic ruin on thousands, possibly millions, of small family farmers. Federal price supports, they said, were needed to keep farm income high enough to sustain the smaller farmers. By the same token, production controls were required to prevent accumulation of unmanageable surpluses.

As it turned out, the farm policy followed during the Eisenhower administration fell between the extremes of *laissez faire* and tight regulation. Income was protected, but at a moderate level, and production was controlled, but not very stringently. The shortcomings of this approach became apparent after the Korean War. Government stocks of wheat (owned outright or under loan) rose from 165.6 million bushels in 1952 to 990.6 million bushels in 1955, and to 1.3 billion bushels in 1960. Feed grain (barley, corn, grain sorghum, oats, rye) stocks also multiplied, from 9 million tons in 1952 to 65.7 million tons in 1960.

The Kennedy administration sought sharply to restrict wheat and feed grain production with a view to paring the massive surpluses that had piled up in the late

1950s. A voluntary land-retirement program for feed grains was introduced in 1961, but farmers rejected strict wheat production controls in a 1963 referendum. A modified version of the rejected wheat plan, providing for land retirement but without controls, was approved by Congress in 1964. These programs, combined with increasing demands from abroad for food, were intended to create a state of equilibrium between supply and demand, a seemingly impossible task by the mid-1980s.

Free Market Debate: 1945-64

Among the major issues of public policy after World War II, none proved more difficult to solve than the farm problem. Its essential characteristic was this: the tendency of production, despite a steady decline in farm population, to increase faster than effective demand, creating heavy agricultural surpluses. In congressional debate, this problem produced some of the sharpest sectional and party clashes repeatedly throughout the postwar period. At the root of the difficulty lay a 20th-century revolution in agricultural technology which, after slacking off during the Depression years of the 1930s, was accelerated by special military needs during World War II and continued apace afterwards. Mechanization, heavy increases in the use of fertilizers, lime, and insecticides, and the spread of specialization and scientific farming were the chief features of the agricultural revolution. Its chief results were sharp increases in productivity and a trend toward concentration of farming in fewer, larger units capable of using the technical advances to best advantage.

During the war and the postwar reconstruction period (1941-48), and during the Korean War period (1950-53), the farm economy's vast increase in productivity did not prove too great a problem, on the whole. Heavy expansion of demand due to special needs provided ready and favorable markets for farm goods.

This situation changed markedly after the Korean War ended. Demand fell off, production continued to increase, and large surpluses began to build up in major crops such as wheat, corn, cotton, and small feed grains.

Many believed that the solution lay in a free market for agriculture. During World War II and the immediately afterward, the government, to stimulate production, had by various means guaranteed high prices to farmers for their produce. The first great debates on postwar farm policy occurred in 1948 and 1949, when demand had started to drop with the end of the postwar reconstruction period and its revival by the Korean War was not foreseen. In those debates powerful arguments (repeated throughout the rest of the postwar period) were made in favor of transition to a free (or relatively free) market in agriculture.

If a free market came into being, its advocates said, the existence of surpluses would drive market prices down; as a result, less efficient farmers, unable to make a profit at lower prices, would leave farming, thus reducing production. At the same time, lower prices would bring about a reduction of capital investments and production inputs by the remaining farmers, additionally decreasing production. These decreases, it was contended, would continue until supply had dropped sufficiently to meet effective demand.

Exponents argued that government pegging of market prices at high levels provided incentives to overproduction. Left to itself, they contended, a free market would automatically end surpluses and obviate the need for major government expenditures. And lower prices, they said, would encourage increased consumption.

Opponents of the free market approach argued that such a policy would mean the collapse of farm prices and the economic ruin of hundreds of thousands, possibly even millions of farm families. The consequences, it was contended, would be an overall national depression, the destruction of traditional social values seen in American family farm life, and the transfer of vast number of persons untrained for other types of work to urban labor markets and unemployment rolls.

This group favored federal management of farm prices and other government policies designed to keep farm income high enough to sustain the smaller farmer, along with production controls to prevent the accumulation of surpluses. The Democratic presidents of this era, Harry Truman (1945-53), John Kennedy (1961-63), and Lyndon Johnson (1963-69), backed this general position.

Ranged between advocates of a free market and supporters of a carefully managed price structure was a broad spectrum of opinion combining features of both positions. Many congressmen, for example, favored some income support for farmers but only at a low level, designed to protect them against precipitate breaks in market prices but not to guarantee a high income permanently regardless of long-term demand and price trends. On the whole, this was the position of Republican president Dwight Eisenhower (1953-61).

In the two decades that followed World War II, a consensus could never be found for a thoroughgoing and permanent policy either of a free market or a sharply managed farm economy. Instead, in the tug and pull of party, regional, and commodity interests, a compromise was worked out to protect farm income, but at moderate rather than high levels, and to limit production, but not very stringently.

Controlling Surpluses

The postwar system of devices for sustaining farm income consisted of two different types of programs. One involved activities not directly affecting the market — technical advice, cheap credit, soil conservation and water supply assistance, and pest and disease control.

The other involved activities and controls aimed at sustaining high prices for farm goods — shoring up farm income. Chief techniques were price supports, "surplus-disposal" programs, and production controls. Under price supports the government stood ready to take off the market at a given price (the support price) all supplies of specified crops. This tended to maintain the market price at about the level of the support price. The support price was fixed by Congress or by the secretary of agriculture within limits set by Congress.

Price supports were used to hold up the price levels of crops accounting for a heavy proportion of farmer income from agriculture. The House Government Operations Committee estimated that in 1959 directly supported products accounted for 42 percent of all cash marketings, while animals fed largely on price-supported feed grains yielded products accounting for another 42 percent of marketings.

Crops supported continuously included cotton, corn, rice, wheat, tobacco, peanuts, small feed grains, dairy products, and beans. From 1945 to 1954, supports for the most important crops were maintained at a high level, 90 percent of parity. Support floors during the Eisenhower administration were dropped to 75 percent of parity for some commodities and to 60 or 65 percent for others.

"Surplus disposal" consisted of enlarging farm marketings, beyond what could be moved in normal commercial channels, through government purchases of farm goods for overseas or domestic welfare donations, or for overseas sale for soft currencies. In the 1950s there was a heavy increase in surplus-disposal programs.

A third device for maintaining farm income was production control, based on acreage allotments and marketing quotas, to prevent the production of surpluses. Production controls were in effect for cotton, rice, peanuts, wheat, and tobacco throughout the post-Korean War period, and for corn during 1954-58.

This system of income aids and production controls was not truly tested until the middle 1950s because special demands resulting from postwar reconstruction and Korean War needs kept market prices high and obviated both production controls and heavy government price-support activities.

When, in the post-Korean War period, the system became truly operative, it proved unable to achieve the ends for which it was constructed: farm income fell, the flow of small farmers out of farming continued, there was overproduction, and federal expenses for price supports and storage and surplus disposal mounted sharply, reaching $3 billion to $4 billion a year by the beginning of the 1960s.

Many observers attributed these results to the halfway-house character of the federal system of assistance. Transition to a free market, it was argued, might have reduced farmer income, but it at least would have permitted supply to drop to the level of demand at little or no cost to the government. Alternatively, a rigid system of production controls, coupled with high price supports (as proposed by President Kennedy in 1961) would have supported the small farmer even if at the expense of higher

market prices and, possibly, the freezing of inefficient patterns of production.

Instead, what appeared to have emerged from congressional battle and constant compromises were price supports at levels not high enough to protect the slender profit margins of most of the smaller farmers, but sufficiently high so that an efficient farmer could make money, provided he was able to find a way to increase his production to maximize his gross income and minimize his per-unit costs.

Production increases were permitted, in turn, by laxity of production controls: these were imposed only on certain crops (cotton, corn until 1959, peanuts, wheat, rice, and tobacco), while others, such as dairy products and small feed grains, received price supports without production limitations during most of the postwar period.

Moreover, the limitations were not fixed in terms of the quantity of the commodity itself, but in terms of acreage allotments: a farmer's quota was simply as much as he could grow on his allotment. And, in addition, minimum national acreage allotments were in existence for much of the postwar era for cotton, wheat, rice, and peanuts, which prevented acreage reductions below the minimum regardless of how great the over-supply was.

Given a statutory minimum price support and an acreage allotment that could be reduced no further, or in some cases, no production limits at all, every farmer was encouraged to maximize his income by raising his yields through increased use of machinery, expansion of operations, and increased use of fertilizers and similar inputs. This was considerably easier for a large-scale farmer with sizable capital resources than for a small farmer lacking capital and, in some cases, with a farm too small to benefit from machinery.

And so, there resulted the paradox of the era: despite lower prices and shrinking profit margins that reinforced the squeeze on small farmers to abandon farming, production on the remaining farms was rising dramatically and surpluses were continuing to increase.

Rural Poverty

One farm problem that received relatively little attention during the postwar era was rural poverty. The term "small farmers," frequently used to justify a policy of high price supports, actually covered millions of farmers, of whom many had small market sales and lived in poverty.

A large portion of such farmers benefitted little from high price supports because their market sales were so small. Of the nation's 3.7 million farms in 1959, about 1.6 million had gross annual sales of less than $2,500 and another 617,677 farms had gross annual sales ranging from $2,500 to $4,999.

It was generally accepted that, for most farmers, agriculture did not offer either decent living standards or a viable occupation, and that to help them to find part-time work off the farm, or to leave farming altogether (a trend already in existence, at any rate, since before the First World War), would aid both in reducing surplus farm production and raising the living standards of those individuals who remained in farming.

Various attempts by Congress to retrain such farmers and guide them to non-farm vocations or to create job opportunities in areas of rural poverty were made on occasion (the 1955 Rural Development Program, the 1961 Rural Area Development Program, the 1962 land conversion and rural renewal programs, the 1964 anti-poverty program), but massive potential retraining costs and the absence of substantial non-farm job opportunities left rural poverty still a major national problem as of the end of 1964.

Economic Trends

Beginning in World War II, there occurred a technological revolution in farming, characterized by heavily increased use of machinery, fertilizers and scientific methods, greater specialization in one crop, concentration of production in larger units, and sharply increased productivity. This trend, which was gradually transforming the American farm into an efficient, modern business, helped accelerate the long-term shift of farm population into non-farm occupations — a shift marked by a steady decline in the percentage of farmers in the total population.

On the whole, farm prices and farm income remained high, partly as a result of heavy demand for farm goods during the reconstruction (1945-48) and Korean War (1950-53) periods, and partly because price supports for the most important farm commodities were kept at a high level.

But in the 1950s, with the Korean War ended and price support levels declining, farm prices and income dropped while, at the same time, costs of non-farm goods rose, producing a cost-price squeeze that had its most serious consequences for the smaller, less efficient farmers. Many observers attributed to the cost-price squeeze a continuation and acceleration in the 1950s of the trends toward larger, more efficient units and toward the flow of small farmers out of farming.

Despite the drop in price support levels during the 1950s, federal outlays for farm programs, particularly for price supports and various surplus-disposal programs such as the school-milk program and PL 480 (the Agricultural Trade Development and Assistance Act of 1954), rose substantially during the 1950s and reached a level of some $5 billion to $7 billion a year in the early 1960s.

Population. Agriculture Department figures show that the number of farms in

Farm population fell as technological advances increased productivity.

the United States declined every year beginning in 1936. In 1935 there were 6,814,000 farms. By 1945, despite wartime prosperity, the number had dropped to 5,967,000. The figure for 1959 was 3,707,973. (The 1959 figure was based on a new census method, but even under the old method the number in 1959 would have been 3.9 million farms.)

Farm population, in numerical terms, had also been dropping since the mid-1930s. As a percentage of the total population, farm population had been dropping annually, with few interruptions, since before the First World War. In 1920 farm population was 30 percent of total population; in 1930, 24.8 percent; in 1940, 23.1 percent; in 1945,

18.1 percent. By 1955 it had dropped to 13.6 percent and by 1959, to 12 percent. Under a new census method adopted in 1960, excluding certain rural residents not actually engaged in commercial farming, farm population was calculated as 12,954,000 in 1964, or 6.8 percent of the total population.

Size of Farms. As the number of farmers dropped, the size of farms increased. Average acreage per farm was 174 acres in 1940. By 1945 it had risen to 194.8 acres; by 1950, to 215.3 acres; by 1954, to 242.2 acres; and by 1959, to 302.4 acres.

Increased Mechanization, Fertilizers. Two of the outstanding trends in the postwar period were increased mechanization and the use of fertilizers and lime. Figures computed by the Agriculture Department, using 1957-59 as a base period, showed the following trend:

Index of Inputs (1957-59 equals 100)

Year	Mechanical Power, Machinery	Fertilizer, Lime
1945	54	45
1964	101	137

Increased mechanization of farming is also indicated by figures showing the value of production assets per farm, the number of trucks, tractors, and other machines in use, and the percentage of farms with given types of machinery. In 1940 the value of production assets per farm worker (this includes productive land and machinery and certain other items) was $3,413. By 1950, it was $9,448; by 1955, it was $13,677 and by 1960, $21,079. The figure for 1964 was $27,005. By comparison, capital production per worker in manufacturing, which was at about the same level as the farm figures in the late 1940s, actually rose somewhat less rapidly than the farm figure in the next dozen years.

In terms of machinery, figures show, in thousands of items of equipment on farms:

	1940	1945	1955	1964
Trucks	1,047	1,490	2,675	2,915
Tractors	1,567	2,354	4,345	4,657
Grain combines	190	375	980	1,010
Cornpickers and picker-shellers	110	168	688	820
Pickup balers	—	42	448	775
Field forage harvesters	—	20	202	345

Source: Agriculture Department

Figures collected in the 1959 Census of Agriculture show even more dramatically the rapid technological changes. The per-

cent of farms with milking machines rose from 6.2 percent in 1945 to 18.0 percent in 1959; grain combines, 6.0 percent to 26.3 percent over the same period; trucks, 22.2 percent to 58.7 percent; tractors, 34.2 percent to 72.3 percent; cars, 61.0 percent to 79.7 percent.

Equities. With so much new machinery, and with farms larger, the value (aided considerably by inflation) of farm land and farm proprietors' equities also rose. The 1959 Census of Agriculture showed that the average value of land and buildings per farm, which was $5,518 in 1940, rose to $7,917 in 1945, to $13,983 in 1950, to $20,405 in 1954, and to $34,825 in 1959. Farm proprietors' equities, meanwhile (physical assets — land, buildings, machinery, stock, etc. — plus financial assets less all liabilities), rose from $43 billion in 1940 to $188.4 billion in 1964.

Specialization. The 1959 Census of Agriculture reported sharp increases in specialization, with fewer "all around" farms, over the period 1954-59, and this merely continued a trend already in operation since the early postwar period. The census report said: "These changes reflect rapid technological advances in production practices, sweeping changes in the organization and operation of individual farms, the rapid increase on many individual farms in the use of non-farm imports (purchased feeds, machine hire, hired labor, fuel, fertilizer, and liming materials), and the discontinuance of production by small producers with small-scale operations.

"Moreover, many farmers found during the last few years that the needs for increased skills, technical know-how, and managerial ability are so great that they have had, by necessity, to specialize. The specialization of farm production on the larger producing units during the last five years has progressed at a faster rate than during any five-year period in history." Thus, the number of farms harvesting cot-

Franklin Roosevelt

flected in higher per acre yields, helped dilute the effectiveness of federal production controls based on acreage allotments.

Division of the Market. U.S. farming during this period was characterized by concentration of large parts of the market in the hands of the relatively few largest producers. The 1959 Census of Agriculture showed, for example, that the 2.8 percent of the nation's farmers with sales of $40,000 or more annually made 31.5 percent of all sales by value, spent 49.9 percent of all funds spent on hired labor, averaged 2,466 acres in size, compared with 791 acres for the next category of farms (those with sales from $20,000 to $39,999). The value of the top 2.8 percent of farms was $220,683 per farm, compared with $93,526 for the next category. Final figures from the 1959 Census of Agriculture divide farms, according to gross annual sales, as follows:

ton dropped from 1.2 million in 1944 to 509,404 in 1959; selling chickens for meat, from 1.7 million in 1949 to 802,853 in 1959; and harvesting white potatoes, from 2.1 million in 1944 to 684,514 in 1959.

Productivity. Heavy specialization and machinery and fertilizer inputs led to sharply increased productivity for many crops. Thus, to cite three of the major grain crops, yields of wheat per harvested acre increased from a 1945 average of 17.0 bushels to 26.2 bushels in 1964. From 1945 to 1964, corn yields increased from 32.7 bushels an acre to 62.1 bushels, and grain sorghums, from 15.2 bushels to 41.1. The story was similar for other crops as well.

The result of this increased productivity was a steady rise in total output despite a drop in acreage harvested. While harvested acreage was decreasing from 346 million acres in 1945 to 293 million in 1964, the index of farm output (1957-59 equals 100) rose from 81 to 111 over the same period. This increased productivity, re-

Class	Number	% of all Farms	% of Sales
Commercial			
$40,000 or more sales	102,099	2.8	31.5
$20,000 to $39,999	210,402	5.7	18.4
$10,000 to $19,999	483,004	13.0	21.9
$5,000 to $9,999	653,881	17.6	15.4
$2,500 to $4,999	617,677	16.7	7.4
$50 to $2,499	348,954	9.4	1.5
Total Commercial	2,416,017	65.2	96.2
Non-Commercial			
Part time (Sales of $50-$2,500 but other work and income also)	884,875	23.9	2.3
Part-retirement	404,110	10.9	1.1
Other (prison farms, Indian reservations, etc.)	3,061	0.1	0.4
Total Non-Commercial	1,292,046	34.9	3.8
Grand Total	3,707,973	100.0	100.0

Farm Income. Overall income of farm operators from farming rose sharply during World War II because of strong demand, continued high in the reconstruction period during the first few years after the war. In 1949 demand slackened off and price (and with them farm income) began to drop; new demands caused by the Korean War, however, were responsible for a new upsurge that lasted into 1952. Then, with demand falling and prices falling, farm income began to drop again. During the 1950s, prices continued low (price supports for many crops were lowered during the 1950s). Gross income picked up toward the end of the 1950s, but, because of higher production costs, net income did not. Net income per farm increased substantially in the 1960s, however.

Chronology of Legislation

As World War II ended in 1945, there already existed most of the major programs that were to be used extensively in the postwar period to shore up production and marketing limitations. Many of the programs had been initially created in 1933, at the behest of President Franklin Roosevelt, as part of New Deal efforts to counter the Depression. The Supreme Court in 1936 held part of the original Agricultural Adjustment Act of 1933 unconstitutional, but within two years nearly all the AAA provisions were re-enacted by Congress. The major programs were:

Soil Conservation and Domestic Allotment Act — 1935-36. Soil Conservation Service was created to give technical and other aid to local soil conservation districts (to be chartered especially for this purpose by the states) in developing soil conservation plans and practices. The 1936 amendments authorized the Agricultural Conservation Program — federal payments to cover part of the costs of soil-conserving practices by farmers — and permitted the government to limit the acreage put to certain soil-depleting crops.

Agricultural Marketing Agreement Act of 1937. Designed to boost the income of producers of milk and fruits and vegetables — perishables that cannot be stored easily — without the use of price supports. Gave secretary of agriculture the right to establish a minimum price that processors in any local marketing area were required to pay farmers from whom they bought milk. For fruits and vegetables, gave the secretary the right to limit the amount of produce that might be sent to market. The limitation might be in the form either of a regulation banning the marketing of low-quality or small-size items, or of a market quota. In either case, the objective was to reduce the supply of fruit and vegetables placed on the market and thereby prevent surpluses from depressing prices.

In a subsequent amendment, the objective was stated as adjusting supplies (or fixing prices, in the case of milk) so as to return a "parity" price to producers. When participants voluntarily signed an agreement with the secretary to meet certain terms on milk prices or on supplies of fruits and vegetables, this was known as a marketing agreement. When the secretary (following a referendum of producers) issued an order making compliance mandatory, this was known as a marketing order. Ordinarily, marketing orders for milk were enforced by obtaining court injunctions against their violation: for fruits and vegetables, by fines.

Agricultural Adjustment Act of 1938. By far the most important New Deal measure in agriculture. Established the basic price-support and production control system for storable (non-perishable) agricultural commodities that, with amendments, was still in effect in the 1960s. The system worked as follows: when it appeared that some major crop covered by the act might be in surplus, causing prices to drop close to or below the break-even point, the secretary could take countermeasures: on the one hand, he could support prices by means of price supports, fixed at a level determined either by Congress or at the secretary's discretion.

The secretary would support prices by standing ready to acquire from farmers, at the support price, all supplies of the commodity in question. On the other hand, he might impose acreage allotments or marketing quotas, or a combination of either with price supports. Acreage allotments and marketing quotas worked in general (with variations for different crops) as follows: the secretary would determine anticipated consumption of the crop in question for the coming year. Then, on the basis of average yields per acre, he would determine how many acres should be planted to produce the desired amount and avoid a surplus. Then, the over-all national acreage allotment would be divided among existing farmers, on the basis of their history of production.

Each farmer was limited to planting only his allotment. Penalties for overplanting varied, and were established for the postwar period in the 1959 Agricultural Act. When acreage allotments were in effect, a farmer who overplanted lost his right to receive price supports for the crops involved. Marketing quotas worked exactly the same way, except that the penalty for overplanting was loss of eligibility for price supports and also a fine. In the postwar period, marketing quotas and acreage allotments were used only for crops on which there were price supports — but some crops whose prices were supported were not subjected to acreage allotments or marketing quotas.

Both under acreage allotments and marketing quotas, the basic method of limiting production was to limit acreage; on his given acreage, a farmer was permitted to produce as much as he could without penalty. His "quota" was whatever he could produce on his allotment. The only major difference between acreage allotments and marketing quotas (a misleading term since it implied limitations in terms of pounds, bushels, and bales) was that fines were imposed on overplanters when marketing quotas were proclaimed in effect.

The Commodity Credit Corp. (CCC), a wholly owned federal agency, already had power under the terms of its charter to support prices (and had done so) before enactment of the AAA of 1938. The new law made supports mandatory for certain crops for the first time and authorized marketing quotas as well. (The secretary operated through the CCC in supporting prices.) It also permanently established the concept of "parity" as the basis of supports.

Parity

The parity concept was an attempt to establish some standard on which to base assistance to farmers. According to this concept, farmers' labors and effort had brought them at some time in the past a "fair" return in terms of their purchasing power and standards of life. The aim of the parity concept was to determine what prices farmers would have to receive currently to enjoy the same relative purchasing power as during the period when things were "fair."

Under the 1938 Act, base periods (1910-14 or 1919-29 for most crops) were established, in which the mythical "fair" relationships had existed, for each crop. Under the parity concept, if the costs of the things farmers must buy had gone up a certain percentage since the base period, the prices of the things they sold should go up an equal percentage, thus keeping the farmers' purchasing power constant. The price of any farm commodity was therefore at full, 100 percent of parity, if it had risen the same percentage as had farmers' costs since the base period. In actual fact, the market prices of most farm commodities in 1938 were far lower than parity prices would have been. This meant farmers had lost purchasing power.

For the farm economy as a whole — that is, for all crops — the relative loss or gain of purchasing power was indicated by a figure called the *parity ratio*. This showed, overall, with various crops weighted according to their volume of sales, the ratio of increases in farmer costs to increases (or drops) in prices received by farmers. If the parity ratio was 100, it meant that farm prices kept pace exactly with farmer costs; if more than 100, that prices rose faster than costs, meaning farm prosperity; if less than 100, that prices had risen slower than costs, meaning a loss of purchasing power by farmers. In 1938 the parity ratio was 78.

The AAA of 1938 made price supports mandatory at 52-75 percent of parity (a sliding scale depending on various factors including the quantities of supplies available) for wheat, cotton, and corn, which were declared to be crops "basic" to the national economy. (These three crops were, and remained, by far the most important individual crops for cash sales and feeding animals.)

The act also permitted the secretary, at his discretion, to support any other farm product, with no upper or lower limits on the range of supports. In addition, it authorized marketing quotas, when necessary, for wheat, cotton, corn, tobacco, and rice. A minimum national allotment for wheat of 55 million acres was established when production controls were in effect; legislation to reduce this minimum permanently was not passed until 1962.

Wartime Changes

From 1921 to 1940 the farm economy was in a depressed or semi-depressed state; the parity ratio reached 90 or over only in six years and never reached 100 during the whole period. It was 78 in 1938, 77 in 1939, and 81 in 1940. World War II changed this. Extraordinary needs for the armed forces (where per capita consumption was higher than for civilians, more meats and high-nourishment foods were eaten, there was waste, losses from sinkings of ships, etc.) and for allies, coupled with higher domestic purchasing power as unemployment ended — all caused demand for food products and fibers to skyrocket. From surpluses, there now were shortages; prices rose; price controls had to be imposed (farmers were then paid direct U.S. subsidies to compensate for income lost through price controls), and the parity ratio jumped to 93 in 1941, 105 in 1942, and was well over 100 throughout the war.

Under conditions of shortage, federal laws changed considerably. The government, instead of curtailing production, now sought to encourage it; first, both acreage allotments and marketing quotas were relaxed. By 1943 they had been removed from all crops by the secretary of agriculture except for certain types of tobacco. None was reimposed until 1949.

Next, the government encouraged farmers to expand production. To do so, Congress raised price supports on many crops to guarantee farmers that once they had expanded, at great cost to themselves, they would not be caught in a surplus market with falling prices. It was not anticipated that it would actually be necessary to make price-support purchases (and by and large it was not, since prices rose so much and shortages continued despite expanded production), but the support minimums were established as a guarantee of protection for the farmer.

For some commodities, supports at high levels were made mandatory; for others, supports were extended through the discretion of the secretary. (One hundred forty non-mandatory crops were eligible for supports during the war.) Third, an additional protective device was provided in the direct subsidy system.

As war's end, this was the support situation:

Basic Crops. The list of "basic" crops, for which supports were mandatory and that were subject to both acreage allotments and marketing quotas when necessary to restrict production, expanded to cover not only cotton, corn, and wheat, but also tobacco, rice, and peanuts. Most of these were supported at 90 percent of parity during the war, and all but cotton were required to be supported at 90 percent for two years beyond the declared end of hostilities (which turned out to be Dec. 31, 1948). For cotton, the support price was set at 92.5 percent. The two-year period of grace was granted to protect farmers from a sudden price collapse after the war (as had occurred in 1920), when demand fell off, and gave Congress time to work out a system for reducing production.

Steagall Commodities. Certain specific crops whose production the War Food Administrator or secretary had asked farmers to raise were protected in a manner similar to the basics. They were required to be supported at *no lower* than 90 percent of parity until two years after hostilities ended. (The basics were simply to be supported *at* 90 percent.) These crops (not subject to marketing quotas) were: hogs, eggs, certain types of chickens, turkeys, milk, butterfat, dry peas, dry edible beans, soybeans, flax-seed and peanuts for oil, potatoes, sweet potatoes, and American-Egyptian cotton. (This was a minor type; the major type, upland cotton, was a basic.) The Steagall commodities were so called after Rep. Henry B. Steagall, D-Ala., sponsor of the legislation to protect those commodities.

Other. The basic provisions of the AAA of 1938 had not been changed by the wartime legislation, merely modified, and the secretary of agriculture retained discretionary power to support any other crops at any price he chose. He also retained power to impose production limitations. The 1941 law making peanuts a basic commodity established a minimum allotment of 1,610,000 acres for peanuts when production controls were in effect, and this was never subsequently changed.

As it turned out, demand for farm goods in relation to supplies continued high after the war ended and through the beginning of 1948 (longer for many foods); therefore, despite the existence of provisions for mandatory support of the basics and Steagall commodities, and even though the secretary on his own was offering supports on many other commodities, government acquisitions of farm goods under support programs were tiny for most goods and nonexistent for many. (Most of the time, market or price-control prices exceeded the support levels, and farmers had no need to use the price-support mechanism.) There was no general price support legislation, therefore, in the postwar period, until 1948.

Crop Limits, Income Aids: 1965-68

The broad direction of basic U.S. farm policy changed very little during 1965-68. Farm production continued in most areas to be highly mechanized, with heavy use of fertilizers and chemicals, steady increases in yields, and a trend toward larger, more consolidated farms.

The farm population continued to decline, as it had been doing for generations, and reached a new low of just over 5 percent of the population. Yet so great was the efficiency of U.S. producers that each farm worker on the average produced enough food in 1967 for more than 42 other persons. Two central problems occupied farm policy makers — overproduction and low rural income.

For some of the nation's most important crops, such as feed grains, wheat, and cotton, there was continual danger that farmers, pouring on the fertilizer and insecticides and using the most modern production methods, would produce more than could be sold at a profit. When that happened, it was feared, farm prices would drop precipitously and eventually drive some farmers out of business. A crisis within the farm community had the potential of increasing rural migration to the cities, creating new welfare problems, and endangering the whole economy with a farm-initiated depression.

The traditional Democratic answer to this threat was a system of production controls and income aids, first tried in the 1930s and kept in effect continuously (except in wartime, when controls were not needed). It applied to about a dozen and a half of the most important crops.

Production controls, in the form of acreage limitations, helped to limit oversupply and prevent price breaks. At the same time the government, through standing ready to buy or offer loans at a fixed price on farm produce with the latter as collateral, could peg the price received by the farmer at some desired rate.

President Lyndon Johnson in 1965 helped put through Congress a revision of the system of production limitations and price support devices. One problem to be faced was that U.S. products might not be able to compete on the international market if price supports were set too high. But if they were set too low, some of the less efficient, smaller farmers might find them inadequate to sustain their income at decent levels.

The 1965 basic legislation was designed to reduce surpluses of cotton, corn, and wheat. It asked farmers to retire a certain portion of their cropland from production of these surplus crops and put it to soil-conserving uses. In return they were made eligible for a price support on their crops plus special, direct cash payments of different types.

The price support was to be fixed at a

level that would result in a market price competitive with overseas prices, but the farmer's income was maintained by giving him the additional direct payments. Thus the U.S. surplus crops could find markets without dropping the farmer's incomes to a disastrously low level.

This system, a new and more sophisticated variation of the basic price support system in effect since New Deal days, was put into effect by the Johnson administration with the assurance that it would reduce surpluses of wheat, cotton, and corn to manageable proportions without costing too much.

By 1968 sponsors were boasting that the program had achieved much of what it set out to do. Corn and wheat surpluses had dropped significantly — aided by large wheat donations to hungry peoples overseas — and cotton surpluses had fallen even more sharply, largely due to a drought that dropped 1967 production to the lowest level (7.4 million bales) since 1895.

At the same time, sponsors said, farm income was at a high level (though dropping somewhat after 1966) and the cost of the overall program was not excessive. The government's costs were running about $2 billion to $4 billion a year — a cheap enough price to pay to guarantee an abundant supply of food and fiber and avoid the dislocations that would occur if too many farmers went broke.

Many Republicans and the nation's biggest farm organization, the American Farm Bureau Federation, sharply disagreed with this diagnosis. They believed that the system of production controls, based on historical acreage rights, had the effect of freezing some of the most inefficient production patterns and preventing expansion of some farms to more efficient size. They saw the Johnson program as a complicated system of market rigging, designed to sustain the income of farmers who could not otherwise successfully compete.

In the long run, they argued, it would be better to move toward a system where the market was the basis for economic decisions. With production controls off and price supports lowered to a level where at best they would merely be a safeguard against disaster — not a market-fixing mechanism or guarantor of high income — supply and demand would automatically adjust and the surplus problem would disappear. The marginal and inefficient farmers would gradually retire or move out of farming. And the $2 billion to $4 billion a year that the government was spending on price support and production control programs would be saved.

Opponents contended also that the Johnson program had not really achieved what it set out to do: farm income was beginning to fall off, the threat of new surpluses of wheat were looming as overseas production rose and export possibilities declined, and people still were leaving farming at a pretty steady rate.

Low Rural Income

The problem of low rural income was related in part to agricultural price and surplus policy. The price and production programs were designed to sustain farm income, but chiefly for the 1.8 million commercial farms with sales of $2,500 a year or more. Even some of these farms, however, clearly were operating on the margin of disaster.

A whole additional category of farmers, about 1.3 million, had sales of under $2,500 a year and could not be considered commercial farms. Some people in this category were actually gentleman farmers or part-time farmers with small holdings. But a large group of them, particularly in the South, were simply impoverished farmers with insufficient land, equipment, credit, or skills to make a living from agriculture.

Income From Farming
(in millions of dollars)

	Realized Gross Income	Production Expenses	Realized Net Income			Parity Ratio**
			Amt.	% of Gross	Per farm, 1957-59 dollars*	
1930	$11,472	$ 6,944	$ 4,528	39.5%	$1,384	83
1940	11,059	6,858	4,201	38.0	1,574	81 (88)
1950	32,271	19,410	12,861	39.9	2,648	101 (102)
1960	38,088	26,352	11,736	30.8	2,904	80 (81)
1965	44,926	30,933	13,993	31.1	3,916	77 (82)
1966	49,597	33,404	16,193	32.6	4,545	80 (86)
1967	49,061	34,820	14,241	29.0	4,005	74 (79)
1968	50,752	35,900	14,852		NA	73 (79)

* Dollars, not millions.
** Adjusted parity ratio, reflecting government payments, shown in parentheses.

For these farmers, and for some of those in the lower echelons of the 1.8 million commercial farm class, government policies were sometimes more welfare-oriented than farm-oriented. Government credits for housing for the rural poor, for retraining, for local economic planning, and for basic water and sewer facilities were among the policies continued in the 1965-68 period. Some of the credits were plainly welfare-type aids. Others were designed to give needy commercial farmers the chance to strengthen their operations by acquisition of new land, machinery, and stock.

Another aspect of rural poverty was the hired farm labor force — a group of about 1 million persons whose pay and living standards were among the lowest in the nation, especially in the case of migratory farm workers. Some welfare programs for these workers were enacted, and about one-third of them were finally given federal minimum-wage protection in 1966, albeit at low pay levels. But attempts to bring them under federal laws protecting the right to organize unions and strike did not succeed.

While the broad outlines of basic policy barely changed during the 1965-68 period, there were a number of new trends on a smaller scale. There was a clear upsurge of resentment among urban congressmen against the large amounts of money being spent on price supports — particularly when it was shown that many large farm enterprises received payments of $1 million or more a year from the government. One such enterprise received $4.1 million.

Urban congressmen resented these payments because some of the farm-area congressmen on committees with jurisdiction over school lunches, food stamps, and other government feeding programs for the poor were holding down appropriations for those programs.

In an attempt to impose a $20,000 annual payment limitation per farm, members of Congress from the cities made common cause with some Republican rural-area members who opposed the whole system of price supports and production controls. The latter believed that imposition of an annual payment limitation would help kill the existing system. Their attempts did not succeed but appeared to portend further efforts of the same sort in the future.

Farm Labor

Despite passage of legislation providing a minimum wage for some farm workers and health, education, and welfare aids for migratory farm workers, the nation's 1.2 million hired farm workers remained among the least privileged and most needy groups of society during the period 1965-68.

Per hour wage rates in agriculture averaged $1.21 in 1968. Migratory farm workers employed for 25 days or more totaled 194,000 in 1967 and earned an average of $1,555 for both farm and non-farm work combined.

Although the regular Mexican farm labor program died in 1964 (Mexican contract workers were brought into the United States in large numbers under this program), many domestic farm workers still faced competition from holders of "green cards." These were chiefly Mexicans holding permanent resident alien cards, making them migrants and permitting them to work in this country, returning over the border at night or living in the United States.

Labor and welfare groups had long contended that the availability of foreign contract labor and green card workers, often at relatively low wages, undermined the wage structure for native American farm workers and helped keep them in a perpetual state of poverty. These labor and welfare groups worked to engineer a congressional situation in which the Mexican farm labor program was allowed to die.

At the same time, Congress, with the farm bloc in the lead, defeated all efforts to give U.S. farm workers the protection to organize and strike, under the National Labor Relations Act, that was enjoyed by most other workers.

The argument against strikes by farm workers — as expressed, for example, at the 1968 convention of the American Farm Bureau Federation — was that perishable commodities such as fruits and vegetables were uniquely vulnerable to work stoppages, and a farmer's entire year's work could be destroyed by only a brief work shutdown.

Nevertheless, a farm worker organization in California had some success in organizing grape workers. Led by Cesar Chavez, in 1966-68, it signed up some of the biggest farms — the Christian Brothers, Schenley — and pressed a national consumer boycott against table grapes that received support from labor unions and welfare groups.

The farm labor force as a whole averaged 4.7 million a month in 1968, but of these, 3.5 million were family workers on their own farms. Only the remaining 1.2 million were hired workers. California, with its huge fruit and vegetable industries, was the largest user of hired farm labor.

The total number of green card holders was estimated in 1967 at 40,000 Mexicans and 10,000 Canadians. Additional foreigners — chiefly West Indians and Canadians — were allowed into the United States for farm work under special temporary-labor provisions of the basic immigration laws. About 15,000 entered for temporary farm work in 1968 — a vast fall-off from the heyday of the Mexican farm labor program in the 1950s when as many as 450,000 workers a year entered for farm work under special conditions.

Administrative action to lessen the competition from imported foreign labor was taken on several occasions by Secretary of Labor Willard Wirtz. In 1964 Wirtz ruled that before farmers could apply to import foreign contract workers under the special provisions of the immigration law, they would first have to seek to hire native American workers by offering them at least $1.15 to $1.40 an hour (depending on location) and various minimum-hour, housing, transportation, and insurance benefits. Wirtz revised this scale upward in 1967 and 1968. *(Migrant workers, p. 37)*

Food for Hungry

Two important sets of agricultural programs were reoriented in the 1965-68 period. Food programs for the hungry had been run for many years as dumping areas for surplus farm goods or as adjuncts to farm support programs. In a series of massive legislative fights during the period 1965-68, Northern congressional liberals, backed by welfare, labor, and philanthropic organizations, made hunger in America a key public issue. They succeeded in winning apparent acceptance of the idea that the problem of hunger deserved to be solved regardless of agricultural surplus problems.

A similar reorientation occurred for the overseas food donation program (PL 480) — the so-called Food for Peace or Food for Freedom plan. It had been started in 1954 as a means of getting rid of surplus production by "selling" it overseas for local currencies.

In 1966 the program was revised to focus on meeting hunger needs among developing nations rather than just getting rid of surpluses. At the same time, it sought to encourage developing nations to improve their own agricultural production and to limit their population increase.

One program in which there was almost no basic change at all was the Sugar Act, that microcosm of agricultural protectionism. First enacted in 1934, the act sustains high prices for domestic beet sugar

Cesar Chavez

growers and cane sugar growers by limiting both domestic production and imports from abroad. Without the import limits, foreign sugar could easily undersell the domestic product.

At the same time, big coastal refineries were protected by the rule that nearly all imports must be in the form of raw sugar, which is then refined in this country. The standard dispute over the Sugar Act was how to divide imports and domestic production, with U.S. mainland beet and cane getting an ever larger share of the total. In 1965 the Sugar Act was extended through Dec. 31, 1971, with Cuba's share of the import quota suspended and the mainland cane and beet producers getting increased shares.

Economic Trends

During the 1965-68 period, U.S. agriculture continued to be highly productive. Wheat, cotton, and corn (with related feed grains) remained the "big three" crops, with soybeans (the number-one export mar-

Acreage Allotments:
Acreage by Crops, United States, 1954-68[1]

Crop year	Wheat[2]	Corn (commercial area)	Cotton Upland	Cotton Extra long staple	Peanuts	Rice	Tobacco Flue-cured	Tobacco Burley
	1,000 acres	*1,000 acres*	*1,000 acres*	*1,000 acres*	*1,000 acres*	*1,000 acres*	*1,000 acres*	*1,000 acres*
1954	62,000	46,996	21,379	41	1,610		1,053	399
1955	55,000	49,843	18,113	46	1,731	1,928	1,007	309
1956	55,000	42,281	17,391	45	1,650	1,653	888	309
1957	55,000	37,289	17,585	89	1,611	1,653	711	309
1958	55,000	38,818	17,555	83	1,612	1,653	712	309
1959	55,000		17,330	71	1,612	1,653	713	309
1960	55,000		17,525	65	1,612	1,653	713	309
1961	55,000		18,458	64	1,612	1,653	714	329
1962	55,000		18,102	100	1,613	1,818	745	349
1963	55,000		16,250	150	1,612	1,818	708	349
1964	49,500		16,200	112	1,613	1,818	638	316
1965	49,500		16,200	78	1,613	1,819	607	287
1966	47,800		16,200	81	1,613	2,001	607	250
1967	68,195		16,200	70	1,613	2,001	607	250
1968	59,300		16,200	70	1,613	2,401	607	250

[1] *National acreage allotments proclaimed by the secretary of agriculture under the Agricultural Adjustment Act of 1938, as amended. In most years, allotments were accompanied by marketing quotas.*
[2] *Excludes increases in allotments granted under special legislation, as for durum for years 1954-57 and 1962, and for small wheat farms, 1964-68.*

ket crop) joining them to make it a "big four." Livestock and dairy products accounted for approximately two-thirds of all cash sales. Cattle and calves alone constituted one-fourth of the market sales.

The feed grain economy underlay all livestock products: a heavy portion of feeds was not sold but fed on the farm to cattle, hogs, and other livestock. Thus, while the government price support program did not include livestock directly (though it did include dairy products), it had profound influence through supports and production controls on feeds.

Federal outlays for programs attributable to agriculture, according to the fiscal 1970 budget, averaged about $5 billion a year over the fiscal 1965-68 period, with a large part of the total going to support prices, make direct crop payments to farmers, or otherwise stabilize farm income.

Outlays to Stabilize Farm Income

Year	Agricultural Outlays (billions)	Portion for Stabilizing Farm Income
1959	$5.365	$4.057
1964	5.186	3.803
1965	4.807	3.234
1966	3.679	1.932
1967	4.376	2.536
1968	5.944	3.934
1969	5.448	4.509

If the Food for Peace outlays, plus certain other items were added, the cost of federal agriculture programs ranged from $6 billion to more than $7 billion a year.

The cost-price squeeze continued to press farmers during the 1965-68 period — that is, the cost of the things they had to buy tended to rise at least as fast as the prices of the things they sold. The farmer's net income as a proportion of his gross fluctuated at around 30 percent for most of the 1960s, dropping to an all-time low of 29 percent in 1967 (compared with a 50 percent figure during the boom years of the World War II period).

Another measure of the cost-price squeeze was the drop in the parity ratio, a measure of "fairness" in farm prices and costs based on historical precedents. A parity ratio of 100 meant that the relationship between the farmer's costs and prices was 100 percent fair. A ratio of 80 meant that the prices the farmer received were less favorable in relation to his costs than they had been during the pre-World War I period (1910-14) used as the historical base used to determine this figure.

The parity ratio — in the 80s during the 1950s — dropped to the low 70s in the 1965-68 period. Farming income, however, rose, and per-operator annual income in terms of constant 1957-59 dollars was substantially higher than in earlier years. Following are some of the statistical measures of these developments. *(Income from farming chart, p. 123)*

Relation to Economy. While farming was one of the biggest, if not the single biggest, occupation in the nation as compared with individual industries such as steel and automobiles, it produced directly only 3 percent of total national income in 1967, the remainder came from non-farming activities. And the per capita personal income of the farm population from all sources — including not only agriculture but dividends, off-farm part-time employment, and pensions — was about 73 percent of the personal income per capita of the population as a whole.

Farm Population. Both the number of farms and the farm population declined steadily over the 1965-68 period, continuing a trend that had been going on steadily since well before World War II.

Year	Farms	Farm Population	As % of Total Pop.
1935	6,814,000	32,161,000	25.3%
1940	6,350,000	30,547,000	23.1
1945	5,967,000	24,420,000	17.5
1950	5,648,000	23,048,000	15.2
1955	4,654,000	19,078,000	11.5
1960	3,962,000	15,635,000	8.7
1965	3,340,000	12,363,000	6.4
1966	3,239,000	11,595,000	5.9
1967	3,146,000	10,817,000	5.4

Size of Farms. The average size of farms increased steadily. In 1940 it was 174 acres per farm. By 1950 it had risen to 215.3 acres, by 1959 to 302.4 acres, and by 1964 to 351.5 acres.

Productivity. The long-term trend of rises in farm productivity due to use of more machinery, fertilizer, lime, and insecticides, continued in 1965-68. Corn yields, which averaged 32.7 bushels an acre in 1945 and 68.3 bushels during the 1962-66 period, reached 78.5 bushels an acre in 1968. Sorghum grain, a feed similar to corn, had average yields of 15.2 bushels an acre in 1945, 47.4 bushels during the 1962-66 period, and 52.9 bushels in 1968. Wheat rose from 17.0 bushels an acre in 1945 to 25.8 bushels in the 1962-66 period and 28.4 bushels in 1968.

Agriculture continued to use heavy machinery inputs. The value of assets per farm worker (land, machinery, etc.), which already in the 1950s was greater than in manufacturing, rose from $27,367 in 1964 to $45,872 in 1968.

Fertilizer use jumped enormously even in the brief 1965-68 period. In 1950 some 2,772,000 tons of the fertilizer nutrients nitrogen, phosphorus, and potassium were used; in 1960, 5,643,000 tons. The 1964 figure was 8,093,000 tons, and by 1968 the total had jumped to 11,649,000 tons.

Importance of Government Payments. Government payments were an important part of farm receipts. They increased as a result of the 1965 Food and Agriculture Act, which reduced price support loan levels but gave farmers direct payments to compensate for the lower loan levels. Direct government payments totaled $1.493 billion in 1961, $2.181 billion in 1964, and $3.079 billion in 1967. Direct payments under the cotton, feed grain, and wheat programs amounted in 1967 to $932 million, $865 million, and $731 million respectively. The soil bank, the agricultural conservation program, cropland retirement, and a few other programs made up the remainder.

Division of Market. The larger commercial farms continued to increase their share of the market. In 1959 some 2.8 percent of the nation's farms had sales of $40,000 or more annually and accounted for 31.2 percent of total farm income from sales. By 1964 farms in the $40,000 or more annual sales class constituted 4.5 percent of all farms and accounted for 42.3 percent of all sales. By 1967 they made up 5.8 percent of all farms, with 47 percent of all sales by value. Agriculture Department figures divided farms in 1967, according to gross annual sales, as follows:

Class	Number	% of All Farms	$ of All Sales
$40,000 and over	183,000	5.8	47.0
$20,000 to $39,999	318,000	10.1	20.8
$10,000 to $19,999	492,000	15.6	17.3
$5,000 to $9,999	446,000	14.2	8.1
$2,500 to $4,999	360,000	11.5	3.4
Under $2,500	1,347,000	42.8	3.4
Total	3,146,000	100.0	100.0

Raised Exports, Reduced Aid: 1969-72

Tension between the Republican administration and the Democratic-controlled Congress produced a halfway step toward a market-oriented national farm policy during President Richard Nixon's first term.

The Agricultural Act of 1970 was the most significant farm legislation passed during the period 1969-72. Enacted after 16 months of controversy, the act constituted a compromise between Democratic advocates of continued crop and price controls and the administration and its allies, who sought a general loosening of government restrictions with increased emphasis on sales abroad. In the act Congress retained the supply-management approach of the preceding Democratic administrations.

The intensified struggle in 1969 and 1970 between the two long-conflicting opinions pointed toward a major confrontation over agricultural policy during the second Nixon term. The stage was set by the scheduled expiration of the three-year price-support act at the end of 1973. *(Production incentives, p. 135)*

Basically, the 1970 act continued policies followed under the John Kennedy and Lyndon Johnson administrations, placing emphasis on keeping a check on supply and maintaining farm income through direct payments to farmers. However, the Republican administration obtained a key concession in what was known as the set-aside feature.

Under this provision, the act permitted a farmer to be compensated for taking a certain amount of land out of production. He was free to raise what he wished on his other land. The set-aside feature constituted a significant step toward giving farmers greater freedom to plant what they desired according to their assessment of market conditions, and it marked a relaxation of restraints imposed under Democratic administrations in the 1960s.

The Nixon administration was prepared to go still further when the time came for another legislative move. It favored eventual elimination of direct government payments on cotton, wheat, and other specified crops and of the crop-by-crop allotments in effect since the 1930s. But it wanted to retain the basic price-support loans and the authority to buy land taken out of production under the new set-aside program. Advocates of the administration approach, including the big American Farm Bureau Federation, pointed to increased farm exports and farm income as supporting their approach toward greater reliance on supply and demand.

On the other hand, a number of Democratic members of Congress from agricultural areas, backed by other farm organizations, argued for continued restraints (in combination with farm income aids) to curb overproduction. They cautioned that increasingly efficient farming methods could,

Farm Program Tools...

A combination of price support loans and direct payments to farmers made up the income-maintenance and supply-control features of the 1969-72 farm program for wheat, feed grains, and cotton.

Basic Price Support Loans. If a farmer could not sell his crop at a favorable price, he could obtain a government loan, using his crop as collateral. Later, if the market price rose, he could sell his crop. If it failed to rise, he could keep the loan money; the government bought his crop. The loan available was placed at a certain dollar figure per bushel of grain or pound of cotton. It was expressed as a percentage of parity, an artificial price designed to reflect a fair relationship between farm income and farm costs. Basic price support loans had been fixed at or near the world price to allow the commodity to move in international trade. The Nixon administration favored keeping the loan administration.

Set-Aside Payments. These were direct payments to a farmer from the government for reducing a specified amount of his total farm from production, except for a small portion of land that must be idled for conservation purposes (the conserving

in the absence of adequate planning and controls along with price supports, produce huge surpluses, drive prices down, eliminate farm profits, and create serious problems for the whole economy.

Resentment that had been rising among urban members of Congress over large farm subsidy payments culminated in the inclusion of a provision in the 1970 bill imposing the first limitation on total payments. After efforts to limit payments to an individual farm to $20,000 a year failed, a compromise ceiling of $55,000 per crop was enacted. A few farmers had received subsidies of as much as $4 million in one year.

Another indication of future controversy came when the House passed a bill by a 12-vote margin in 1971 amended to raise price-support loan levels for wheat and feed grains by 25 percent. The bill, which would have established a national reserve purchased by the government to reduce oversupply of grains, died without action in the Senate. The issue, however, was far from dead.

In other actions during the four-year period, Congress extended the sugar quota program under the much-lobbied Sugar Act and continued such existing programs as those providing for food stamps, school lunches and Food for Peace — also called Food for Freedom.

Economic Trends

As the first Nixon term ended, the intensified debate over farm policy, and whether to move further away from the basic support-controls programs of some three decades, took place against a background that included:

● Record exports of farm products, including grains and soybeans, accompanied by the opening of a previously untapped market in the Soviet Union and a growing

...Price Supports and Payments

base). On the rest of his land, a farmer was free to plant whatever crop he desired, even though payment formulas and production restrictions still took into account a farm's historic allotments for individual commoditites. The administration favored continued authority to make set-aside payments, but it wanted a clean break from historic allotments.

Wheat Certificate Payments. These were special payments to a farmer participating in the program to assure him "full parity" on the wheat he produced for use in the United States. A payment amounted to $1.34 a bushel in 1972. To help finance the program, millers were required to purchase certificates from the government for 75 cents a bushel for the wheat they processed for human domestic consumption. The administration classified this payment as the type of "income supplement" it wanted to phase out.

Cotton Payments. A cotton grower who participated in the program received a payment of 15 cents a pound calculated on the acreage he planted up to his share of the national allotment on a yield in past years. The administration wanted to phase out this "income supplement" as well as the wheat payments.

interest in underdeveloped countries.

● Record realized net farm income in 1972 of $19.2 billion.

● A continued trend toward fewer farms and a declining U.S. farm population, both in real terms and in relation to the overall population.

● A pronounced swing away from the family farm and toward larger farms that produced an ever larger share of the total farm production, required larger capital, and directed increasing attention to the term "agribusiness."

● Continued increases in mechanization and steadily rising production per acre.

Relation to Economy. While farming was one of the principal occupations in the nation, it continued in the early 1970s to produce directly only 3 percent of total national income. Both the number of farms and the farmer population declined over the 1969-72 period, continuing a trend that had been going on before World War II.

Year	Farms	Farm Population	As % of Total Pop.
1935	6,814,000	31,161,000	25.3%
1945	5,967,000	24,420,000	17.5
1955	4,654,000	19,078,000	11.5
1960	3,962,000	15,635,000	8.7
1967*	3,146,000	10,875,000	5.5
1968	3,054,000	10,454,000	5.2
1969	2,971,000	10,307,000	5.1
1970	2,924,000	9,712,000	4.8
1971	2,876,000	9,425,000	4.6

* Revised Agriculture Department figures.

Size of Farms. The average size of farms increased steadily. Government figures reflecting changes in farm definitions and revised counts showed that the average farm size rose from 167 acres in 1940 to 213 acres in 1950. By 1959 it had increased to 288 acres, by 1964 to 333 acres, and by 1969 to 378 acres. In 1971 the average farm size was 389 acres and preliminary 1972 figures indicated a rise to 394 acres.

Productivity. The long-term trend of increases in farm productivity, due to use of more machinery, fertilizer, lime, and insecticides, continued in 1969-72. Corn yields, which averaged 32.7 bushels an acre in 1945 and 68.3 bushels during the 1962-66 period, reached 78.5 bushels an acre in 1968 and 86.8 bushels in 1971. Sorghum grain, a feed similar to corn, had average yields of 15.2 bushels an acre in 1945, 47.4 bushels during the period 1962-66, 52.9 bushels in 1968, and 53.9 bushels in 1971. Wheat rose from 17.0 in 1945 to 25.8 bushels an acre in the 1962-66 period, 28.4 bushels in 1968 and 33.8 bushels in 1971.

Exports. Agricultural exports showed a steady and accelerating climb. In 1961-65 they averaged $5.6 billion a year. In the period from 1966-70, farm exports averaged $6.5 billion annually. In 1970 they totaled $7.4 billion and in 1971, $7.9 billion. Exports passed $8 billion in 1972 and were expected to hit $10 billion in 1973.

In 1970 official figures showed that the United States produced 13 percent of the world's wheat and provided 36.8 percent of the world's wheat exports. The 1.1 billion bushels expected to be exported in 1973 greatly exceeded the previous U.S. record wheat export of 867 million bushels in 1966. This country produced 41.4 percent of the world's corn for grain in 1970 and supplied 50.5 percent of world corn exports, 73.0 percent of world soybean production and 93.5 percent of world soybean exports, 19.1 percent of world cotton production, and 22.5 percent of world cotton exports.

Division of Market. The larger commercial farms continued to increase their share of the market and to grow in number. In 1959 some 2.8 percent of the nation's farms had sales of $40,000 or more annually and accounted for 31.2 percent of total farm income from sales. By 1967 they made up 5.8 percent of all farms, with 47 percent of all sales by value. By 1971 these farms made up 8.8 percent of all farms, with 59.3

percent of all sales by value. Agriculture Department figures divided farms in 1971, according to gross annual sales, as follows:

Class	Number	% of All Farms	% of All Sales
$40,000 and over	253,000	8.8	59.3
$20,000 to $39,999	365,000	12.7	19.2
$10,000 to $19,999	392,000	13.6	10.9
$ 5,000 to $ 9,999	385,000	13.4	5.5
$ 2,500 to $ 4,999	409,000	14.2	3.0
Under $2,500	1,072,000	37.3	2.1
Total	2,876,000	100.0	100.0

Major Legislation

The most important farm legislation of the 1969-72 period was enacted in 1970. That year saw passage of the Agricultural Act of 1970, establishing three-year price-support programs for wool, wheat, feed grains, and cotton, beginning in January 1971.

The bill was a compromise between the Nixon administration's request for more flexible price supports based on world market and the demand by many farm state members of Congress and farm organizations for higher parity guarantees. The 1970 act extended for three years, through 1973, the PL 480 (Food for Peace) program which made farm products for sale and donation available to underdeveloped countries.

Congress also enacted in 1970 a bill providing free food stamps to families of four with monthly incomes under $30, and a bill expanding and improving the program of free and reduced-price lunches for school children.

Congress in 1971 extended the Sugar Act of 1948, as amended, for another three years through 1974. The legislation, traditionally the center of much lobbying and attention from domestic and foreign sugar interests, extended the import quota system, adjusted production quotas for producers and made changes in some import quotas. Controversy in 1971 centered on the inclusion of a sugar quota for South Africa's apartheid regime.

In other action, Congress expanded the authority of the farmer-owned cooperative lending system to make loans to farmers and other rural residents and established a rural telephone bank to finance rural telephone facilities.

The president's nomination of Earl L. Butz as secretary of agriculture to succeed retiring Clifford M. Hardin led to a struggle over confirmation in the Senate. Butz found he was caught in the economic discontent that gripped farmers and their representatives in a lean year for agriculture. His close ties to corporate farming interests made some members fear he would be unwilling to use government policy to protect the small family farmer in time of need. However, after Butz met with senators in his own behalf, only four Republicans joined Democratic foes in opposing him on the floor. Butz was confirmed Dec. 2 by a 51-44 roll-call vote.

Congress cleared a major bill — the Rural Development Act of 1972 — in August. The act, designed to improve agricultural job opportunities and rural life, followed presidential messages in 1971 and 1972 calling for rural community development.

Agricultural interests joined in successful opposition to a measure to raise the federal minimum wage. The bill would have affected certain farm workers and was fought by producers of many commodities.

Increased Production Incentives: 1973-76

A major change in U.S. agricultural policy, which had been expected for several years, finally occurred in 1973. The Agriculture and Consumer Protection Act of 1973 represented the achievement of a long-sought Republican goal of moving farmers away from dependence on federal subsidies and "freeing" them to grow as much as they wanted for the open market.

Arguments about the two approaches had been advanced for years and were only temporarily stilled in 1970 when compromise legislation, the Agricultural Act of 1970, was passed. *(Legislation, p. 127)*

But circumstances had changed by 1973. Instead of the huge commodity surpluses that had been common during the previous two decades, in 1973 there were empty storage bins, rapidly rising consumer prices, and what appeared to be unceasing world demand for U.S. commodities.

The 1973 farm bill replaced the old support prices for the major commodities of cotton, wheat, corn, and other feed grains, with lower "target prices" that would reimburse farmers only if market prices should drop precipitously. Farmers responded eagerly to the new system, planting "fence-row to fence-row" in 1974 and raising record crops in succeeding years.

The increased agricultural production helped abate somewhat the inflation-produced, high consumer food prices that had been facing the American public. From a dramatic jump of 14.5 percent in both 1973 and 1974, retail food prices increased only 8.5 percent in 1975 and an estimated 3.1 percent in 1976.

Yet, during this period of rising production, farmers complained that inflation was eating away their profits. Because of the increased cost of fertilizer, equipment, and land, they said, their production costs were rising faster than their income.

"Cost-price squeeze" was a rallying cry for farmers who were becoming increasingly sophisticated in politics. Livestock producers sought and received a government-guaranteed emergency loan program in 1974 — extended in 1975 and 1976 — to help them stay in business without slaughtering their foundation herds. Dairy farmers, however, were unsuccessful in three attempts to obtain increases in dairy price supports in the 1973-76 period. Unprecedented numbers went into bankruptcy, claiming they could not afford to keep their cows at the high cost of feed.

Grain Production

In becoming the world's principal supplier of grain, the United States had difficulty first in creating and then in sticking to a viable grain export policy. Huge grain purchases by the Soviet Union in 1972 were largely responsible for depleted grain bins in the United States in 1973. Continued

The Reasons for ...

The law of supply and demand can throw agriculture out of kilter, creating a need for some kind of intervention to stabilize production.

Take wheat, for an example, and assume that market forces alone will determine the price.

Each of 1.3 million wheat growers is an independent decision-maker. Each has high fixed costs in land and equipment, which he naturally wants to use to produce as many bushels as he can.

The trouble is that 1.3 million wheat growers, operating on the same premise, will often overshoot demand by producing massive surpluses that have the potential to drive prices below production costs.

Contrast the situation of those 1.3 million wheat growers with three or four major U.S. automobile manufacturers who can make a survey of expected demand for cars and adjust supply accordingly and who moreover can attract sales with new styles and models. Wheat growers have neither option, because by themselves they cannot control supply, and because they produce a uniform or homogeneous product.

Wheat growers have the additional problem that consumer demand for bread and other wheat products (and for food in general) is relatively stationary — inelastic, in economic terms. A consumer in good times might buy more food, but not much more. He can eat only so much. The effect is that oversupply causes exaggerated price drops. A rule of thumb among agricultural economists is that a 1 percent increase in excess supply will result in a 3 to 4 percent drop in price to farmers.

In times of undersupply, as in 1973, exactly the opposite situation prevails. Because people always have to eat, they will bid up food prices to an exaggerated extent.

Because wheat growers (and other producers) are helpless in adjusting supply to demand in the short run, they have looked to the federal government for help in bringing

world demand made careful husbanding of the U.S. grain supply a major concern.

Congress in 1974 expanded federal regulation of all commodity futures markets. The huge grain sale to the Soviet Union had dramatized the possibility of manipulation of U.S. commodities markets by large grain companies or even by foreign countries. The legislation Congress approved brought all trading in commodity futures under regulation by a five-member Commodity Futures Trading Commission.

The U.S. government in 1975 negotiated a five-year purchase agreement with the Soviet Union that was expected to control that country's volatile purchases and help the United States stabilize its exports.

Another problem appeared in the grain industry in 1975 — corruption in the lucrative U.S. grain trade, including short-weighting of shipments and bribing of inspectors. Congress responded in 1976 with legislation that provided greater federal control over the grain-inspection process.

By 1976 the heady days of the 1973 shortages seemed very far away to American farmers, many of whom began to wonder if the "new era" created by the 1973

... Price Support System

supply and demand roughly into balance. The farm program basically is a cooperative effort of government planners and farmers to perform an economic function the free market cannot perform without severe disruption of the structure of the agricultural economy.

In February 1973, the Agriculture Department spelled out the consequences of abolishing the farm program: "... production increases, sharp drops in farm product prices and even greater drops in net farm incomes in the immediate years after removal of controls ... many marginal farm units (would) go out of production ... it is by no means certain that farm prices and incomes at the end of the decade would have recovered to the levels of recent years. In addition, the social consequences ... could be a source of considerable public concern ... a free market system would be less equipped to cope with such unpredictable phenomena as the 1970 corn blight and the recent unusually strong export demand."

As ingenious as wheat growers — and other producers — have been in adapting new knowledge to increase their productivity, they have been singularly unsuccessful in getting together voluntarily to adjust total supply to demand. Their sheer numbers have prevented such cooperation. So have the conflicting interests of producers of different commodities and in different sections of the nation.

There are trends under way that may make it possible for producers to achieve supply and price stability other than through government programs. Increased farmer-processor bargaining and long-term contracting could assure guaranteed prices and reasonable production geared to expected demand, with planned reserves for such outside factors as bad weather. Agricultural economists think that such alternatives may be down the pike, possibly covering many farm products in the 1980s.

bill would be able to bring stability in bad times. Although American farmers again produced a bumper grain crop in 1976, so also did much of the rest of the world, including the Soviet Union. U.S. farmers saw their prices drop, as traditional foreign customers disappeared enjoying their own good harvests, and U.S. grain stocks began to mount.

The World Food Conference in 1974 had accepted a proposal by Secretary of State Henry A. Kissinger for a system of nationally held but internationally coordinated grain reserves to help stabilize prices and achieve greater world food security. Many American farmers opposed such a reserve, fearing its presence would tempt the government to dump stocks in times of rising consumer prices, causing farmers' income to drop. International negotiations on a reserve proceeded very slowly during 1975-76, indicating the issue would be alive for some time to come.

In an atmosphere of dramatic rising retail sugar prices, Congress in 1974 surprised almost all observers by permitting the nation's 40-year-old sugar program to expire. The program had set foreign and domestic sugar quotas and provided subsidies for domestic producers. The House Agriculture Committee, deaf to arguments that the sugar program, which was designed in a period of world surplus, had become obsolete in a period of world shortage, had voted 30-5 to extend the Sugar Act of 1948. But the House decided by a 175-209 vote not to extend the provisions of the law beyond Dec. 31, 1974.

Economic Trends

The period 1973-76 saw a continuation of the trend toward fewer farms and a smaller farm population growing a greater amount of commodities, as the following Agriculture Department figures indicate:

Year	Number of Farms	Farm Population	As Percentage of total population
1971	2,908,950	9,425,000	4.6
1972	2,869,710	9,610,000	4.6
1973	2,843,890	9,472,000	4.5
1974	2,830,490	9,264,000	4.4
1975	2,808,480	8,864,000	4.2

Size of Farms

While the number of farms continued to decline, the average size continued to increase. From 377 acres in 1971, the average farm size increased to 383 acres in 1973, 387 acres in 1975, and an estimated 389 acres in 1976.

Productivity

Although yields rose during the 1950s and 1960s, yields per acre for major crops during 1973-76 showed a leveling and in some instances a decline. The rising cost of fertilizer and equipment during the four-year period, as well as some years of bad weather, had a depressing effect on yields:

Average Yields Per Acre

(in bushels per acre)

Year	Wheat	Corn	Soybeans
1971	33.9	88.1	27.5
1972	32.7	97.1	27.8
1973	31.7	91.2	27.7
1974	27.4	71.4	23.2
1975	30.6	86.2	28.4

Total production of wheat and corn remained steady during the period:

Years*	Wheat	Corn
	(in billion bushels)	
1971/72	1.62	5.64
1972/73	1.54	5.57
1973/74	1.70	5.65
1974/75	1.80	4.66
1975/76	2.13	5.80

* *The wheat marketing year runs from June 1 to May 31. The corn marketing year runs from Oct. 1 to Sept. 30.*

Agricultural Exports

American farmers faced a demanding world market during much of the 1973-76 period, and agricultural exports increased dramatically:

Year	Agricultural Exports	Year	Agricultural Exports
1971	$ 7,693,000	1974	$21,999,000
1972	9,401,000	1975	21,884,000
1973	17,680,000	1976	22,996,000

Of those totals, grain accounted for the following amounts:

Year	Grain Exports	Year	Grain Exports
1971	$ 2,431,000	1974	$10,311,000
1972	3,484,000	1975	11,619,000
1973	8,481,000	1976	10,875,000

Grain Embargo, Crop Insurance: 1977-80

President Jimmy Carter continued farm policies established by his Republican predecessors, stressing low price supports and minimum interference in farmers' planting decisions. That lean, low-cost approach displeased those who expected more from the peanut-farmer-turned-president. A new, militant farmers' lobby, the American Agriculture Movement, surfaced in 1978 and sparring between farm-state members of Congress and administration representatives continued throughout Carter's four years in office.

Still, by 1980 it was clear that the farm community generally had moved away from reliance on old Depression-style farm programs, which once coupled high price supports with strict limits on what and how much a farmer could produce. For example, participation in a 1979 production control program — which in turn made farmers eligible for disaster payments and other benefits — was only 24 percent.

For farm groups judging the presidential candidates in 1980, anticipation of omnibus farm legislation in 1981, inflation, government regulation, and other matters beyond the reach of farm legislation often overshadowed price supports and other specific agriculture issues.

Farmers in 1976 had voted in significant numbers for Carter because they were then very angry with Republican grain embargos, imposed in the early 1970s to counter inflation in consumer food prices.

And many were nervous about Republican "free market" policies that increased farm vulnerability to the vagaries of markets and weather.

Four years later, similar discontent prompted a shift in farm voting from Carter to Ronald Reagan, despite Reagan's obvious unfamiliarity with agriculture issues. In one widely reported campaign incident, Reagan amiably conceded to a farm audience that he did not understand parity — the controversial farm price index that had been at the center of farm policy debates for decades. But the Republican candidate recouped any lost support with a promise to end Carter's unpopular grain embargo against the Soviet Union.

Less Federal Involvement

Two key features of Carter's farm policies illustrated his efforts to continue the trend of the last decade away from federal involvement in agriculture. Carter proposed, and Congress finally agreed in 1980, to end direct payments to farmers whose crops were damaged by drought or other natural disasters and instead to offer a greatly expanded federal crop insurance program. Though the insurance premiums were federally subsidized, the change meant that farmers themselves would have to contribute substantially to future compensation payments, instead of relying on

139

Bob Bergland

the disaster payments as a form of "free insurance."

Carter also rarely used his standby authority to curb surplus production by paying farmers not to grow, relying instead on the farmer-held grain reserve to strengthen market prices. Under that program, farmers could borrow against the value of their crops, as with conventional price support loans. Those in the reserve program, however, had to agree not to sell their crops to repay the loans until market prices reached certain high levels set by law. The program was meant to serve as a marketing tool while allaying farmers' traditional suspicions that government-held reserves would be used to quash high prices.

Although farmers began to accept the reserve program by the end of Carter's term, there was lingering doubt that the newly expanded crop insurance program gave them enough protection from the ravages of natural disasters.

Uneasy Relations

Carter's disputes with farmers began early in his term when he repeatedly threatened to veto the 1977 omnibus farm bill on the grounds that it was too expensive. Yet many producers thought the bill's spending levels were too low to help them. In reauthorizing basic farm programs, Congress significantly increased target prices, the basis for one type of price support that provided direct payments to producers. Even those higher target prices seemed inadequate to farmers who measured them against their soaring costs for diesel fuel, petroleum-based agricultural chemicals, machinery, and land. Carter grudgingly signed the farm bill without resolving the underlying conflict between the goals of producers and federal policy makers.

Farmers who used federal farm programs saw them as sources of operating capital because the primary form of aid was the price support loan. Farmers used their crops as collateral for the loans, which, they argued, should fully reflect the costs of producing those crops. They believed the Carter administration inappropriately chose the lowest permissible levels for the loans.

Farm production costs were growing more rapidly than the prices farmers received for their crops. Between 1979 and 1980, the per-acre cost of producing the 10 major crops grew by 20 percent. In that period of time, fertilizer prices rose by 23 percent, the cost of agricultural chemicals increased by 18 percent, and the interest rates on some short-term commercial loans reached 20 percent — perhaps a third more than interest rates of the previous year. Yet, the average market price for wheat grew by 6 percent. *(Production expenses, chart, p. 141)*

Carter's Agriculture Department (USDA), headed by former farmer and member of the House, Bob Bergland, D-Minn. (1971-77), insisted that farmers should look to market prices, not the federal government, for their income. Federal programs, Bergland believed, should promote orderly and predictable market behavior by moderating abrupt swings to very high or very low prices. High price supports would artificially inflate the price of American farm products and distort the market, he said.

Disagreements between farm-state members of Congress and the administration over the proper level of federal involvement in agriculture continued throughout Carter's term, and it did not differ significantly in tone from debates of earlier years. But in one respect, Carter broke new ground, to the displeasure of many farmers and food industry executives.

Carter placed in key positions at USDA such prominent environmental and consumer activists as Carol Tucker Foreman, the former head of the Consumer Federation of America. As assistant secretary for food and consumer services, Foreman backed controversial nutritional guidelines issued jointly in 1980 by USDA and the Health and Human Services Department.

Dairy, egg, and livestock producers were particularly distressed by the guidelines, which advised Americans to cut down their consumption of saturated fats, cholesterol, sugar, and salt, and to eat more fiber and starch. Similar findings had been issued in 1977 by Sen. George McGovern's, D-S.D., Select Committee on Nutrition and Human Needs.

Foreman also initially supported — and then backed off from — a proposed ban on the use of sodium nitrite to preserve sausage and other pork products. She provoked the food industry by urging fuller food labeling, for both ingredients and nutrient value.

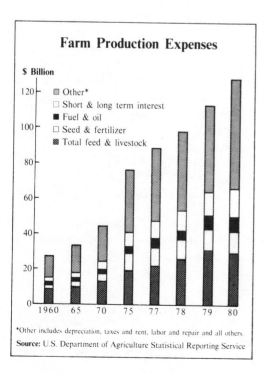

Farm Production Expenses

$ Billion

☒ Other*
☐ Short & long term interest
■ Fuel & oil
☐ Seed & fertilizer
☒ Total feed & livestock

1960 65 70 75 77 78 79 80

*Other includes depreciation, taxes and rent, labor and repair and all others.
Source: U.S. Department of Agriculture Statistical Reporting Service

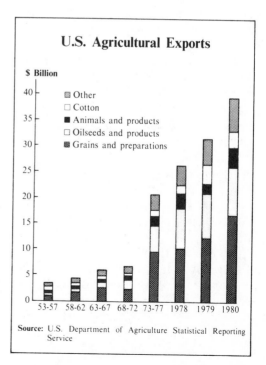

U.S. Agricultural Exports

$ Billion

☒ Other
☐ Cotton
■ Animals and products
☐ Oilseeds and products
☒ Grains and preparations

53-57 58-62 63-67 68-72 73-77 1978 1979 1980

Source: U.S. Department of Agriculture Statistical Reporting Service

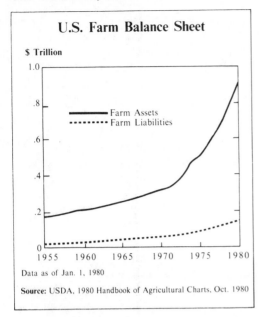

U.S. Farm Balance Sheet

$ Trillion

— Farm Assets

········ Farm Liabilities

Data as of Jan. 1, 1980

Source: USDA, 1980 Handbook of Agricultural Charts, Oct. 1980

The department's annual "yearbooks," traditionally devoted to farm statistics and technical information, took on a distinct consumer orientation under Bergland. One year the book was a colorful, cartoon-filled discussion of eating habits aimed at children. Members of Congress who liked to distribute the conventional version to farm constituents were displeased.

Bergland himself criticized a basic thrust of USDA-supported agricultural research, which he said had stressed development of mechanized farming at the expense of farm worker jobs. He endorsed a favorable 1980 department report on "organic" or non-chemical farming.

In all, established farmers practicing high-technology agriculture believed unhappily that "their" department had been leased out to their political opponents. Moreover, Carter's labor officials trod on producers' toes while enforcing migrant labor laws. And his environmental appointees sought to revive a dormant statute that greatly restricted the size of farms benefiting from federal irrigation projects.

Grain Embargoes

Carter put the final seal on his disturbed relationship with farmers in January 1980 when he abruptly embargoed most sales of American grain to the Soviet Union to protest that nation's invasion of Afghanistan. Farmers bitterly recalled Carter's campaign pledge "never" to use an embargo, and they watched with dismay as grain prices plunged — and stayed low — for months after the announcement. They did not accept the conclusion of many economists, in and out of government, that their income was damaged more by a 1979 surplus and rising production costs than by the long-term impact of the embargo.

Congressional agriculture committees reported bill after bill dramatically boosting price supports for the duration of the embargo, but the only significant change approved was a higher loan rate for the farmer-held reserve.

Uncertain Future

As Congress began in late 1980 to look forward to the following year's reauthorization of farm programs, it appeared that legislation could not reach many factors that spelled the difference between financial success and distress for ranchers and farmers. Foreign food needs, domestic monetary and tax policies, deregulation of the trucking and rail industries, and energy prices profoundly affected farm income. None of these factors, of course, was within the jurisdiction of congressional agriculture committees.

There were, also, growing challenges to the philosophy underlying the Depression's legacy of federal price support and production control programs. For more than four decades, federal farm law had been written to deal with the risks of overproduction, chronic surpluses, low commodity prices, and farm income.

But in 1980 USDA analysts were predicting that the nation's major farm "problem" of the coming decade "could well be frequent shortages, highly volatile prices, and unstable farm incomes," as one economist told the department's annual outlook conference. The major policy question of the future would be how to allocate food supplies between growing domestic and foreign trade needs and the new demand for grain to produce alcohol fuel. A related issue, the official predicted, would be "wise use of production resources," particularly easily erodible land that was being drawn into production as farmers sought to meet mounting demands.

Every year since 1970, U.S. food exports had hit record highs — exceeding $40 billion by 1980. The expansion into world markets meant higher incomes for farmers, but it also greatly magnified the uncertainties of markets and weather. Untimely rains in Russia and Japanese investments in the Brazilian soybean industry ranked with domestic drought and farm politics as determinants in farm income. *(Exports and subsidies, p. 89)*

Other challenges to the nation's basic farm programs surfaced in 1980 with the publication of two important studies suggesting that those programs had outlived their usefulness. Both the conservative Washington-based research group, the Heritage Foundation, and a hefty "agriculture structure" study completed for Bergland suggested that federal farm policies had hastened the demise of small farms, while encouraging consolidation and growth of larger operations.

Economic Trends

Farmers' income during the four years of Carter's term was comparable with that of middle-class Americans living off the farm. In 1979, for example, the per-capita disposable income of the farm population was $7,535 or 102 percent of the per-capita disposable income of non-farm individuals. That was a high but during the period farm income did not dip much below the earnings of non-farm families.

The closeness between the two groups' earnings was a dramatic change from earlier decades. In the 1930s the farm population earned between 32 and 45 percent of the amount earned by non-farm workers, while as late as the 1960s their earnings averaged about 75 percent of non-farm income. Increasingly, owners of smaller farms were supplementing sales of farm products with income from a range of other jobs not related to agriculture. The average per-farm income in 1979 was $26,254; of that, an average of $14,728 came from off-farm sources.

As farming became increasingly dependent on capital, farmers also expressed concern about their growing indebtedness. The ratio of total farm assets to indebtedness fluctuated between 16 and 17 percent during this time. But the problem seemed to be more one of cash flow than of net worth, because the total value of assets also grew during this period. In 1977 total farm assets were valued at $614.7 billion, while by 1980 that figure had jumped to $918.9 billion. *(Farm balance chart, p. 142)*

Reagan Farm Policies: 1981-84

Ronald Reagan, campaigning as the Republican presidential candidate, admitted that he did not understand parity, but still received the farm vote because he vowed, if elected, to end the grain embargo against the Soviet Union imposed by President Jimmy Carter in January 1980 in retaliation against Russia's invasion of Afghanistan. Reagan fullfilled his campaign promise three months after taking office, but the good will between the farm community and the administration quickly dissipated when the administration proposed its omnibus farm bill.

In that proposal it became clear that Reagan wanted to end production controls and target prices, and to lower commodity loan rates and dairy subsidies — in other words, to wean the farm community from government support.

Despite the administration's intentions, federal expenditures for farm programs reached new heights in 1982, only to surpass those records again in 1983. The large increase in federal outlays reflected an attempt to balance commodity surpluses against increased production capabilities and highly competitive foreign markets. But the administration's policies did not solve the growing issues surrounding the farm community. Already in 1984 farmers were preparing a lobbying strategy to influence favorable congressional action on the omnibus farm bill up for renewal in 1985.

POST-ELECTION FARM PROPOSALS, LEGISLATION

Ronald Reagan's first year as president brought stormy debates in Congress over his insistence on low-cost farm programs and major reductions in federal loans to farmers and rural communities. In the end, the president generally got what he wanted from Congress.

Reagan won a strategically important victory over the well-financed dairy lobby in March when lawmakers canceled a scheduled increase in dairy price supports. The president painted the victory as an important first step on the road to his more wide-ranging aim of balancing the budget and bringing down the massive deficit. The fight divided the dairy lobby internally and also helped set up stresses among commodity groups that later aided the administration's drive for a low-cost omnibus farm bill.

Reagan's appointments to the Agriculture Department, his massive tax-cutting and budget-reduction bills, his deregulation policies, and his cancellation of the unpopular embargo on the sale of grain to the Soviet Union generally pleased the agricultural community. Still, the "profits" Reagan had promised farmers during his 1980 presidential campaign continued to be elusive.

Reagan told farmers that net farm income had dropped during Jimmy Carter's presidency to "the lowest level since the... depths of the Great Depression." Yet, as Reagan's first year came to an end, the Agriculture Department predicted that net farm income would slide below the level of Carter's last full year in office. That made 1981 the third consecutive year that U.S. farmers' income declined below the previous year's level. Parity, the decades-old measure of farmers' purchasing power, was 61 percent in 1981, perilously close to the all-time low of 58 percent in June 1932. (One-hundred percent of parity would give farmers the same purchasing power they had had during the prosperous 1910-14 period.)

Income per farm for 1981 was expected to average approximately $24,000, nearly $1,000 less than in 1979. Of the 1981 figure, only $7,950 was earned on the farm, with the remainder gleaned from outside jobs and other non-farm sources of income.

As in previous years, farmers found in 1981 that market prices for their commodities rose less rapidly than the prices they had to pay for fertilizer, credit, machinery, and similar items.

Their cash expenses and total production costs increased about 9 percent in 1981, compared with a 5 percent increase in cash receipts. Interest rates reached record highs in August — 20 percent for commercial loans in some regions.

The Farmers Home Administration reported a sharp upsurge in delinquencies on farm loans. Private lenders voiced worries that, unless farm income improved signficantly, they too might have trouble collecting on their loans in 1982.

The chronic imbalance between market prices and farm expenses was worsened by several developments during 1981. Bumper crops — particularly in wheat and corn — depressed prices, and crop production was up 14 percent.

Foreign sales of U.S. farm commodities hit a record high of $43.3 billion, but gloomy farm leaders said the total should have been even higher and did not adequately offset low prices to individual farms. A stronger U.S. dollar and inflation abroad had eroded the purchasing power of foreign buyers, as American commodities became more expensive for them to buy. At the same time, Australia, Argentina, and other U.S. agricultural competitors had increased their production and taken a larger share of the market during the 15 months of Carter's grain embargo.

Yet another depressant on farm prices was administration talk, at the end of the year, of new economic reprisals against the Soviet Union if that nation intervened in the troubled political situation in Poland. But those fears were assuaged by the fact that Reagan had pledged to promote farm exports. Moreover, officials announced Oct. 1 that the United States was extending the expired U.S.—U.S.S.R. grain agreement for one year. The agreement would permit the Russians to nearly triple the quantity of U.S. wheat and corn that they could buy.

By the year's end, however, Soviet purchasers had committed themselves to only half the 23 million metric tons alloted, and they were not expected to purchase much more. The Soviets ordered American grain only after they had bought as much as they could from other suppliers.

Reagan's cancellation of the grain embargo was one of a number of moves that filled campaign pledges and pleased farmers. He also kept his promise to rid the Agriculture Department of "activists," an apparent reference to Carter's controversial appointments from consumer and environmental groups.

Bureaucratic Changes

Reagan's choice of an Illinois hog farmer, John R. Block, as secretary of agriculture was popular. Block split or combined a number of department agencies and functions in June, and in the process Carter's special offices for environmental quality and human nutrition disappeared.

Critics complained that those issues would get little attention without the visibility that the special offices had provided. But Block declared that the functions of the offices would be redistributed to the appropriate department agencies.

The department, having distributed approximately seven million copies of its controversial 1980 pamphlet *Dietary Guidelines*, decided not to pay for more reprints. Budget pressures dictated the move, a department spokesman said. The pamphlet had offended egg, meat, and dairy producers.

On another front, the Interior Department under Secretary James G. Watt did not enforce new regulations that would have severely limited the size of farms that could benefit from federally subsidized irrigation projects. Some owners of massive Western farms that depended on cheap federal water said the new rules, derived from a 1902 act, were out of step with modern agriculture.

Regulations Scrutinized

As part of Reagan's government-wide review of regulations, about a half-dozen Agriculture Department rules came under scrutiny. Standards for grading beef and labeling processed meat that included pulverized bone fragments were changed in accord with the wishes of producer groups.

The most controversial review, marketing orders for fruits and vegetables, was not completed during the year. Farm groups defending the rules said that they assured consumer quality while permitting farmers to share the costs of promoting their produce. But Reagan's Office of Budget and Management was exerting strong pressures against the use of such orders to control

prices by restricting the volume of a crop that could come to the market.

Reagan's landmark tax bill included rate reductions and liberalized depreciation allowances that were expected to benefit farmers. Its provisions permitted tax-free transfer of farm assets between spouses, by gift or by will, and thus ended the so-called "widow's tax" that had been a sore point in the farm community.

The new law also eased transfer of farms within families by tripling the value of gifts that could be made without tax penalties and by revising rules for determining the value of farmland for calculating estate taxes.

Omnibus Farm Bill

Just before adjournment Dec. 16, 1981, a reluctant House by a two-vote margin cleared the four-year farm bill the administration wanted. Conflicting demands from a divided farm community, the Reagan administration, consumer advocates, and food processors had kept the outcome in doubt until the final House vote of 205-203 adopting the $11 billion conference agreement.

The Senate had approved it by a 68-31 vote Dec. 10. The bill renewed basic food and farm programs for four years, replacing the 1977 law that had expired Sept. 30.

Coalition Shattered. The House action on the Agriculture and Food Act of 1981 capped a long and painful process. It was the first year that legislators had to craft farm programs to fit within a total dollar amount specified by the budget. That constraint forced commodity groups to compete directly for shares of a smaller federal pie and shattered their vote-trading relationships.

At critical points during the year, many farm-state members abandoned their logrolling habits and voted against programs — such as dairy or sugar or peanuts — that were of minimal interest to their own constituents. The resentment spawned by those votes meant that there was rarely a smoothly functioning coalition to move the farm bill along. Nor was there a united farm front against administration pressures to keep spending levels down.

Stirring up the longstanding rivalries within the farm coalition was a deliberate administration tactic, according to administration budget director David A. Stockman. It enabled Reagan to block what he viewed as budget-busting farm demands.

Other sources of pressure on farm groups during the year were record high interest rates and sagging commodity prices caused by bumper crops and rumors of renewed economic sanctions against the Soviet Union.

Compromises. The Republican Senate reluctantly complied with Reagan's demands for price support increases that were less generous than the commodity groups wanted. House farm interests shepherded a far more costly bill all the way to conference, and the conference itself dragged on for six weeks until House members bowed to administration pressures for cost reductions.

The final agreement generally continued the price support, research, Food for Peace, and other farm programs. It included an $11.3 billion one-year extension of the food stamp program.

Except for the dairy program, whose minimum support level was significantly reduced from existing law, the bill increased major crop price supports, but it did not permit those supports to rise as rapidly in future years as many farmers wanted. Substantial changes were made in the tightly regulated peanut program and a new sugar price support program was created.

The bill set minimum support levels for dairymen in dollars instead of linking them to a parity index as in the past. The contro-versial new inflation index was to come into play only if government purchases of dairy products, as required by law, exceeded certain levels.

Reagan Request

As Congress began deliberating the renewal of farm programs that had survived since the 1930s, the situation resembled that of four years earlier: Farm interest groups clamored for financial relief in a troubled economy, and the new administration signaled that it wanted to lower farm program spending. In 1977 Congress had demanded substantially higher price support levels than the new Democratic president, Jimmy Carter, wanted. Congress won after a difficult struggle that permanently soured relations between farm-state members and Carter and his agriculture secretary, Bob Bergland.

Reagan's economic message to Congress urged hefty cuts in such deeply entrenched programs as the Farmers Home Administration (FmHA) and the Rural Electrification Administration (REA). The reductions were in line with the belief of Reagan's economic advisers that federal lending, including federal guarantees of private loans, distorted free-market forces.

Jesse Helms, R-N.C., new chairman of the Senate Agriculture Committee, and House Agriculture Committee Chairman E. "Kika" de la Garza, D-Texas, at first predicted that committee members and their constituencies would be willing to make do with less. "Farmers understand that unless this inflation is cured, they don't stand a chance no matter what kind of farm bill we pass," Helms said.

However, as the extent of the revisions the president had in mind became clear, both committees rebelled. Senate Democrats and Republicans — including Helms — introduced competing bills departing markedly from key administration proposals.

Reagan had asked Congress to eliminate target prices, a major form of price support, and to drop a number of production control programs. For basic price support loans, whose minimum levels were traditionally fixed in law, the president asked for broad, discretionary authority to set loan rates as supply and demand dictated. He also requested substantial changes in the farmer-held grain reserve.

The versions brought to the floor by the House and Senate Agriculture committees largely ignored those requests.

Divisions in the Farm Alliance

As Agriculture Secretary John R. Block was sounding the threat in August of a presidential veto of the developing farm bill because of budget constraints and objections to dairy and certain grain provisions, there were signs that the farm alliances were so shaky that the president's cost-cutting drive might prevail.

The pressures of the budget sent farm interests scrambling to protect their shrinking shares of the federal pie. An every-man-for-himself attitude threatened years of mutual accommodation in which lobbyists and members were inclined to look after each other's interests. *(Farm lobby, p. 77)*

"It used to be that everybody could get their piece of the pie, and if the pie was too small, they [Congress] could just make it bigger," one lobbyist explained. In 1981, he added, "There's not enough to go around." Sen. Robert Dole, R-Kan., remarked that farm coalitions always had been unstable but that in 1981 "It's worse. It's sort of dog-eat-dog." The well-financed dairy lobby was isolated early in the year when Reagan persuaded Congress to cancel a scheduled price support increase.

The peanut and tobacco programs were in particular trouble in both chambers, and the sugar price support program drew strong opposition in the House. Part of the opposition to the tightly controlled peanut and tobacco programs was attributed to an anti-regulation mood. Both programs operated under rigid allotments and quotas that limited growing rights to a select few. Critics called the system "feudalistic."

All three programs survived, but the tobacco program narrowly missed extinction in the Senate, the peanut program was modified against the wishes of peanut producers, and the sugar program came through with somewhat lower support prices than those approved in committee.

One potentially explosive issue was defused April 24 when Reagan ended the embargo of sales of U.S. grain to Russia. Farmers had chafed under the embargo ever since it was instituted by Carter in January 1980 to express disapproval of the Soviet invasion of Afghanistan.

Even without the embargo, the 1981 crops were so large that farm prices fell far short of predicted highs, and pressures built quickly for higher price supports. In a move to strengthen prices, Block announced in September that the government would ask wheat farmers to cut back their acreage. The authority that Block proposed to use was one of the production controls that Reagan had asked Congress to cancel six months earlier.

Dairy Price Supports

An administration bill to cancel a scheduled April 1 increase in the dairy price support provided President Reagan with one of his first legislative victories on Capitol Hill.

Two years later Congress enacted legislation that overhauled federal dairy policy and further reduced federal price supports. That bill, however, met with strong administration objections because it contained provisions paying dairymen for not producing. *(Dairy program, p. 160)*

The dairy bill was the first piece of

The government owns a large surplus of dry milk as a result of federal dairy programs.

Reagan's ambitious economic program to go before Congress. The president's allies and tacticians managed to blunt strong efforts by the dairy industry and some Democrats to make changes that were unacceptable to the White House.

The 90-cent-per-hundredweight increase in the federal price support for dairy products had been required by a provision in the 1977 farm law, which was extended for two years in 1979. Administration officials contended that the increase would cost consumers an additional 8 cents a gallon for milk. They also maintained that the dairy program stimulated overproduction and that eliminating the April 1 increase would save the federal government $147 million in 1981 in purchase and storage costs for dairy products.

The program required the government to buy, in the form of butter, dried milk, cheese, and all the milk that dairy farmers could not sell at the price support level. If the April 1 adjustment had not been blocked, the price support would have risen from $13.10 to $14.00 per hundredweight.

Dairy spokesmen countered that inflation had so increased the expenses of dairymen that they needed the April 1 adjustment badly. They contended that low feed-grain prices and relatively low beef prices — not the federal support program — had prompted high dairy production. Without the adjustment, they warned, small- to moderate-sized dairy operations would simply fold. Industry officials were divided and did not attack the basic bill. Instead, they pressed for changes that could have delayed passage beyond the April 1 deadline.

Farm Loan Interest Rates

The 1981 budget reconciliation bill brought higher interest rates for many federal farm loans and new charges for grading and inspecting cotton, tobacco, and grain.

The massive budget-cutting bill cleared by Congress July 31, also gave dairymen price supports at least 5 percentage points above the 70 percent parity level the Reagan administration wanted. The legislation explicitly stated that the dairy program would be reconsidered during deliberations on the farm bill reauthorizing agricultural programs for four years. But controversy delayed enactment of the farm bill, and separate measures were passed to prevent dairymen from reaping a bonus throughout the year.

The reconciliation cuts were felt through much of the Agriculture Department (USDA). Chairman de la Garza of the House Agriculture Committee noted that USDA programs were cut by $8.8 billion in fiscal 1982-84, some $3 billion more than was required.

The House-passed dairy program that the reconciliation conferees retained was strongly opposed by the administration. Because Reagan believed that the statutory support price of 80 percent of parity encouraged farmers to produce more milk than Americans could consume, he already had persuaded Congress to cancel a scheduled April 1 adjustment in the support price for dairy products.

That action left payments at $13.10 per hundredweight — a figure that was about 75 percent of parity in the spring but dropped to about 72 percent of parity by the end of the year.

Under the dairy program, if a farmer was not able to sell his dairy products at a price equivalent to the percentage of parity set by law, the government had to buy the excess stocks at that price and store them.

In 1980 the government bought 579 million pounds of butter, cheese, and non-fat dry milk at a cost of $1.2 billion, excluding interest and storage charges.

Lowering the stipulated percentage of parity would decrease the government's costs. Reagan wanted Congress to give the agriculture secretary broad discretion to set the support level at 70 percent of parity, or even less, to discourage production.

The dairy provisions of the reconciliation measure set a 75 percent minimum price support but postponed semiannual adjustments until fiscal 1983. Legislators intended that the dairy program be reappraised during consideration of the four-year reauthorization of farm programs.

But the House and Senate became embroiled in controversy over the farm bill, and the 1977 law setting the existing level of supports expired Sept. 30. With that expiration, the reconciliation provision came into play, raising the price support from the existing $13.10 per hundredweight to $13.49.

The missed deadline set off a legislative scramble to block the price support hike. On Oct. 1, by a 328-58 vote, the House approved legislation delaying the increase until Nov. 15, by which time the new farm bill with lower price supports was to have been enacted. The Senate by voice vote Oct. 19 cleared the bill for the president, who signed it into law Oct. 20. When it became clear that farm bill conferees would not reach agreement by Nov. 15, an unrelated bill was amended to postpone the increase until the end of 1981.

In 1982 Congress passed a budget reconciliation bill that froze, and even provided for cutting, dairy price supports. The supports were further reduced in 1983.

Embargo Loans

Less than a year after it approved certain interest-free loans for farmers to compensate for the embargo of grain sales to Russia, Congress reinstated the charges. President Reagan signed the bill into July 23.

The act ended a mandatory interest waiver established in December 1980 on loans for 1980 and 1981 grain crops stored in the farmer-held reserve. The 1980 legislation was intended to aid farmers adversely affected by President Carter's Jan. 4, 1980, announcement establishing the embargo. Under the legislation, farmers borrowed from the government, using their crops as collateral, and could not sell them to repay the loan until certain market prices were reached. The program was intended to stabilize grain prices by keeping potential surpluses off the market.

Reagan lifted the embargo April 24. The administration then asked Congress to end the interest waiver, and the Agriculture Department refused to admit 1981 grain into the reserve program and make loans until the request was approved. The cancellation was expected to save the government $165 million in fiscal 1982.

The grain reserve was opened the same day the president signed the bill.

FARM POLICY REVERSAL, 1982

The deteriorating farm economy forced the Reagan administration to make a striking change in its farm policy in 1982. By the end of the year, the administration was poised to offer farmers both cash and "payments in kind" of surplus crops to not plant wheat, cotton, and other major crops in 1983. The goal of the program was to retire as much as half the nation's cropland.

Administration officials insisted that the program was a temporary expedient to eliminate the enormous surpluses of major commodities that had accumulated in the nation's storage bins and warehouses. No previous administration, Democratic or Republican, had attempted a production cutback of such magnitude.

Top Agriculture Department officials, such as deputy secretary Richard E. Lyng, acknowledged that when they took office they hardly expected to launch sweeping — if temporary — production curbs. Secretary Block had come to Washington advocating all-out production by farmers, with minimum government intervention.

Estimates of farm income for 1982 were so grim that early in the year USDA stopped publishing them. When pressed to defend that move, Block and his economists usually said that income predictions were meaningless because it was so difficult to anticipate weather, world markets, and other variables. But Block also told a Senate subcommittee, "The truth is, the department doesn't want to give validity to the horror stories. The forecasts give credence to what farmers around the country are saying and feeling."

What farmers were saying was that 1982 was the worst year for agriculture since the Depression of the 1930s. Farm income and parity figures, dipping to 50-year lows, seemed to bear that out. Parity, the economic index of farmers' purchasing power, stood at 57 percent in December; the previous low of 58 occurred in 1932. The final 1981 figure had been 61 percent.

The underlying problem was that world markets had gone sour while farm production peaked. Global recession and aggressive competition for markets by other agricultural exporters lessened demand for American commodities. The continuing strength of the U.S. dollar, compared with other currencies, was also damaging. It meant that even though U.S. commodities were selling for bargain-basement prices, their cost in foreign currencies kept rising to uncompetitive levels.

For more than 10 years, U.S. farm policy and individual farmers' decisions to gear up production had been based on an assumption that the world would buy as much as America could grow. But in 1982, for the first time in a decade, U.S. farm exports instead declined in value, to $36.6 billion, from a record 1981 level of $43.3 billion.

The slump coincided with the second year in a row of record high yields. USDA officials reported that the United States was ending the year with surpluses unequaled in magnitude for 20 years. "Ending stocks" — commodities for which there was no commercial demand at the end of the year — were estimated at about 150 million metric tons. That was nearly enough to meet the nation's domestic needs for a full year.

There were other disheartening statistics too. Farm loan delinquencies rose. Private banks expected that as many as one-fourth of their farm customers would fail to qualify for financing another year.

The growth in farm land values, which had supported much farm borrowing for expansion during the 1970s, turned around. Agricultural land values registered a 1 percent decline in March 1982.

Farm Income Declines

Farm income for 1982 fell to $22.1 billion in 1982. That was a sharp drop from a 1979 high of $32.3 billion, and about the same as 1981. During the year, however, unofficial department estimates and projections by private economic forecasters had placed net farm income as low as $15 billion to $16 billion. The department did not publish its total until September, when it could include some $4 billion in early payments to farmers. The advance payments were for one type of price supports known as deficiency payments, and for farmers promising to retire farmland in the coming crop year.

The pre-election injecton of cash had been proposed by the administration and approved by Congress, which increased the amount that could be paid out before customary dates.

In all, the government spent an unprecedented $11.9 billion in fiscal 1982 to prop up farm income; that included the $4 billion in advances for deficiency and land diversion payments, price support and reserve loans to farmers, and about $2 billion in payments under the surplus-swollen dairy program. The total was about four times the annual average for the preceding decade.

USDA historians said that while total farm income figures, adjusted for inflation, were the same as those of the Depression, the comparison was not totally valid. Fifty years earlier there had been more farmers to divide up the income and no federal programs such as farm loans and price supports, they said. And, by 1982, off-farm jobs had become a major source of income for farm families. Nevertheless, as one department publication observed in November, "Pretty generally, it was a bad year."

Other Developments

The president extended the U.S.S.R.—U.S. grain sales trade agreement for one year, but Soviet buyers showed little interest and instead concluded major agreements with competing suppliers.

Reagan sought to stimulate sales when he announced Oct. 15, 1982, that if Soviet buyers completed contract and delivery agreements by specified deadlines, he would guarantee delivery for 23 million metric tons of grain. The grain sales agreement's basic guarantee had covered a minimum of six million tons. The offer had little visible effect on depressed grain markets.

Europeans, incensed at Reagan's efforts to cut off sales of technology and equipment for a Soviet natural gas pipeline, criticized the grain offer.

Ronald Reagan

Sugar Quotas. The administration departed conspicuously from its advocacy of free trade in May when the president announced an immediate restriction on the amount of sugar imported into the United States. A world glut had pushed sugar prices so low that the federal government was faced with program payments to sugar producers of as much as $800 million. The quota survived an unsuccessful lawsuit by outraged sugar refiners.

GATT Talks. High-level trade talks in Geneva, Switzerland, in November failed to produce any change in European farm export subsidies. American farmers believed the subsidies were a contributing factor to their financial problems. *(Exports and subsides, p. 89)*

American delegates to the meeting of the General Agreement on Tariffs and Trade (GATT) sought unsuccessfully to win a freeze and then a gradual elimination of subsidies by all producing nations. But European officials refused even to discuss their commodity subsidies. When USDA officials returned to Washington they renewed threats of retaliation but later softened their statements after resuming discussions with European trade officials.

Blended Credit. Using funds appropriated to promote exports, the administration launched what it called a "blended credit" program, in which interest-free federal loans could be used in combination with federally guaranteed commercial loans to provide lower-interest financing for farm exports.

Farm Program Cuts

Two farm policy changes aimed at reducing grain and dairy surpluses were included in the 1982 budget-cutting reconciliation measure passed by Congress Aug. 18. President Reagan signed the legislation Sept. 8.

One provided new advance payments to farmers who agreed not to grow major crops. The theory was that the reduced production would lead to higher market prices and subsequently decrease the amounts the government would have to pay in the future for price supports to bolster farm income.

The final measure required early payments to farmers of one type of price supports known as deficiency payments for fiscal 1982 and 1983. Deficiency payments were paid by the government to farmers when the market price of a commodity failed to reach a higher target price set by law. It required the secretary of agriculture to offer a 20 percent diversion for wheat, 15 percent for corn, and 20 percent for rice. In each case, a producer had to retire the specified acreage to qualify for price supports and other farm programs, and for special diversion payments on 5 percent of his land.

The second change had the effect of cutting up to $1 from the existing dairy price support of $13.10 per hundred pounds, unless dairymen reduced milk production sharply. That change, however, was dropped in 1983.

The final bill did not include controversial House-passed dairy provisions establishing an industry-dominated board that in some cases could have set the level of price supports and could have levied assessments on farmers to pay for promotional programs.

The measure also reduced projected increases in major farm and food stamp programs by $6.6 billion over fiscal 1983-85, according to Congressional Budget Office estimates.

Tobacco Act

Congress in 1982 approved legislation aimed at eliminating costs to taxpayers of the federal tobacco program. Passage of the bill represented a critical victory for tobacco interests, who hoped that it would defuse criticism of the controversial program. The legislation, sponsored by Rep. Charlie Rose, D-N.C., was in response to a mandate contained in the 1981 omnibus farm bill that the tobacco program be run at no net cost to taxpayers, other than administrative expenses.

The tobacco act obligated growers who used the program to reimburse the federal government for losses resulting from the price support loans that were provided to farmers. They were required to make new "contributions" for this purpose to special funds run by their cooperative marketing associations. The provision was repealed in 1983 as part of legislation making major revisions in the tobacco program.

The measure also directed institutional owners of acreage allotments and marketing quotas for flue-cured tobacco to sell these federal "licenses to grow" to farmers who would use them. The act did not disturb allotment and quota leasing arrangements among individuals.

The industry-backed package of changes in the tobacco program was criticized by an anti-smoking coalition of health groups because it continued federal involvement with a product that endangered human health. Other opponents, including Rep. Paul Findley, R-Ill., said the measure did not go far enough in charging tobacco farmers for the cost of their program. The act did not require farmers to pay for administrative costs, estimated at $15.9 million in fiscal 1983.

PIK Bills

The Reagan administration failed to win congressional endorsement in 1982 of a major change in farm policy involving payments of federally owned commodities to farmers who reduced acreage. However, the administration announced in early in January 1983 that it would proceed without legislation.

Bypassing its Agriculture Committee, the Democratic House approved a bill Dec. 18 involving the so-called Payment-in-Kind (PIK) program. However, a more elaborate Senate version, approved by the Agriculture Committee Dec. 13, became bogged down by deadline pressures.

Both the House and Senate bills were intended to address what the agriculture secretary called relatively minor changes in the law needed to protect the program from potential lawsuits. Block said the changes would clarify authority he already had.

One change would have exempted commodity payments in kind from a $50,000 limit on federal farm program payments to an individual farmer. The second would have exempted the PIK payments from a requirement that commodities owned by the Commodity Credit Corp. (CCC) could not be sold for less than 110 percent of the price at which grain could be sold out of the farmer-held reserve.

The CCC was the Agriculture Department agency that operated price support programs. It became the owner of wheat, corn, and other farm commodities when farmers defaulted on federal loans. The reserve program permitted farmers to borrow from the federal government if they agreed to keep their crops in storage and not sell them until market prices reached a fixed "release" level.

A General Accounting Office report criticizing the multimillion-dollar PIK payments to individual farmers — and the congressional reaction it provoked — prompted the Agriculture Department to announce Dec. 21, however, that it would impose a $50,000 limit on payments to individuals participating in the 1984 program. Only wheat farmers could qualify for PIK payments on 1984 crops.

Commodity Futures

President Reagan Jan. 12, 1983, signed into law a bill reauthorizing the Commodity Futures Trading Commission (CFTC) through Sept. 30, 1986. The bill contained a controversial "contract sanctity" amendment requiring the president to guarantee the delivery of American farm exports for up to nine months even if he subsequently decided to impose a trade embargo.

Contract Sanctity Issue. Sponsored by Sen. Dave Durenberger, R-Minn., the contract sanctity provision had been adopted by voice vote before the Senate passed its version of the bill Oct. 1. The House-passed bill had no similar language. The amendment barred imposition of restrictions on the export of any agricultural commodity under contract at the time an embargo was imposed if delivery was scheduled within 270 days. Supporters said the guarantee was needed because the United States' reputation as a reliable supplier of food had

been damaged severely by the 1980 embargo on grain sales to the Soviet Union and by previous trade restraints. Despite an earlier threat of a veto, conferees on the bill agreed Dec. 9 to retain the provision.

The rider drew objections from the State Department because it restricted the president's freedom to act in the future. But because the trade guarantee had wide support within the financially troubled farm community, administration officials had avoided making public objections to it.

Sen. Robert Dole, R-Kan., told conferees Dec. 9 that he and other supporters of the provision had offered to soften the language in conference if the State Department would agree to negotiate a long-term grain sale agreement with the Soviet Union. Although department officials did not respond to his offer, Dole said, "Now, at the last minute, they're calling frantically and saying, 'you've got to change this.' "

Administration officials sought, without success, to convince farm lobbyists and their congressional allies that they did not need the statutory guarantee because Reagan repeatedly had pledged to avoid trade embargoes, except in extreme circumstances. But supporters insisted a statutory guarantee was needed to assure foreign purchasers that U.S. export commitments would be honored despite an embargo or other foreign policy action.

Other Provisions. Other provisions of the bill were intended to strengthen the hand of state law enforcement officials and individuals against fraudulent commodity operators. The bill also ratified an important jurisdictional agreement between the CFTC and the Securities and Exchange Commission (SEC).

In addition, under a compromise worked out between the commodities industry and the Office of Management and Budget, the final legislation affirmed CFTC authority to charge the industry fees for such services as approval of contracts. Both the House and Senate had rejected attempts to include administration-backed fees on individual commodities transactions, but conferees added the "service fee" language to avert another veto threat to the bill. The fees would return about $3 million a year to the Treasury, according to Richard G. Lugar, R-Ind., chairman of the Senate Agriculture subcommittee with jurisdiction over the CFTC.

The administration originally had wanted Congress to authorize transaction fees to raise enough revenue to cover most of the CFTC's annual $23 million budget. But the industry objected that the fees would drain financial support from its new, self-regulatory group, the National Futures Association (NFA), and neither the House nor the Senate included the transaction fees in their CFTC bills. The bill set a deadline by which the NFA must actively share regulatory responsibilities with the CFTC.

Background. Congressional committees struggled throughout 1982 to revise the regulation of an industry whose rapid growth in new directions made some members uneasy. At issue was how to treat the fast-growing trade in new hybrid financial instruments. The new instruments based so-called "forward" or future contracts on conventional stocks or bonds that were used by corporations and units of government to raise capital. Future contracts typically set a price for a given commodity on a specified date in the future. An option permitted an owner to buy or sell at a certain price in the future but imposed no obligation to do so.

Those types of contracts had been used for decades by speculators as well as buyers and sellers of agricultural commodities as a form of insurance against price changes. Inflation made the contracts attractive to dealers in non-farm goods, and the market responded with ingenious new variations. Futures or options were available, for example, on foreign currency, Treasury bonds, housing bonds and stock indexes.

Congress fueled the trend in 1974 when it wrote an unusually inclusive definition of "commodity" into the statute creating the CFTC. But fierce competition over new products between securities and futures industries continued to inspire occasional congressional plans for dismembering the CFTC.

The commission almost went out of business in 1978, when it came under fire for alleged ineffectiveness at screening firms and individuals for registration, slowness in moving against manipulations of the market and its lack of internal structure. In the end, however, Congress granted the CFTC a four-year reauthorization.

In December 1981 the CFTC and SEC voluntarily divided up much of the disputed turf, deciding which types of transactions would be regulated by each agency. The major features of the agreement were incorporated in the CFTC reauthorization legislation.

Pesticide Law Revisions

Congress was unable in 1982 to reconcile conflicts surrounding a rewrite of federal pesticide law, despite nearly a year of negotiations among interested groups.

Although the House passed a two-year reauthorization of the Federal Insecticide, Fungicide and Rodenticide Act (FIFRA) Aug. 11, sharp conflicts among environmentalists, pesticide makers, and farmers kept the measure from reaching the Senate floor before the 97th Congress adjourned. Meanwhile, the Environmental Protection Agency (EPA), which administered federal pesticide programs, was able to continue its activities with appropriated funds. Congress finally cleared a one-year authorization Nov. 18, 1983. The act was again renewed in 1984.

The programs involved the registration with the federal government of chemicals used to kill insects, rodents, fungi, and plants. To obtain registration — in effect a license to sell a product — manufacturers had to submit data to EPA. The last major rewrite of the law was in 1978.

Key controversies in 1982 were whether stricter state registration laws could pre-empt federal statutes, whether individuals would be able to sue to stop violations of pesticide laws and the confidentiality of industry information filed with state and federal governments.

Migrant Farm Worker Relief

Congress in late 1982 approved a major revision of federal laws governing the treatment of migrant farm workers. The bill replaced the existing Farm Labor Contractor Registration Act (FLCRA) with a new set of federal protections for migrant and seasonal workers.

The measure was a compromise that enjoyed support from the Reagan administration, unions, and agricultural employers. *(Migrant workers, p. 37)*

Agricultural groups had pushed for the legislation because farmers resented the burdens imposed on them by FLCRA, which was passed by Congress in 1963 to prevent abuses by "crew leaders" — independent contractors who recruit and transport migrant workers from farm to farm. Its most important provision required contractors to register with the Labor Department. Congress in 1974 enacted amendments that broadened the coverage of the 1963 act and toughened its penalties.

The Labor Department in recent years had required many farmers to register under the law as farm labor contractors. The bill would prevent that by exempting "fixed-site" farm employers from the registration requirements imposed on farm labor contractors.

However, farm employers as well as farm labor contractors would have to satisfy other requirements in the bill involving treatment of workers. The bill required that workers receive adequate housing, safe transportation and correct information about their pay.

PRICE SUPPORT HIGHS, RECORD DROUGHT

For American agriculture, 1983 was a year of extremes: record drought, grandiose farm programs, and startlingly high spending to prop up the farm economy.

Federal expenditures for price supports and other farm subsidy programs reached an extraordinary high of $18.8 billion. That figure did not include the value of the surplus commodities — about $9.8 billion — used to pay farmers in the administration's ambitious Payment-in-Kind program. Farm income for 1983 slid to a low estimated at $16 billion by the Agriculture Department. That figure, adjusted for inflation, was the lowest farm income total since 1933.

The high program costs were blamed on the large surpluses of major crops that existed at the beginning of the year and depressed market prices — as in the previous three years. Like food stamps and welfare, farm programs cost more during times of economic stress, when more people depended more heavily upon them.

The surpluses signaled the continuing mismatch between high farm productivity and export markets too weak to siphon off much of the U.S. surplus. Farm exports slid downward in 1983, totaling $36.1 billion in value. The decline continued the downward trend from the 1981 high of $43.3 billion.

In an attempt to prop up exports, the Reagan administration offered subsidized credit and bonuses of commodities to promote foreign sales of U.S. commodities. It also signed a new, long-term grain trade pact with the Soviet Union.

On July 28, Agriculture Secretary Block and U.S. Trade Representative William E. Brock III announced that under the terms of the five-year grain sales agreement the United States would sell, and the Russians would buy, at least nine million metric tons and as much as 12 million tons of wheat and corn each year. The deal also made special arrangements for soybean sales. The expiring U.S.-U.S.S.R. pact called for annual sales of six million to eight million metric tons, without provision for soybeans.

Politics of Program Costs

Privately and publicly, budget director Stockman attacked the high costs of the farm programs. At a May congressional hearing, he complained that "We are spending more for farm subsidies than we are for welfare for the entire poverty population of this country."

Agriculture Department officials turned on the programs they administered, publicly adding to Stockman's complaints. They said that farm programs were in political trouble that could only get worse. They repeatedly reminded audiences, in Congress and elsewhere, that the hefty infusions of federal farm money were going to a relatively small number of people.

According to the most recent Census Bureau figures, the farm population dropped to 5.6 million people in 1982, just 2.4 percent of the total population. Within that number, a still smaller group actually produced the bulk of the nation's food. USDA estimated in 1983 that about 12 percent of the nation's farms marketed about two-thirds of all farm products.

Because of the way farm programs operated, the larger the size of a farm, the larger the federal farm benefits it could

collect. The benefits came in many forms, among them loans on favorable terms, cash payments for price supports, and subsidies for storage facilities, and crop insurance.

The Reagan administration in 1983 swallowed its aversion to meddling in the farm economy and ran the largest crop-reduction program in the history of federal farm programs. The president also managed to ignore his free-market philosophy long enough to sign legislation authorizing first-time-ever payments to dairy farmers for not making milk. These two developments seemed clear evidence of the enduring political power of farmers, despite their shrinking numbers.

The PIK program paid farmers for idling part of their crop land; the payments were in the form of wheat or other stocks, not cash. The assumption was that federally owned surpluses would "finance" the program.

As it turned out, the government did not own enough surplus crops to meet its PIK commitments. To make many of these payments, the government simply forgave price support loans. In effect, the government gave back to farmers full title to crops they owned, but had obligated to the government for loans. (In the price support loan programs, farmers borrowed from the federal government, using crops as collateral.)

According to participation figures, the PIK program was popular. Approximately 47.3 million acres were idled under PIK and an addition 28.3 million acres under the acreage diversion program. The total of 75.6 million acres taken out of production represented nearly 43 percent of the farm land eligible for the two programs.

The PIK program appeared to put the United States at a disadvantage in world markets. In October, Secretary Block told a congressional committee that the large production cuts at home had stimulated extra production by nations that compete with the United States in agriculture. "While U.S.

grain production for 1983-84 is expected to be down by 129 million tons, foreign production is expected to rise by 43 million tons to a new record," Block said.

Nevertheless, Block and other administration officials generally declared the PIK program to be a one-shot success that had headed off yet another surplus and put some badly needed money in farmers' pockets. A scaled-down version of PIK operated in 1984 for wheat producers. *(PIK program, p. 15)*

Drought Impact

Another exceptional event for agriculture was an unusually broad and long-lasting spell of hot, rainless weather that devastated corn, soybeans, and other major crops. The drought, the worst in 50 years, began in July and affected production in at least 28 states across the Southeast, Midwest, and Southwest. Drought damage was estimated at about $7 billion.

This natural "production cut" greatly magnified the impact of the PIK program. Corn production was cut in half; carryover stocks — those left over at the end of the year — were reduced by about four-fifths, compared with the previous year. The short supplies produced substantial increases in market prices. In mid-September, according to USDA, the farm price of corn was up more than 50 percent, compared with the September 1982 price; soybeans were up more than 60 percent; cotton prices were up about 15 percent.

Wheat prices, however, did not show the same strong recovery. Wheat producers brought in their winter wheat before the drought hit, harvesting the second largest crop in the nation's history. The PIK program had cut the acreage planted in wheat — from 79 million acres to 60 million acres between 1982 and 1983. Yet, because yields rose markedly, the 1983 wheat harvest declined only 14 percent, to 2.4 billion bush-

els, from the 2.8 billion all-time high of 1982.

Dairy, Tobacco Programs

President Reagan in late 1982 signed into law landmark changes in federal dairy policy despite his strong objections to the new program. The legislation, intended to curb dairy surpluses, authorized payments to dairymen, partly financed by dairy farmers themselves, for producing less milk.

The bill also reduced dairy price supports and included changes in the federal tobacco program, an authorization for egg producers to coordinate marketing, and authorization for livestock producers to buy damaged federal stocks of feed to help them cope with the 1983 summer drought.

Some economic and farm officials in the administration objected strongly to the new dairy plan. Reagan himself protested that paying farmers for not producing violated his free-market philosophy. But Agriculture Department officials advised the president to sign the bill, arguing that existing law was worse. Moreover, a veto would have dealt a serious blow to one of Reagan's early Southern supporters, Sen. Helms. The tobacco provisions were critically important to Helms, up for re-election in 1984. The tobacco sections, in fact, had been viewed by dairy lobbyists and their congressional allies as solid-gold "insurance" of enactment.

Dairy Program. Since the Depression a regional system of dairy quotas had limited the quantity of fresh milk for which an individual farmer could receive federal support payments. But there never had been payments to dairy producers on a national scale for producing less milk.

The 1983 bill was meant to reduce surplus dairy production, which had been running about 10 percent more than demand. The program required the government to buy surplus dairy goods at the established support price.

The existing dairy price support program guaranteed that the government would buy dairy products at a set price — at $13.10 per 100 pounds of milk equivalent in mid-1983 — if producers could not sell them elsewhere. The government was buying about 10 percent of the milk produced in the United States, at a cost of nearly $3 billion a year. If no changes were made in the dairy program, the government would buy and store about 16 billion pounds worth of milk, in the form of butter, cheese and non-fat powdered milk.

Major regional dairy cooperatives split over how to cope with the swelling dairy surplus. On one side were those who wanted strict production limits for individual dairy farms to reduce the surplus. They included the National Milk Producers Federation, an umbrella organization for all co-ops, and the Associated Milk Producers Inc. (AMPI), a major Midwestern cooperative. AMPI spokesman Jim Eskin said that about 80 percent of the industry supported production limits, "and we think that's a pretty good showing of unity."

But other elements of the industry, led by the Southeastern cooperatives of Dairymen Inc. and joined by consumer and industrial user groups, objected to production controls. They wanted hefty across-the-board cuts in federal price support levels.

The final bill reduced to $12.60 per hundred pounds of milk, from $13.10 per hundred pounds, the federal dairy price support. It authorized two further reductions of 50 cents each on April 1, 1985, and July 1, 1985, if federal purchases of milk in 1985 were estimated to exceed six billion pounds (as of April 1) or five billion pounds (as of July 1). However, the bill would authorize an increase of at least 50 cents on July 1, 1985 if federal purchases were estimated at below five billion pounds and more milk was needed.

The legislation authorized a 15-month paid diversion program, from Jan. 1, 1984, until March 31, 1985. Producers who participated would cut production by 5 percent to 30 percent from their previous yields and would be paid at a rate of $10 per hundred pounds.

Changes in dairy assessments also were authorized by the landmark legislation. It repealed the second of two controversial assessments that Congress had approved in 1982 in an attempt to discourage overproduction in the dairy industry, while offsetting costs of the federal dairy program. The 1982 law had provided for two 50-cent assessments on every hundred pounds of milk equivalent (as measured in butter, cheese and dry milk) produced by dairy farmers above certain levels.

The fee enraged dairymen and generated several lawsuits, one of which blocked the Agriculture Department in December 1982 from collecting the assessment. The department began collecting the first assessment in April 1983 and announced its intentions to collect the second 50-cent assessment if Congress provided no acceptable alternative.

When the legislation overhauling the federal dairy program and replacing the two assessments with a single assessment became entangled in disputes over other farm issues, Congress Aug. 4 abruptly passed a measure postponing the second assessment from Sept. 1 to Oct. 1.

President Reagan vetoed the measure on Aug. 23. His veto message said the $60 million the assessment would yield during September would help offset the $2.4 billion it was estimated the federal dairy program would cost in 1983.

Tobacco Program Changes. The legislation also included major revisions in the tobacco program, some of which negated features of a major industry-backed tobacco bill cleared by Congress in 1982.

The bill temporarily froze tobacco

Surpluses, Quota Costs, ...

There's more to growing tobacco than scratching up the dirt and throwing in a few seeds. Unless a farmer had had what amounted to a federal "license" to sell all but three of the nearly 20 types of tobacco grown in America, he had been subject to heavy financial penalties if he tried to sell tobacco.

And because of legislation passed in 1982, he had to help pay the storage and other costs for any excess tobacco left unsold at the end of the season. But record surpluses had distorted the federal tobacco program, making per-farmer costs rise to uncomfortably high levels for many growers. It was those increases and the certainty that they would continue that were behind the drive for legislation to change the government tobacco program in 1983.

The "licensing" system consisted of federal allotments that specified the number of acres that could be planted in tobacco, together with quotas that limited the number of pounds a farmer could sell. A farmer selling tobacco at auction had to show a card obtained from a county Agricultural Stabilization and Conservation Service office listing his quota.

There was a fixed number of allotments, originally assigned to the land on which farmers were growing tobacco decades ago. Active growers without such land had been able to rent the use of the allotments and quotas from their owners. However, with the passage of the 1983 legislation, "off-farm" leasing of quotas would end after 1986 for flue-cured tobacco and was greatly reduced for burley tobacco.

For the two major types of American tobacco — flue-cured and burley — the number of allotment owners dramatically outnumbered the number of growers. Burley was grown largely in Kentucky and Tennessee, while flue-cured tobacco was grown primarily in the Carolinas. The Agriculture Department (USDA) estimated in 1983

price supports, ended double payments by growers to special tobacco support funds, and phased out the renting of tobacco quotas to land away from the farms to which they were assigned. (Most tobacco could not be sold without a federal quota.) *(Tobacco costs, box, above)*

Drought Relief. The bill also directed the agriculture secretary to let farmers and ranchers in areas affected by the devastating drought buy, at 75 percent of the existing price support loan rate (about $2 per bushel), federally owned surplus feed corn that was in poor condition.

PIK Tax Breaks

Despite the administration's belief that the Payment-in-Kind program required no legislative action, Congress did enact special tax legislation when it appeared PIK participants could lose tax benefits normally enjoyed by farmers.

Under the PIK program, announced Jan. 11, 1983, farmers who agreed not to plant wheat, corn, cotton, and rice were paid by the government in surplus stocks of those crops.

Questions soon arose concerning

... and Tobacco Levies Growing

there were 40,000 to 50,000 actual producers of flue-cured tobacco and approximately 200,000 owners of allotments and quotas. For burley, the proportion of active farmers who owned their allotments and quotas was higher — approximately 150,000 active growers to 300,000 owners.

The system was subject to referendums every three years in which owners and growers could vote whether to continue it. Farmers within the system were eligible for federal price support loans set by law at a specific per-pound rate, which increased automatically every year unless Congress legislated otherwise, which it did in 1983. Whatever tobacco they could not sell on the market for a price that equaled or exceeded the loan rate, they could use as collateral for loans from the government. In 1982 the loan rates were $1.70 per pound for flue-cured tobacco and $1.75 per pound for burley.

A number of cooperative growers' groups administered the loan program and held the surplus tobacco put up as collateral for later sale. Once farmers consigned their surplus to a cooperative, they could keep the loan money, and the cooperative was responsible for reselling the crop and repaying the government loan.

The assessment against tobacco farmers approved by Congress in 1982 was meant to pay for any losses that occurred if the cooperative sold the surplus for less than the loan rate, and for interest and other costs. Until 1982, such losses were borne by the federal government. To cover anticipated losses from the 1982 crop, the government collected $29.5 million from flue-cured growers and quota-owners, and $7.7 million from burley growers and quota-owners.

That did not prove to be enough, so in 1984, to cover "catch-up" 1982 costs and anticipated losses from the 1983 crop, the department expected to collect at least $32.5 million from burley growers and $85 million from flue-cured growers.

---

whether farmers had to pay taxes on the commodities in the year in which they received them, or could defer tax payments until the commodities were sold. Farmers were not taxed on their crops until they sold them, even if that occurred several years after the harvest.

However, the Internal Revenue Service viewed the PIK commodities as the equivalent of income, liable to taxes in the year in which the commodities were received. Without the change, farmers could have faced tax payments on two crops in the same year — crops they raised and sold and

PIK commodities. They also would be shoved into higher tax brackets. In addition, it was unclear whether land idled in return for commodity payments still would be eligible for special treatment under federal estate tax law.

Fearing the tax liability would make farmers shy away from PIK, the administration pressed for changes in tax law for program participants. Though some members were skeptical, the tax changes received swift congressional approval and were signed by the president March 11.

Congress was less compliant when the

administration sought to extend the tax changes for a second year to cover a 1984 wheat PIK program the Agriculture Department unveiled in August. As reports circulated of farmers reaping large payments for not planting crops, PIK drew scathing criticism from several quarters, and the tax break was not extended in 1983.

PIK Cotton Program

Congress July 29 enacted legislation modifying the terms of cotton farmers' participation in the government's Payment-in-Kind program after the cotton growers complained they were being treated unfairly.

The PIK provision — reopening cotton bidding on the same terms offered producers of feed grains — was included in a fiscal 1983 supplemental appropriations bill. Administration objections to the additional costs generated by the cotton program — estimated at $75 million to $100 million — were not strong enough to threaten enactment of the supplemental. President Reagan signed the measure July 30.

The PIK section of the supplemental appropriations bill was meant to rectify a problem that arose when the administration found it did not own enough surplus cotton, wheat, and corn to make promised payments to PIK farmers. Under PIK, producers were paid with surplus crops to take farm land out of production in an effort to reduce the unsold surpluses that were depressing market prices. The Agriculture Department did not own enough of the surplus to meet its commitments to farmers because much of it was being used as collateral for federal price support loans and thus was still owned by individual farmers. In addition, because the department in an attempt to save money offered less favorable terms for cotton than for other commodities, it failed to acquire enough cotton.

Consequently, USDA invoked a clause in the farmers' PIK contracts requiring them to take out price support loans on their 1983 crop. The plan was to foreclose on the loans, so the farmers would keep the loan money and the government would take possession of the cotton.

But changing market conditions made such forced "sales" extremely costly to producers. A large, unexpected Soviet cotton purchase and poor weather had shrunk market supplies and hiked prices well above the "price" farmers would receive from compulsory sales to the government.

Moreover, many farmers had contracted to sell both their PIK cotton and their 1983 crops — crops that would be taken over by the government. They had gone ahead with the contracts after receiving repeated assurances from department officials that the PIK contract clause was not likely to be used.

The cotton language in the bill permitted farmers to offer again to sell their cotton to the government, but on more attractive terms than in the first round of bidding.

Export Subsidy Program

The Senate Agriculture Committee March 16 reported legislation to establish an aggressive export subsidy program for U.S.-produced food and fiber. The Senate Foreign Relations Committee subsequently considered the bill and reported it March 24, but the full Senate did not take up the measure in 1983. No agricultural trade subsidy legislation made it out of the House Agriculture Committee.

The Senate Agriculture Committee members almost unanimously put a large share of the blame for sagging U.S. farm exports on what they viewed as predatory trade practices by the 10-nation European Community and a handful of other nations. They contended that American farmers had been unfairly undersold in foreign markets

Major changes in the federal tobacco program were passed in 1983

and that U.S. agriculture had to retaliate in kind to regain those markets.

The bill required the secretary of agriculture to sell at least 150,000 metric tons of federally owned surplus dairy stocks abroad annually in fiscal years 1983, 1984, and 1985, at prices not below those established by an international dairy agreement. Those prices were substantially lower than the domestic level set by the federal dairy price support program.

The bill also explicitly authorized export Payment-in-Kind arrangements in which bonuses of federally owned surplus commodities could be used to lower prices of exported goods. The measure required the secretary to use half the receipts from the mandated dairy sales and all of the $190 million authorized in the 1982 budget reconciliation bill to subsidize loans and prices of export commodities.

It earmarked portions of the reconcilia-tion money for exports of poultry and eggs, raisins, and canned fruit — all, according to members, inappropriately subsidized by European nations. Other sections provided for extra PIK bonuses to foreign purchasers who expanded their capacity to take imports by investing in processing and similar facilities.

In addition, the bill expanded Food for Peace (PL 480) programs of donations and low-cost loans for food purchases by impoverished foreign nations.

U.S. - U.S.S.R. Grain Pact

Agriculture Secretary Block and U.S. Trade Representative Brock announced July 28, 1983, that the United States and the Soviet Union had concluded a new, five-year grain sales agreement.

The pact, to take effect Oct. 1, committed the United States to sell — and the Soviet Union to buy — at least nine million metric tons and up to 12 million metric tons of wheat and corn each year. It also permitted the Soviet Union to substitute a purchase of 500,000 metric tons of soybeans or soy meal for one million metric tons of wheat or corn; in a year when that occurred, the minimum combined sale of wheat and corn would be eight million tons. The expiring U.S.-U.S.S.R. grain pact called for annual sales of six million to eight million metric tons, with no provision for soybean sales.

Block said the new pact generally followed the terms of the U.S.-U.S.S.R. agreement that expired in 1983. That pact guaranteed delivery of the specified minimums and permitted either side to opt out of its commitment under certain conditions, such as a short supply in the United States. It was the guarantee that continued some grain shipments to the U.S.S.R. during President Carter's grain embargo, imposed after the Soviet invasion of Afghanistan.

President Reagan ended the unpopular Carter embargo in April 1981 but, to protest the establishment of martial law in Poland, refused until 1983 to negotiate a new long-term pact. Instead, the existing agreement was continued on a year-to-year basis. Farm-state critics said that practice encouraged the Soviet Union to find other, apparently more reliable sources of grain.

Part III:

Appendix

Selected Bibliography on U.S. Farm Policy

Articles

"Agriculture in America." *Wilson Quarterly* (Summer 1981).

American Association for the Advancement of Science. *Science.* Selected issues.

American Farm Bureau Federation. *Farm Bureau News.* Selected issues.

The American Federation for Immigration Reform. "FAIR — Immigration Report." Selected issues.

Barnett, Mary, and Janet Marinelli. "Medfly Madness." *Environmental Action* (September 1981).

Batie, Sandra S., and Robert C. Healy. "The Future of American Agriculture." *Scientific American* (February 1983).

Boraiko, Allen A. "The Pesticide Dilemma." *National Geographic* (February 1980).

"The Border: A World Apart." *Newsweek,* April 11, 1983.

Brady, C. Nyle. "Chemistry and World Food Supplies." *Science,* November 26, 1982.

Cook, Kenneth. "Slip, Sliding Away." *Environmental Action* (November 1981).

Cox, Meg. "Farm Crisis Falls Short of Depression Agony But There Are Parallels." *Wall Street Journal,* October 18, 1982.

Farm Journal Inc. *Farm Journal.* Philadelphia, Pa. Selected issues.

Gunby, Phil. "Military Looks Toward 1985 in Ongoing Defoliant Study." *Journal of American Medical Association,* April 27, 1984.

Johnson, Richard S. "Our Historical Abuse of Farm Workers." *Denver Post Empire Magazine,* March 1, 1981.

Larson, W. E., et al. "The Threat of Soil Erosion to Long-Term Crop Production." *Science,* February 4, 1983.

Lyman, Francesca. "Industry to Government: 'Let Us Spray.'" *Environmental Action* (November 1981).

Marcellin, Roger. "New Tools for A New Agriculture." *OECD Observer* (September 1980).

Maugh, Thomas H. II. "The Day of the Locusts Is Near." *Science,* August 14, 1981.

"A Move to Franchise 'Vegetable Factories.'" *Business Week,* December 29, 1980.

"The New Migrants: Struggles in an Alien Land." *Miami Herald,* March 22-27, 1981.

Press, Aric. "Agent Orange in the Dock." *Newsweek,* May 14, 1984.

Ripton, John. "The Surprising Truth about Farm Workers." *New Jersey Reporter* (May 1982).

Rawls, Rebecca L. "Dioxin's Human Toxicity is Most Difficult Problem." *Chemical and Engineering News,* June 6, 1983.

Reaves, Lynne. "Agent Orange Megatrial." *American Bar Association Journal* (May 1984).

Robbins, William. "Some Farmers Thriving as Others Go Under." *New York Times,* February 19, 1983.

Satchell, Michael. "Bent, But Not Broken." *Parade,* October 10, 1982.

Scrimshaw, Nevis S., and Lance Taylor. "Food." *Scientific American* (September 1980).

Sinclair, Ward. "An Endless Season, Migrants of the East." *Washington Post,* August 23-27, 1981.

Soil Conservation Society of America. *Journal of Soil and Water Conservation.* Selected issues.

Sprague, G. F., et al. "Plant Breeding and Genetic Engineering: A Perspective." *BioScience* (January 1980).

Steinhart, Peter. "The Edge Gets Thinner." *Audubon* (November 1983).

Tamarkin, Bob. "The Growth Industry." *Forbes,* March 2, 1981.

U.S. Department of Agriculture. *Agricultural Research.* Selected issues.

U.S. Veterans Administration. *Agent Orange Review.* Selected issues.

Vietmeyer, Noel D. "A Wild Relative May Give Corn Perennial Genes." *Smithsonian* (December 1979).

Walsh, John. "Medfly Continues to Bug California." *Science,* December 11, 1981.

Wehr, Elizabeth. "Conservation Policy Faces Far-reaching Shift." *Congressional Quarterly Weekly Report*, September 17, 1983.

Wehr, Elizabeth. "Diverse Critics Attack Amendments to Extend Plant Patent Protection." *Congressional Quarterly Weekly Report,* April 19, 1980.

"Why the Recovery May Skip the Farm Belt." *Business Week,* March 21, 1983.

Books

Batie, Sandra S., and Robert C. Healy, eds. *The Future of American Agriculture as a Strategic Resource.* Washington, D.C.: The Conservation Foundation, 1980.

Bennett, Hugh Hammond. *Soil Conservation.* New York: McGraw-Hill, 1939.

Brown, A. W. A. *Ecology of Pesticides.* New York: John Wiley & Sons, 1978.

Brown, Lester R. *Building a Sustainable Society.* New York: W. W. Norton & Co., 1981.

___. *Seeds of Change: The Green Revolution and Development in the 1970s.* New York: Praeger, 1970.

___. *The Twenty-Ninth Day: Accommodating Human Needs and Numbers to the Earth's Resources.* New York: W. W. Norton & Co., 1978.

Brown, Lester R., et al. *State of the World, 1984.* New York: W. W. Norton & Co., 1984.

Brown, Michael. *Laying Waste: The Poisoning of America By Toxic Chemicals.* New York: Pantheon Books Inc., 1980.

Carson, Rachel. *Silent Spring.* New York: Fawcett Books, 1962.

Chou, Marylin, and David P. Harmon, Jr., eds. *Critical Food Issues of the Eighties.* Elmsford, N.Y.: Pergamon Press, 1979.

Coles, Robert. *Migrants, Sharecroppers, Mountaineers.* Boston: Little, Brown & Co., 1967.

___. *Uprooted Children.* Pittsburgh: University of Pittsburgh Press, 1970.

Crosson, Pierre R., ed. *The Cropland Crisis: Myth or Reality?* Baltimore, Md.: Johns Hopkins University Press, 1982.

Dies, Edward Jerome. *Titans of the Soil: Great Builders of Agriculture.* Westport, Conn.: Greenwood Press, 1976.

Emerson, Robert D. *Seasonal Agricultural Labor Markets in the United States.* Ames, Iowa: Iowa State University Press, 1983.

Goldfarb, Ronald L. *Migrant Farm Workers: A Caste of Despair.* Ames, Iowa: Iowa State University Press, 1981.

Gunn, D. L., and J. G. R. Stevens. *Pesticides and Human Welfare.* New York: Oxford University Press, 1976.

Hadwiger, Don F., and William P. Browne, eds. *The New Politics of Food.* Lexington, Mass.: Lexington Books, 1978.

Hadwiger, Don F., and Ross B. Talbot, eds. *Food Policy and Farm Programs.* Montpelier, Vt.: Capital City Press, 1982.

Hurt, R. Douglas. *The Dust Bowl: An Agricultural and Social History*. Chicago: Nelson-Hall, 1981.

Levy, Jacques. E. *Cesar Chavez*. New York: W. W. Norton & Co., 1975.

Lindecker, Clifford, with Michael Ryan and Maureen Ryan. *Kerry: Agent Orange and an American Family*. New York: St. Martins, 1982.

Merk, Frederick. *History of the Westward Movement*. New York: Alfred A. Knopf, 1978.

Paarlberg, Don. *Farm and Food Issues of the 1980s*. Lincoln, Neb.: University of Nebraska Press, 1980.

Sampson, R. Neil. *Farmland or Wasteland: A Time to Choose*. Emmaus, Pa.: Rodale Press, 1981.

Uhl, Michael, and Tod Ensign. *GI Guinea Pigs*. Chicago: Playboy Press, 1980.

Whiteside, Thomas. *The Pendulum and the Toxic Cloud: The Course of Dioxin Contamination*. New Haven, Conn.: Yale University Press, 1979.

Wilcox, Fred A. *Waiting for an Army to Die: The Tragedy of Agent Orange*. New York: Vintage, 1983.

Government Publications

U.S. Bureau of the Census. *Statistical Abstract of the United States 1982*. Washington, D.C.: Government Printing Office, 1982.

U.S. Department of Agriculture."Final Regulatory Impact Analysis," January 11, 1983.

____. "A Time to Choose: Summary Report on the Structure of Agriculture." Washington, D.C.: Government Printing Office, 1981.

____. Division of Economic Indicators and Statistics. *Agricultural Outlook*. Selected issues.

Reports and Studies

Bottress, Dale R. "Integrated Pest Management." Council on Environmental Quality, 1979.

Council on Environmental Quality and the Department of State. "The Global 2000 Report to the President: Entering the Twenty-First Century," vol. 1, 1980.

Dow Chemical Co. "Dioxin, Agent Orange and Human Health." (April 1984).

Eckholm, Erik, and Lester R. Brown. "Spreading Deserts: The Hand of Man." Washington, D.C.: Worldwatch Institute, August 1977.

Editorial Research Reports. vol. 2, p. 543. "Europe's Foreign Laborers." Washington, D.C.: Congressional Quarterly, 1975.

____. vol. 2, p. 807. "Farm Policy and Food Needs." Washington, D.C.: Congressional Quarterly, 1977 .

____. vol 1, p. 233. "Farm Policy's New Course." Washington, D.C.: Congressional Quarterly, 1983.

____. vol. 2, p. 945. "Genetic Business." Washington, D.C.: Congressional Quarterly, 1980.

____. vol. 1, p. 233. "Genetic Research." Washington, D.C.: Congressional Quarterly, 1977.

____. vol. 2, p. 903. "Genetics and the Life Process." Washington, D.C.: Congressional Quarterly, 1967.

____. vol. 1, p. 219. "Green Revolution." Washington, D.C.: Congressional Quarterly, 1970.

____. vol. 2, p. 549. "Hispanic America." Washington, D.C.: Congressional Quarterly, 1982.

____. vol. 1, p. 105. "Migratory Farm Workers." Washington, D.C.: Congressional Quarterly, 1959.

___. vol. 2, p. 825. "World Food Needs." Washington, D.C.: Congressional Quarterly, 1974.

General Accounting Office. "Agriculture's Soil Conservation Programs Miss Full Potential in the Fight Against Soil Erosion." November 28, 1983.

___. "The Department of Agriculture Can Minimize the Risk of Potential Crop Failures." April 10, 1981.

Legislative Research Commission Report to the 1983 General Assembly of North Carolina. "Migrant Workers." (January 1983).

MacNeil-Lehrer Report. "Grain Paybacks," January 11, 1983, PBS-TV transcript no. 1902.

Monsanto Co. "Why Monsanto Settled the Agent Orange Case." May 21, 1984.

Mooney, P. R. "The Seeds of the Earth." International Coalition for Development Action, 1979.

National Academy of Sciences. "Conservation of Germplasm Resources: An Imperative." 1979.

___. "Genetic Vulnerability of Major Crops." 1972.

National Association of Conservation Districts. "1983 National Survey: Conservation Tillage Practices." (February 1984).

North, David S., and Marion F. Houston. "The Characteristics and Role of Illegal Aliens in the U.S. Labor Market." New TransCentury Foundation (March 1976).

Office of Technology Assessment. "Impacts of Applied Genetics: Micro-Organisms, Plants, and Animals." (April 1981).

___. "Impacts of Technology on U.S. Cropland and Rangeland Productivity." (August 1982).

___. "Pest Management Strategies in Crop Protection." (October 1979).

Porter, Patricia A. "Health Status of Migrant Farm Workers." The Field Foundation (March 1980).

Presidential Commission on World Hunger. "Overcoming World Hunger: The Challenge Ahead." (March 1980).

Reichert, Joshua S. "The Agricultural Labor System in North Carolina: Recommendations for Change." North Carolina Department of Administration, Division of Policy Development (June 1980).

Rural America. "Pesticide Use and Misuse: Farm Workers and Small Farmers Speak on the Problem." (September 1980).

U.S. Congress. House. Subcommittee on Government Operations. *Administration of Laws Affecting Farm Workers.* 96th Cong., 1st sess., 1979.

___. Senate. Select Commission on Immigration and Refugee Policy. *Temporary Worker Programs: Background and Issues.* 96th Cong., 2d sess., 1980.

U.S. Department of Agriculture. "Biological Agents in Pest Control." (February 1978).

___. "A National Program for Soil and Water Conservation: 1982 Final Program Report and Environmental Impact Statement." (September 1982).

___. National Plant Genetic Resources Board. "Plant Genetic Resources: Conservation and Use." 1979.

White House Agent Orange Working Group. "Fact Sheet on Scientific Research of the Federal Government." April 15, 1984.

Index